FINDING BATTLESTAR GALACTICA

AN UNAUTHORIZED GUIDE

SOURCEBOOKS, INC.®
NAPERVILLE, ILLINOIS

LYNNETT[illegible] [illegible]VID LAVERY,
& [illegible]SON

Published by Sourcebooks, Inc.
P.O. Box 4410, Naperville, Illinois 60567-4410
(630) 961-3900
Fax: (630) 961-2168
www.sourcebooks.com

Library of Congress Cataloging-in-Publication Data

Porter, Lynnette R.
Finding Battlestar Galactica : an unauthorized guide / Lynnette Porter, David Lavery, and Hillary Robson.
p. cm.
Includes bibliographical references and index.
1. Battlestar Galactica (Television program : 2003-) 2. Battlestar Galactica (Television program : 1978-1979) I. Lavery, David II. Robson, Hillary. III. Title.
PN1992.77.B354P67 2008
791.45'72--dc22

2008009288

Printed and bound in the United States of America.
VP 10 9 8 7 6 5 4 3 2 1

TABLE OF CONTENTS

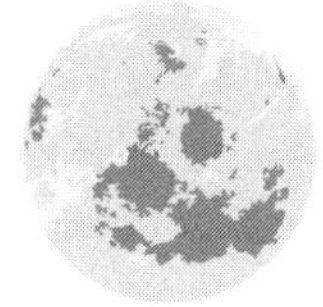

Part Three: The *Battlestar*verse

Part Four: Episodes

Acknowledgments

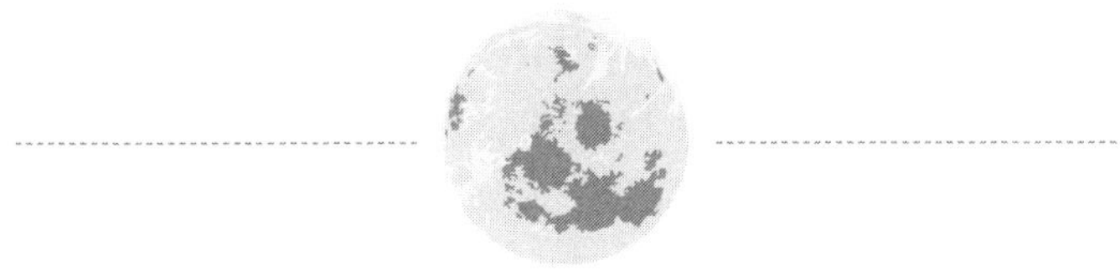

Special thanks to Bart, who shares my interest in and knowledge of the original series, as well as more than forty years' enjoyment of TV sci fi (and numerous SF conventions).

As always, thanks to my co-authors, David and Hillary, who brilliantly navigate the SF and publication universes, and to Peter Lynch at Sourcebooks, who suggested this book.

Finally, but never least, thank you to Jimmie, Nancy, and Heather, who make the journey home worthwhile.

—Lynnette Porter

Thanks go, of course, to Lynnette Porter and Hillary, who made this book, the fourth we have worked on together, fun. Many thanks to Ian Mauli for his careful proofing of the galleys. Thanks as well to Peter Lynch, our editor at Sourcebooks, and Uwe Stender, our agent. As always, thanks, too, to my wife, Joyce, who defended the home planet while I have been at academic fantasy camp in London working on books like this one.

—David Lavery

I would be remiss to not first thank my fabulous co-authors, beginning with David, who told me I should watch *Battlestar* time and time again before I finally took his advice and fell in love with such a deeply creative and wonderfully imaginative series. Thank you for bringing so many great and wonderful things to my life, for your friendship, and for being one-third of the best collaborative team in the world. Of course, the other third of this glorious team is Lynnette, who has been a friend, mentor, collaborator, hotel-mate, conference pal, and a million other incredible things in the time I've known her. The two of you are my inspiration, and I thank you for giving me the opportunity time and time again to work with you both!

To all the people who helped make this book happen, thank you: from the authors who contributed their inspired pieces, to the guidance of Peter Lynch, and the efforts of the great Uwe Stender. Your efforts are a major of part of why this book is so great.

And finally, I'd like to thank Don, who gladly embarked on "another TV show with me" (and I'd like to add that, just like *all* the others, fell in love with this one too!). You bring me so much love and laughter, and have my heart for always.

—Hillary Robson

Contributors

Heather E. Ash graduated from Northwestern University with a degree in radio/TV/film and a minor in creative writing for the media. She has written for *Stargate SG-1* and *Glory Days.* Her original spec pilot, *Square One*, was featured in *Written By*'s "Unproduced" issue.

Justin Door is an undergraduate at Embry-Riddle Aeronautical University. He is pursuing a degree in aerospace engineering, but between time spent researching airfoil control systems and rocket propulsion systems, he enjoys science fiction and fantasy.

Sean Hockett recently graduated with honors in film and television at Brunel University in the UK. He co-authored the chapter on "Comic Book *Heroes*" in *Saving the World: A Guide to* Heroes.

Ewan Kirkland received his doctorate at the University of Sussex and lectures in media studies at Buckinghamshire New University in the UK. He organized a 2007 conference on *Battlestar Galactica*. He has published on *Buffy the Vampire Slayer*, heterosexuality in romantic comedies, masculinity in the work of Robin Williams, and video games.

Currently serving as the president of the Affiliated Faculty of Emerson College union, David Kociemba has taught at Emerson and at four other colleges and universities for the past seven years. Past courses include introductory media history classes and seminars devoted to exploring topics like American film censorship, the representation of physical disability, video art, and *Buffy the*

Vampire Slayer. In addition, he has taught talented fourth- through twelfth-grade students the principles and practice of parliamentary debate at College Academy and the Roxbury Boys and Girls Club. He won the 2007 Mr. Pointy Award for his article "'Actually, it explains a lot': Reading the Opening Title Sequences of *BtVS*."

David Lavery is the author of numerous essays and reviews, and author, co-author, editor, or co-editor of more than a dozen books (including three with Lynnette Porter and Hillary Robson) on such TV series as *Twin Peaks*, *The X-Files*, *Buffy the Vampire Slayer*, *The Sopranos*, *Seinfeld*, *Deadwood*, *Lost*, *Heroes*, and *My So-Called Life*. He co-edits *Slayage: The Online International Journal of Buffy Studies* and is one of the founding editors of *Critical Studies in Television*. He has lectured around the world on the subject of television.

Lynnette Porter teaches humanities courses at Embry-Riddle Aeronautical University, in Daytona Beach, Florida, where she is an associate professor. She frequently collaborates with David Lavery and Hillary Robson to create books about other TV series, including *Lost* and *Heroes*. She also has published numerous papers, essays, chapters, and a book about Tolkien's *The Lord of the Rings* and currently is working on additional *LotR*–themed book projects, as well as chapters in David Lavery's forthcoming *Cult TV.*

Hillary Robson works as an academic advisor and teaches adjunct courses in composition at Middle Tennessee State University. Her major areas of interest include fandom, popular culture, and TV studies. She is the author of chapters in *Investigating Alias: Secrets and Spies* and a textbook on using popular culture in the composition classroom and co-author (with Lynnette Porter and David Lavery) of *Lost's Buried Treasures: The Unofficial Guide to Everything* Lost *Fans Need to Know* and *Saving the World: A Guide to* Heroes. She is co-editing (with Cynthia Burkhead) a collection of essays on *Grey's Anatomy* (forthcoming from Cambridge Scholars Publishing).

Christopher Smiley recently graduated from Brunel University in London.

PREFACE

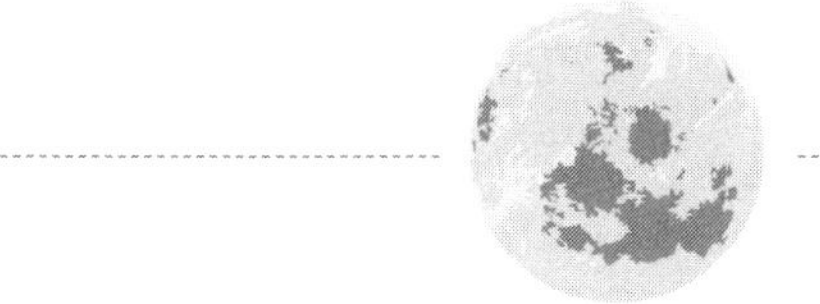

CONFESSIONS OF A LONG-TIME *BATTLESTAR GALACTICA* FAN

—LYNNETTE PORTER

My co-authors, the special contributors to this book, and I enjoy and appreciate on a number of levels the "reimagined" *Battlestar Galactica*. But unlike most of my colleagues (some who are too young to have seen the original series when it was first broadcast), I was and still am a fan of the 1978–79 version. When I see those "ancient" episodes today, I sometimes cringe at the costumes, hair-styles, or special effects, but I also fondly recall Sunday evenings when my brother and I bonded over Starbuck's many romances and adventures. Bart wanted to be a guy's guy like Starbuck; I just wanted to be with him. (I almost hate to admit how excited I was to finally meet Dirk "Starbuck" Benedict more than fifteen years later. Almost. After all, I've talked with "Starbuck"!)

Ever-faithful *Battlestar* fans, Bart and I read Glen Larson's 1978 novelization of the pilot episode and, over the years, followed Richard Hatch's further explorations of *Battlestar*'s storylines in his novels. When the pilot episode was resurrected as a full-fledged theatrical movie, we were in the audience. When I moved to a new city near the end of the 1978–79 TV season, during Bart's first visit we discussed *Battlestar* over a cigar, à lá Starbuck. When Dirk Benedict (starring as Curly) toured Ohio in a Kenley Players' 1979 production of *Oklahoma*, we cheered from the audience.

When *Battlestar* ended, we commiserated over what we (and most fans) considered an abysmal *Galactica 1980* (with the exception of the Starbuck episode), and we gave up cigars. Of course, we never completely gave up our fascination with *BSG* (although Bart eventually agreed not to name his child Starbuck, for which daughter Heather is eternally grateful). To everyone else's chagrin, we still occasionally pepper our conversations with "frak," a word back in vogue in recent years.

In the intervening decades since the original series, I've talked with several original cast members at fan conventions and watched Richard Hatch's short "pilot" trailer. It was intended to bring *Battlestar* back as either a movie or TV series but unintentionally became an on-screen memorial to John Colicos, the original Baltar.

When word of a new *Battlestar* arrived in early 2003, I was skeptical when I learned that Starbuck would be played by Katee Sackhoff. I saw the photo op between "old" and "new" Starbucks but didn't think I'd ever accept the new Starbuck, or series—until one of my students handed me the first season's DVD set. (Thank you, Justin.) Although the story begins with the same premise, this new series quickly became (to me, and many fans of the original) an entirely different entity. The reimagined story captures not only the essence of current global problems but presents its often dark vision in extremely realistic ways. It elevates science fiction (and the Sci Fi Channel) as a benchmark of excellent storytelling and entertainment; it even alludes to "messages" or "meanings" without hitting audiences over the head with morality tales. If anything, *Battlestar* illustrates moral dilemmas without clear-cut resolutions; it can make everyone squirm. I understand the complaints of those who dislike GINO (*Galactica* in Name Only), but I find a lot to like about both the old and the new.

So yes, I still smile fondly when I see the original series; it's part of my past—and that of sci-fi television. But I'm riveted by the new series, even when its violence becomes difficult (for me) to watch. It is, dare I say it, relevant television that sneaks in political and social commentary while providing one heck of a daring ride.

Of course, science fiction isn't (and probably never will be) embraced by mainstream audiences, which is a shame. Mediocre or bad sitcoms come and go, but they're more likely to be accepted by the public than a high-quality, mentally and visually stimulating sci-fi program such as *Battlestar*. In defiance of most critics' lower expectations for a sci-fi show, *Battlestar* has received more nominations and garnered more critical accolades than anything in recent sci-fi history.

This book is a bridge between old and new, although the majority of chapters present insights into the reimagined series. In early chapters we discuss the significance of Glen Larson's original *Battlestar Galactica* and its impact on fandom, the fans' refusal to let the series die, the mind of series co-creator Ronald D. Moore, and the reinvention of the story as the remarkable sci-fi series in the 2000s.

Authors in the second section, Reimagination at Work, analyze reasons behind the new series' success and discuss the work of some of *Battlestar*'s most creative minds: series creators Moore and David Eick, Jane Espenson, and Michael Rymer. This section also tackles *BSG*'s place within sci-fi television.

So many themes to choose from—the third section, The *Battlestar*verse, introduces some of the most intriguing, from religion to sex. Just what in god's/gods' name(s) is going on? A look at humanity's many religions and Cylon monotheism offers some answers to that question. Religion isn't all that's on the Cylons' minds; red hot, spine-tingling sex steams up the screen. Gender issues, quite naturally, are also a hot topic, and two chapters unravel the female mystique (or lack of). What makes humanity and their Cylon children laugh or cry, love or hate, and how those actions and emotions translate visually on television shape the *Battlestar*verse.

Although the *Battlestar* universe is vast, individual episodes give us our bearings and, arrow of Apollo-like, point us in the right direction in understanding the series' mythology. "Kobol's Last Gleaming" and "Final Cut" are discussed in the Episodes section. Not all episodes are shining stars, however; what happens when one "fraks up" also makes an interesting essay.

Fanfare, please: Marita Grabiak, director of *Battlestar*'s "Water" (as well as many other series' episodes and films), graciously agreed to talk with us; her interview provides insider information about what it's like to direct *Battlestar*.

Buckle up, and prepare the FTL drive: Throughout the book are Jumps—short but insightful leaps into new topics. What makes science fiction worthwhile, who's steering *Battlestar*, what's funny about a post-apocalyptic society—these and other Jumps explore new territory.

Near the end of the book, an episode guide, bibliography, and index help you navigate the *Battlestar*verse from 1978 onward. A catalog of R & D logos—those amusing cartoons at the end of the closing credits—shows just how creative (and darkly funny) Moore and Eick can be to the very end.

Throughout the book we explore what *Battlestar* means to us and our culture. The journey from 1978 to 2008 takes us through many iterations of the *BSG* saga, culminating in the recent *Razor* special episode and Season Four's twenty-two episodes. Although Moore and Eick swear there are no plans for *BSG* beyond that, I doubt if fans are ready for the story to be over. In another thirty years we'll see where the saga stands; my bet is that *Battlestar Galactica* will still be around.

Part I

IN THE BEGINNING

This section examines *Battlestar Galactica*'s origin myth in three chapters. "That Was Then" contrasts the reimagined *BSG* with its 1970s predecessor. Heather E. Ash's "The Next Generation: *Battlestar Galactica* Creator Ron Moore Reimagines Deep Space," an essay originally published in the official journal of the Writers Guild of America, offers an interview with and commentary on the role of Ronald D. Moore in the rebirth of the series. "Piloting a Series" takes as its subject *BSG*'s pilot.

Chapter One

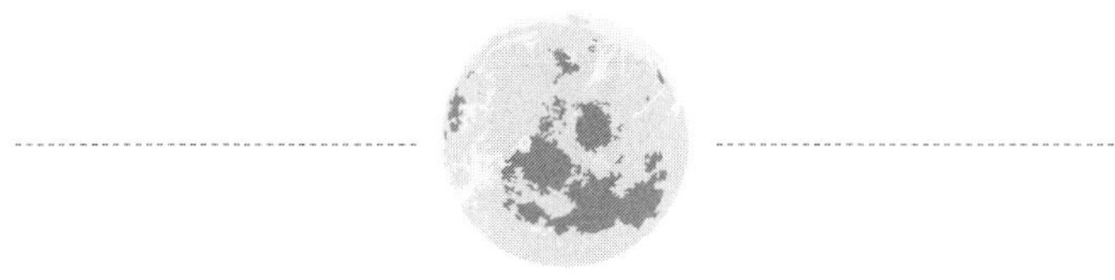

THAT WAS THEN …

We must understand history or be doomed to repeat it. At least that's the adage often repeated by historians. Being "doomed" to revisit *Battlestar Galactica* decades after the original series isn't such a bad idea, especially when Ronald D. Moore and David Eick became determined to "reimagine," not just "repeat" or "remake," the original. So to better understand the popularity of and creativity within Moore's and Eick's *Battlestar Galactica*, we should know something about its famous predecessor, Glen A. Larson's original series of the same name.

Battlestar's history is long and sometimes convoluted but always interesting. Those who enjoyed the 1978–79 series initially feared changes to the characters and story they remembered and loved, but the new series has won over some original series fans while gaining a large new audience. Especially during the 2000-era version's introduction, many fans of the earlier series scorned the new as "GINO"—*Galactica* in Name Only. Websites decried the new series for destroying a sci-fi favorite, especially when its most beloved character, Starbuck, was turned into a woman. (More about that later, both in this chapter and Ewan Kirkland's.) Why did—and do—so many fans care about a late 1970s series that has long since been superseded with better science fiction, especially in the quality of special effects and depth of characterization? With a widely acclaimed reimagined version available on the Sci Fi Channel (and on DVD), why not let the old series quietly die?

But that hasn't happened. If anything, the original series' release on DVD and its continuing syndication (including periodic broadcasts on the Sci Fi Channel) have increased its popularity, especially with a new audience wondering what all the fuss was about. In 2003, the newly released DVD set of the original series, *Battlestar Galactica: The Complete Epic Series*, received critics' and fans' applause; in 2004, it was nominated for a Saturn award for Best DVD Television Release. The original obviously still holds a fond place in fandom and TV history. To appreciate the new series, with its nods to the original as well as its many changes from it, we should first look at *Battlestar*'s long history, which, perhaps surprisingly for its short run on ABC, now spans almost thirty years on screen and in print.

The Original Series

During its one-season lifespan (1978–1979), the original *Battlestar Galactica* developed quite a loyal fan following. Much of that fandom resulted from Dirk Benedict's winning portrayal of Starbuck, the handsome, charismatic "bad boy" who wasn't too bad and usually came out a winner. He played cards, smoked cigars, enjoyed a drink, and liked to look at the ladies, even if his encounters with Athena and Cassiopeia remained chaste by current TV standards. (TV execs even required a steamy early scene between Starbuck and Cassiopeia be reshot so that his shirt remained on while the couple canoodled in a launch tube.)[1] Starbuck was one of the great TV characters that season, so popular that long after the series ended and Benedict went on to other roles, most notably in *The A-Team*, fans wanted more.

Of course, the series initially was pitched to maximize more than just a good-looking cast of young actors. *Star Wars* played a huge role in getting this sci-fi space drama off the ground;

Battlestar looked much more like the action-adventure, buddy drama (with lighthearted moments) of *Star Wars* than TV predecessors *Star Trek* (1966–1969) or lesser-watched but still fan-friendly *Lost in Space* (1965–1968). An October 1978 *Us* cover story explained ABC's high hopes for the series:

> Early on, the network converted it [from a seven-hour miniseries] to a weekly series. A two-hour version of 'Galactica' opened in Canada in a north-of-the-border sneak preview—and without fanfare grossed a healthy $3.8 million in two months. ABC bet a record $7 million—for the first seven hours—that the phenomenon of the smash film *Star Wars* could be converted into a small-screen spectacular.[2]

The theatrical version, later released in the U.S. and Europe, also brought in healthy ticket sales throughout 1979.

As creator Glen A. Larson admitted,[3] *Battlestar* wouldn't have been possible without the success of *Star Wars*. The new series even used the movie's special effects studio, leased from 20th Century FOX, and hired *Star Wars*' special-effects genius John Dykstra. (The reimagined *BSG*, in the same vein, used the same FX house as Joss Whedon's *Firefly*.) FOX also sued ABC and Universal for copyright infringement,[4] a lawsuit later settled and now mostly forgotten. Today's *Battlestar Galactica* is far more modern in content and tone than anything in the *Star Wars* franchise, but back in 1978, the comparison seemed much stronger to fans and studios.

Apollo and Starbuck in some ways resembled Luke Skywalker and Han Solo, with the link between Starbuck and Solo especially strong: Both are lovable rogues who often get into and out of scrapes because of their charm; they love the ladies but find romance baffling at times; they are daring pilots who end up becoming freedom fighters; they enjoy scheming and frequently attempt shady dealings but are more entrepreneurs than pirates or scoundrels. Some critics, however, considered Starbuck and Apollo space cowboys more along the lines of "an extraterrestrial Butch Cassidy and the Sundance Kid."[5] In fact, a few years earlier, Larson had been accused of "borrowing" the premise for his buddy Western series *Alias Smith and Jones* (1971–1973) from the hit *Butch Cassidy* (George Roy Hill, 1969); Larson's ability to develop small-screen ideas from big-screen hits brought a touch of the space epic and the Western to *Battlestar*.

Like many science fiction series before it, *Battlestar Galactica* could've been a space Western—hadn't *Star Trek* creator Gene Roddenberry first pitched his series as "*Wagon Train* to the stars"?[6] People traveling into a new (to them) frontier, facing unknown dangers along the trek—whether in the American West or outer space—has enduring televisionary appeal. Part of *Battlestar*'s initial appeal included the casting of Lorne Greene, former patriarch of the Ponderosa, as Commander Adama. Greene led the refugees with the same serious, gentle, but commanding presence he displayed as Pa Cartwright. ABC likely anticipated another *Bonanza* with *Battlestar Galactica*; both were Sunday night series meant for the whole family, although *Battlestar* would be marketed as more of a children's program.

Fans today, even those who loved the series back in 1978–79, often find these early special effects and storylines cheesy; in hindsight, especially after the reimagined series gained popularity, the original series seems ancient TV history, hardly relevant either to modern sociopolitical situations or the expected quality of TV dramas. Like such fondly remembered but often laughable (by current standards) series as *Buck Rogers in the 25th Century* (1979–1981, also a Larson production) or *Lost in Space*, which never gained the number of fans or respect accorded classic *Star Trek* or its first, best spin-off *Star Trek: The Next Generation* (1987–1994), *Battlestar Galactica* nevertheless captured fans' imagination because of its story.

Like *Star Wars*, people—in this case the sole survivors of the human race—are threatened by an evil empire seeking to wipe out anyone in its way. In the *Star Wars* saga, a few stalwart individuals, among them Obi-wan Kenobi, Luke Skywalker, Princess Leia, and, eventually, Han Solo and Chewbacca, take a stand against the empire and, against all odds, win their freedom and that of all other species downtrodden by the evil regime. *Battlestar* made this basic concept more personal. The "rag-tag fleet fleeing Cylon tyranny" pulled together to search for Earth, a planet from legend or scripture (take your pick) where other humans may have settled. Just as fangirls and fanboys believed in the possibility of a *Star Wars* (with lots of teens seriously acting out their Jedi-wannabe fantasies), *Battlestar*'s premise suggested that humans on Earth aren't alone—other species, perhaps even more beings just like us, travel across galaxies and might one day show up at our door. That premise was appealing to those who grew up during the late 1950s and 1960s' space race, stayed up late to witness the moon landing on television, and watched *Star Trek*'s first-run or syndicated episodes.

Even TV critics and industry pros praised *Battlestar Galactica*. Its sole season garnered several technical nominations: Saturn Award for Best Costumes (1980), American Cinema Editors (the "Eddie") for Best Edited Television Special (1979), even a Grammy (1979) for Best Album or Original Score Written for a Motion Picture or Television Special. Although the series didn't win in these categories, professionals across the industry recognized the quality of many different aspects of the series' production. In 1979 the series did well at the more prestigious Emmy Awards. The pilot episode, "Saga of a Star World," won an Emmy for Outstanding Individual Achievement—Creative Technical Crafts, and former *Star Wars* special-effects guru Dykstra was one member of the team picking up the award. Jean-Pierre Dorléac won an Emmy that year for Outstanding Costume Design for a Series, and *Battlestar* was also nominated for Outstanding Art Direction for a Series.

As with most science fiction series, *Battlestar Galactica* received more critical recognition for its technical merits, but at least a few actors weren't overlooked.[7] In 1979 Richard Hatch (Apollo) received a Golden Globe Best Actor nomination, and the series was nominated as Best TV Series—Drama. Little Boxey, Noah Hathaway, also received a Young Artists Award nomination as Best Juvenile Actor in a TV Series or Special.[8]

The series developed such a following that fans and *Battlestar Galactica*'s actors believed it was a shoo-in for renewal. At a 2000 Vulkon convention, Laurette Spang (Cassiopeia) recalled during a fan Q&A session that she was shocked at the cancellation. She first learned of it by watching an entertainment news program while on a family visit to Michigan; she fully expected to be back in her role for the next season.[9] The final episode, "The Hand of God," ends with the promise that Earth isn't all that far away; Apollo, searching the universe for some signal from other humans, leaves his observation post moments before Neil Armstrong's famous moon-landing pronouncement finally makes it across space and time to *Galactica*. On the personal front, Starbuck and Cassiopeia seem well established as a "dating" couple, and Sheba finally musters enough courage to really kiss Apollo. The series seemed ready to take on a new season and open storylines for more character development; the last episode hardly provided a satisfying conclusion.

Like Spang, fans felt a definite lack of closure. Unfortunately, ABC chose to solve the problem with a weak spin-off, *Galactica 1980*. In this even shorter-lived series, Boxey, now known by his grown-up name of Captain Troy, tries to act much like his father Apollo (who is not in this series). Lorne Greene reprised his role as Adama, as did a few others from the original series: Herbert Jefferson, Jr. (Boomer) and, in one memorable guest appearance, Dirk Benedict (Starbuck). In this series, the would-be colonists find Earth and have to 1) learn to mingle with the natives like normal earthlings and 2) protect the planet from Cylons while trying to be as unobtrusive as possible. The spin-off never caught on, but some episodes, including the Starbuck special, were more generally appreciated. This series' final episode (number 10), "The Return of Starbuck," revealed what happened to most fans' favorite Viper pilot. Marooned on a planet with no hope of rejoining the fleet, Starbuck eventually becomes friends with an abandoned Cylon centurion he nicknames Cy. Starbuck even gains a makeshift family, a pregnant woman who gives birth to his "spiritual son," and the former warrior then protects his new family from invading Cylons. After he manages to help the woman and child later escape the planet, Starbuck is once more alone.

As with the original series, *Galactica 1980* lacked a clear ending. The Starbuck episode seemed poised to take the story in a new direction, one badly needed after the series floundered once *Galactica* found Earth. Book and comic series, as well as competing visions of what *Battlestar* should be if it returned to television, gave fans hope for a better conclusion in the future.

Novels and Novelizations

While *Battlestar Galactica* and *Galactica 1980* were still on the air, series creator Glen A. Larson began publishing a series of novelizations that ultimately kept the story before fans in one form or another from 1978–1988. Berkley Science Fiction published fourteen official novelizations, the first books arriving in stores shortly after ABC broadcast the episodes on which they were based. The book series, however, long outlasted both TV series.

The novelizations carried a fine authorial pedigree. Larson not only created the series but wrote several episodes. His novelizations have also been reprinted as "classic" paperbacks, the latest reissued in 2003. As well as directing episodes, Donald Bellisario also wrote some of the original series' scripts, which formed the basis of a few early novelizations; he went on to create more military-themed series such as *JAG* and *NCIS* but made his greatest contribution to sci-fi television with *Quantum Leap*.

The first few books closely followed the plot of original series episodes: *Battlestar Galactica* (the pilot episode and theatrical movie with additional scenes); *Battlestar Galactica 2: The Cylon Death Machine* (based on the two-part episode "The Gun on Ice Planet Zero," albeit with a sexy space opera cover showing three warriors who bear little resemblance to the series' actors); *Battlestar Galactica 3: The Tombs of Kobol* (based on the episode "Tombs of Kobol" but also more directly reflecting the series with cover art of TV's Apollo and Starbuck in action poses); and *Battlestar Galactica 4: The Young Warriors* (based on the episode "The Young Warriors" and showcasing an intriguing cover of Apollo firing a weapon and a young woman and unicorn in the background). By the time the fifth novelization, *Galactica Discovers Earth*, was published, the books moved into *Galactica 1980* territory and summarized key events from several spin-off episodes. Table 1 lists the official novelizations and other novels written by Richard Hatch, who played Apollo in the 1978–79 series.

TABLE 1. *BATTLESTAR GALACTICA* (ORIGINAL SERIES) NOVELS AND NOVELIZATIONS

Title	Author(s)
Originally published 1978-1988, official publications from a division of parent studio Universal	
Battlestar Galactica	Glen A. Larson & Robert Thurston
Battlestar Galactica 2: The Cylon Death Machine	Glen A. Larson & Robert Thurston
Battlestar Galactica 3: The Tombs of Kobol	Glen A. Larson & Robert Thurston
Battlestar Galactica 4: The Young Warriors	Glen A. Larson & Robert Thurston

Title	Author(s)
Battlestar Galactica 5: Galactica Discovers Earth	Glen A. Larson & Michael Resnick
Battlestar Galactica 6: The Living Legend	Glen A. Larson & Nicholas Yermakov
Battlestar Galactica 7: War of the Gods	Glen A. Larson
Battlestar Galactica 8: Greetings from Earth	Glen A. Larson & Ron Goulart
Battlestar Galactica 9: Experiment in Terra	Glen A. Larson
Battlestar Galactica 10: The Long Patrol	Glen A. Larson & Ron Goulart
Battlestar Galactica 11: The Nightmare Machine	Glen Larson & Robert Thurston
Battlestar Galactica 12: Die Chameleon	Glen Larson
Battlestar Galactica 13: Apollo's War	Glen Larson & Robert Thurston
Battlestar Galactica 14: Surrender the Galactica!	Glen Larson & Robert Thurston
Novels not affiliated with Universal or their publishing subsidiaries but based on the original series	
Battlestar Galactica: Armageddon	Richard Hatch
Battlestar Galactica: Warhawk	Richard Hatch
Battlestar Galactica: Resurrection	Richard Hatch & Stan Timmons
Battlestar Galactica: Rebellion	Richard Hatch & Alan Rodgers
Battlestar Galactica: Destiny Paradise	Richard Hatch & Brad Linaweaver
Battlestar Galactica: Paradise	Richard Hatch & Brad Linaweaver
Battlestar Galactica: Redemption	Richard Hatch

The novels and novelizations from the original *Battlestar Galactica* span more than three decades, and a new batch of novels provide further adventures of characters from the reimagined version. Characters from the new series, such as Laura Roslin, are featured in a recent book series.

Then there are the comic books launched by Dynamite Entertainment in 2006, featuring the original series' characters and those in the new series.[10] A single-issue special about the *Pegasus*, published in October 2007, preceded the Sci Fi Channel's *Razor* special episode of November 2007. By late 2007, Dynamite Entertainment had released several titles related to both series: *Battlestar Galactica*, *Classic Battlestar Galactica*, *Battlestar Galactica Zarek*, *Battlestar Galactica Origins*, *Battlestar Galactica Season Zero*, and *Battlestar Galactica: Cylon Apocalypse*, in addition to the *Pegasus* issue. The comic series features film, TV, and comics writers, including Marvel's rising star, Greg Pak, and Javier Grillo-Marxuach, acclaimed TV scriptwriter (recently of *Lost*) and author of Viper Comics' The Middleman series, as well as those in the know behind the scenes, such as *Battlestar Galactica*'s writer's assistant Kevin Fahey.[11] Although these additional print stories have helped satisfy fans' appetite for more *Battlestar*, nothing could compare to more video versions of the rag-tag fleet's adventures. Fans held out hope for a return to the series or at least a new movie.

Multiple Potential TV Series or Films

Even with the demise of the original series and spin-off, *Battlestar Galactica* stayed alive through publications and fan activities, including convention appearances by various actors. Even more significantly, Richard Hatch became determined to keep the series alive or, better yet, bring it back in a new form. As *Starlog* noted in 2005, Hatch "has worked tirelessly to keep the show in the public eye through novels, comic books and an attempt to revive the show with the original cast members."[12]

Hatch's novels moved the story forward in time and further developed the major characters. His interest (some would say obsession) in the series focused on bringing back the characters twenty-five years after the original series' time frame (roughly corresponding to the actors' ages in the present), as well as introducing the next generation of *Galactica* crew. His efforts culminated in a four-and-a-half-minute video that he showed to fans during conventions. Hatch even involved John Colicos (the original Baltar), whose death a few months after filming made the rough trailer even more poignant.[13] Hatch's efforts ultimately were in vain, but they illustrated his and fans' deep interest in reviving the series.

Part of Hatch's problem was bad timing; Glen Larson also wanted to make a new series at about the same time Hatch funded his short film. Whereas Hatch primarily was an actor-turned-writer-turned filmmaker, Larson's expertise spanned years in television as a producer, writer, director, and composer; he created dozens of series, including science fiction such as the previously mentioned *Buck Rogers in the 25th Century*, *Knight Rider* (a series redeveloped in 2007), and *The Six Million Dollar Man* (whose spin-off, *The Bionic Woman*, is another series the new *Battlestar*'s Eick "reimagined" for television in 2007). A 1999 *Cinescape* article summarized the competition with its announcement that Glen Larson and *Wing Commander* producer Todd Moyer planned "to shoot a $40 million film based on the infamous television program. Meanwhile, series star Richard Hatch (Capt. Apollo) is trying to entice Hollywood with his own BG project, which he calls *Battlestar Galactica: Second Coming*."[14]

Larson's project centered on what happened to the *Pegasus*, an undeveloped plot possibility from the original series. (Interestingly, Sci Fi Channel's special episode between Seasons Three and Four of *Battlestar Galactica* also focused on the *Pegasus*.) Larson's *Pegasus* story in the original series introduced

Admiral Cain, played by Lloyd Bridges, in a two-part episode, "The Living Legend." As is typical of Moore and Eick, who like gender-switching characters, Admiral Helena Cain is portrayed by Michelle Forbes in the later series. In both series the commanders take charge of the fleet from Adama, but Bridges' Cain, and the *Pegasus*, disappear during a battle and aren't heard from again (in that series, at least). Forbes' Cain suffers a more violent end—murdered by Gina, a Six—but she receives more screen time in *Razor*, explaining just what happened onboard *Pegasus* after the first Cylon attack and before its reunion with the *Galactica*. Because Larson's movie never was made, his story of the *Pegasus* remains a mystery to fans, but in 1999, his version was the one fans eagerly awaited.

Despite Hatch's enthusiasm for his own movie or TV series, it too would never be made. After all, Universal and Larson, not Hatch, owned the rights to the characters and had a much more likely chance of bringing them back. Obviously, Moore and Eick, after some wrangling over Larson's rights as the original series creator, became the winners in this competition, and their vision differed from both Larson's and Hatch's.

GINO or Brilliant Reimagining?

For better or worse, how does the Moore-Eick version created for the Sci Fi Channel, beginning in 2003, compare with the Larson version created for ABC in 1978? Some obvious character similarities and changes are shown in Table 2. (See Chapter 2 for a detailed comparison of the original pilot episode/theatrical movie and the new pilot miniseries, as well as changes to Baltar, and Chapter 3 for a fuller explanation of Moore and Eick's series development.)

Table 2. Characters in Glen Larson's Original *Battlestar Galactica* and David Eick and Ronald D. Moore's Reimagined *Battlestar Galactica*

Original Character Name	Starbuck	Apollo
Originally Played By	Dirk Benedict	Richard Hatch
Revised Character Name	Kara Thrace, call sign Starbuck	Lee Adama, call sign Apollo
Now Played By	Katee Sackhoff	Jamie Bamber
First Incarnation	Charming card-playing, cigar-smoking, fun-loving womanizer who is also an ace Viper pilot; gender: male	Charming if standoffish Viper captain, excellent pilot, Adama's son, Serina's husband (briefly), Boxey's stepfather, Sheba's "boyfriend"
Reincarnation	Card-playing, cigar-smoking, hard-drinking, hard-partying manizer who is also an ace Viper pilot; gender: female	Charming if self-doubting Viper pilot (frequent CAG, promoted and demoted at various times from major to commander), Commander Adama's son, Dee's husband, Kara's sometimes lover

Original Character Name	Commander Adama	Colonel Tigh
Originally Played By	Lorne Greene	Terry Carter
Revised Character Name	Bill Adama, former call sign Husker	Saul Tigh
Now Played By	Edward James Olmos	Michael Hogan
First Incarnation	Paternal commander, member of the governing Colonial council, father of three, serious but gentle	Adama's friend and advisor, generally a background character, race: African-American
Reincarnation	Fearsome commander, father of two, military strategist and leader of the Colonial fleet, counselor to the president	Adama's friend and advisor, a major character, a hard-drinking man who has difficulty making sound command decisions, revealed to be a Cylon, race: Caucasian

Original Character Name	Athena	Cassiopeia
Originally Played By	Maren Jensen	Laurette Spang
Revised Character Name	Sharon Agathon, renamed call sign Athena	N/A
Now Played By	Grace Park	N/A
First Incarnation	Adama's daughter, Apollo's sister, Starbuck's sometimes "girlfriend"; *Galactica*'s communications officer	First a socialator, then a nurse/counselor, always with an eye for Starbuck
Reincarnation	Cylon, a Viper pilot who chooses a new name to establish a new persona, although this Sharon/Athena looks just like the former Sharon/Boomer	N/A

Original Character Name	Sheba	Boomer
Originally Played By	Anne Lockhart	Herbert Jefferson, Jr.
Revised Character Name	N/A	Sharon Valerii, call sign Boomer
Now Played By	N/A	Grace Park
First Incarnation	Commander Cain's daughter (Cain was a man in this version), ace Viper pilot, Apollo's "girlfriend"	Starbuck's and Apollo's friend, an ace Viper pilot, but still a background character, gender: male, race: African-American
Reincarnation	N/A	A Raptor pilot, an activated "sleeper" Cylon who attempts to kill Commander Adama, killed on board *Galactica* only to download her consciousness into another body, gender: female, race: Asian

Original Character Name	Jolly	Boxey
Originally Played By	Tony Swartz	Noah Hathaway (as an adult character in Galactica 1980 played by Kent McCord)
Revised Character Name	Call sign Jolly	Boxey
Now Played By	N/A	Connor Widdows
First Incarnation	Background character, a Viper pilot	Serina's son, Apollo's step-son, a cute child best known for playing with his pet daggit and getting into trouble
Reincarnation	Only mentioned in Starbuck's communication, obviously another Viper pilot but without other character development	Appearing in only three episodes, a boy Boomer rescues from Caprica shortly after the Cylon attack

Original Character Name	Serina	Baltar
Originally Played By	Jane Seymour	John Colicos
Revised Character Name	N/A	Dr. Gaius Baltar
Now Played By	N/A	James Callis
First Incarnation	Widowed during the Cylon attack, falls in love with Apollo shortly after the exodus, becomes his wife before dying in another Cylon attack; listed as a reporter from Caprica in the pilot episode's novelization	Traitor who collaborates with the Cylons in the hopes of being made ruler of the humans surviving the Cylon attack, beheaded by the Cylons in the revised pilot–theatrical movie, living with the Cylons (and occasionally the humans) throughout the TV series
Reincarnation	The closest character to Serina would be D'Anna Biers (Lucy Lawless), a Cylon masquerading as a human reporter who makes a documentary about *Galactica*'s pilots.	Cylon collaborator whose guilt or innocence is frequently debated throughout the series, lives with the Cylons at different points in the story, a brilliant researcher, literally a Cylon lover

These changes to individual characters also changed the series' tenor and emphasis. Alterations to characters' vocabulary and theme music further separated the new from the old and helped shift *BSG* from a sometimes corny family series into a hard-edged adult drama.

Watching Their Language

To make the original series more "sci fi," *Battlestar Galactica* introduced TV audiences to words from the Colonial vocabulary: *felgarcarb* ("bs"), *daggit* (dog), *yaron* (year), and the ever-popular *frak* (f***). Time measurements included *centons* (minutes) and *centars* (hours), as well as the aforementioned *yaron*. Although the vocabulary of non-English words was limited, variations made characters sound more like they came from outer space than next door: Cassiopeia affectionately referred to lover/client Cain as an "old war-daggit," and calling someone's comments "daggit dribble" indicated serious doubt about the speaker's veracity.

The absence of most of these words in the reimagined version—except for the frequently used *frak*, which now has entered the modern lexicon[15]—makes it seem less hardcore science fiction and more typical drama. Although the original additions to Colonial vocabulary may have been superficial and, yes, cheesy, they had been another way to make *Battlestar Galactica* science fiction, its characters literally a world away from viewers; the story could be more epic if its battle glories against a fearsome enemy and its quest for a new home took place in a distant place and time, more like the stuff of *Star Wars* or the legendary quests scrutinized by Joseph Campbell.

One more change, this time in catchphrases, also signals a shift in the respective series' tone. The Cylon mantra, "By your command," typically ended a conversation between a lower-level Cylon and his superior. The Imperious Leader reigned supreme, and his command took precedence over any other programming. In fact, the 1979 *Encyclopedia Galactica: From the Fleet Library Aboard the Battlestar Galactica* calls the Cylons "computers," further indicating their mindless adherence to a fixed set of rules. Artificial intelligence, especially among the Centurions, wasn't evident. Blind allegiance to an authority, in this case the Imperious Leader (which is an interesting title choice itself), became the norm for the Cylon empire.

The new series gives us a very different breed of Cylons sharing governance via a council and often debating just what they should do; they obviously are self aware and plot or take orders according to personal choice. Even individual models, such as the Threes, Sixes, or Eights most often shown, invite individuals to think on their own and display some personality differences (e.g., baby Hera recognizes her biological mother, even though other "Sharons" look just like her). "By your command" would be a laughable catchphrase for these Cylons.

The new series' human affirmation "So say we all" indicates humanity's attempt to indicate unity. As the series progresses, it is used to help reinforce a democracy, although this rallying cry often belies dissent bubbling just below the surface. Its origin is primarily religious, to indicate believers' unified agreement with their scriptures. Because the language is inclusive and indicates common agreement, military- and politically savvy Adama co-opts this phrase; he uses it to pull everyone together at key times. It becomes a group chant, an invigorating cheer, a political statement.

Both catchphrases are used for political conformity. The early series uses "By your command" to indicate almost a "heil Hitler" allegiance to a dictator kept in power by military might—rhetoric being just one more way to keep the troops in line. Although a similar argument might be made for the way military leader Adama uses "So say we all" to unify civilians and military personnel under appointed-later-elected President Roslin, the new series' rhetoric at least attempts to be inclusive, uniting people who may (and sometimes do) choose to shift their allegiance from one politician to another.

Music Sets the Tone

Star Wars is well known for its rousing main fanfare composed by John Williams for the original 1977 film. The multiple award-winning soundtrack[16] for *Star Wars*, later renamed *A New Hope*, ushered in a new sound for movies, especially those epic in scope.

To emulate *Star Wars* in music as well as story, the original *Battlestar Galactica* employed a similarly "large" orchestral theme with a fanfare well known to series fans; it too is still iconic thirty years later to sci-fi aficionados. Composer Stu Phillips, who worked frequently with Larson during the 1970s and 1980s on *Buck Rogers in the 25th Century*, *Knight Rider*, and *Galactica 1980*, created the opening and closing themes, with Lorne Greene's deeply authoritative voiceover intoning "Fleeing the Cylon tyranny, the last battlestar, *Galactica*, leads a rag-tag fleet toward a shining planet known as Earth." The effect was indeed the stuff of cinematic epic.

The reimagined series radically departs from trumpet fanfares and large orchestras in its more minimalist music. Like costuming, lighting, and settings, the music helps create a much darker, bleaker atmosphere better suited to chaos in a post-9/11 world. Although composer Richard Gibbs does introduce strings for some heart-tugging moments, the main theme is hardly something that fans hum after seeing the miniseries, even if the music does infiltrate their minds. Gibbs' *Battlestar* is eerie and haunting, with a distinctly Middle Eastern-sounding series of chord progressions or the odd tone standing out among softly wailing/moaning voices. His soundtrack mirrors current sociopolitical angst, distinct from Phillips' upbeat "of course we'll win" orchestration. The difference in soundtracks also illustrates the composers' different backgrounds: veteran TV composer Phillips also scored, among other shows, *The Monkees* (in the mid-1960s), whereas Gibbs played keyboard with New Wave band Oingo Boingo (in the early 1980s) and worked with bandmate Danny Elfman, who also successfully entered the world of TV and film composing, becoming a major, thrice-Oscar-nominated figure, perhaps best known for his themes for *The Simpsons* and *Desperate Housewives* and his collaborations with Tim Burton.

The completely different musical themes become evident in the miniseries "tribute" to the old: as the about-to-be-decommissioned *Galactica* makes one last public appearance, the old TV theme heralds its arrival. (In a later episode, "Final Cut" [2.8], D'Anna Biers uses the old *Galactica* theme in the background of her documentary about life onboard.) Although the re-introduction of the original fanfare most likely was meant as a fond tribute to the original series, its style, like the battlestar about to become a museum piece, seems far out of date and at odds with the darker ambiance of the reimagined series.

Out with the Old, In with the New: Significant Changes to Canon

Beyond these (to most fans) less significant changes, the primary differences discerned by fans and critics center around changes to Starbuck and the mythology itself.

Discrepancies in canon between old and new (e.g., Cylons as reptilian-based species/Cylons created by humans) can't be easily explained away, and so fans who embrace *Galactica*'s second coming either ignore these changes or, across the decades, have forgotten them. Even Larson, who might be expected to object to some serious literary license taken with his original series' scripts, was brought into the fold with a writer's credit,[17] even if it took litigation to do so. The Writers Guild of America awarded Larson a "consultant" credit as the writer on whose work the original story is based; he also is listed as a "consulting producer" for the series.[18]

The following sections detail the more important changes

made to the original series and provide the rest of the story for those familiar with only the Moore-Eick version.

Changes to the Original Characters

The biggest (and most widely publicized) change for fans of the original series was to Starbuck's gender. Of course, in hindsight, Kara "Starbuck" Thrace is her own woman and a highly watchable character in her own right, not merely a shadow of her male predecessor; the development of Kara/Starbuck during *Battlestar*'s first three seasons took the character far beyond what Larson or Benedict was able to do in a single season.

Sure, both characters drink, swear, play cards, and carouse, but, like the general tone of the original series, Benedict's Starbuck is much more innocent, his fights bloodless, his lust contained, and his charm maximized. Certainly part of that apparent "innocence" came from ABC executives concerned about making the program less adult and more child friendly; as well, ABC as a national network could (and still can) get away with far less graphic depiction of any adult activity than cable-network Sci Fi. In contrast, for many reasons, Sackhoff's Starbuck seems far from innocent although still capable of vulnerability, but all her activities are portrayed more graphically, and she has been given far more to do.

Boomer and Cain also changed from male to female characters during the reimagining, but fans didn't seem to notice or care. Furthermore, Boomer and Tigh shifted from African-American characters to Asian and Caucasian, respectively, but again, fans didn't protest. Grace Park (Boomer) confided that she almost wished she had faced some of the same backlash as Katee Sackhoff (Starbuck) in the series' early days: "I don't think I experienced any backlash at all. ... I feel very spared and very lucky in that way. But I also feel bad I didn't get to share that burden with [Sackhoff]—it was just all her."[19] Like Sackhoff, Park wasn't familiar with the earlier series and thus was never tempted to model her character on the old Boomer.

Although former Starbuck Dirk Benedict at first seemed all right with changes to the character he brought to life, posing (appropriately) with Sackhoff at a Starbucks, later he bitterly complained about the female Starbuck as only one example of the many (he felt) detrimental changes from the original series. In a well-written diatribe that he later admitted got him in trouble,[20] Benedict fired an angry salvo toward the reimagined *Battlestar*:

> [W]hat a problem the original Starbuck created for the re-imaginators. Starbuck was all charm and humor and flirting without an angry bone in his womanizing body. Yes, he was definitely 'female driven', but not in the politically correct ways of Reimagined Television. What to do, wondered the Re-imaginators? Keep him as he was, with a twinkle in his eye, a stogie in his mouth, a girl in every galaxy? ... He would stick out like, well like a jock strap in a drawer of thongs. ... It matters not to Suits [television executives and businesspeople] if it is Starbuck or Stardoe, if the Cylons are robots or lingerie models, if the show is full of optimism and morality or pessimism and amorality. What matters is that it is marketed well ....[21]

Moore and Eick clearly had more in mind for Starbuck than they saw in the original character. Beyond the gender shift, Starbuck's personality also underwent great change. Although both Starbucks have issues with their same-sex parent, the situations and outcomes are very different. Both Starbucks serve well in the military, but each has a different perspective on his/her role there. Both are involved in love triangles that reveal different aspects of their personality and belief in love. Despite these similar situations, original Starbuck's and his reimagined counterpart's differences are even more significant than a gender switch.

The original Starbuck, introduced as an orphan, first confronts a man who might be (and later is revealed to really be) his father. In the 1970s series' episode "The Man with Nine Lives" (1.17), Starbuck meets an aging con man (played by Fred Astaire). He goes by the name Chameleon, although three men on a "blood hunt" track him down because of shady business dealings they have had with this "Captain Dmitri." By the end of the episode Cassiopeia and Chameleon know that he really is Starbuck's biological father, but Starbuck isn't yet told, leaving that option open for a follow-up episode that never took place. Viewers can see similarities in personality, if not physical resemblance, between Starbuck and his father. They share a twinkle in the eye, a healthy appreciation of women, and an urge to obfuscate during deal making. The episode's tone is family friendly: Starbuck helps save his father from the hunters on his trail, but the father also risks his life for his son. Even though he's been an absent father—in fact, Starbuck is called an orphan—Chameleon intuitively understands his son and confides to a giggling Cassiopeia that someday Starbuck will be ready to settle down. The episode concludes with Chameleon promising to be Starbuck's friend.

The 2000 series' episodes "The Farm" (2.5) and "Maelstrom" (3.17) show a very different parental dynamic between Kara "Starbuck" Thrace and her mother Socrata. Again, only one parent, the same gender as the child, is portrayed. In "The Farm," a doctor tending the wounded Starbuck (and sizing her up as a potential baby maker for the Cylons) asks about her x-rays, which indicate her fingers have been broken, more than once, in the same places. Starbuck angrily responds to the accusation that she was an abused child, but she admits she doesn't want children, a fact the doctor notes is likely if she had an abusive parent.

During "Maelstrom," audiences see her abusive childhood through a series of flashbacks and strange visions supplied by Leoben. (Kara drifts in and out of consciousness as her damaged

Raptor descends ever closer to a planet surface, and her "visions" may be of her own making, or perhaps a Cylon-instigated series of images in her mind.) Kara remembers being a child who takes revenge on her mother by playing to her greatest fear—bugs. After Kara releases a particularly nasty spider near her mother, Socrata retaliates by smashing her daughter's fingers between the door and frame. Apparently this is how Kara's fingers became broken. Flashbacks to the adult Kara show her mother's verbal abuse, which ultimately drives her away. Although she knows her mother is dying, she refuses to visit. In the "do over" created by Leoben, Kara sees her mother once more before she dies and learns that her mother really is proud of her. Her mother gives her the confidence to know she can do whatever she must to claim her destiny (which is what Leoben has wanted all along, because he says he knows exactly what Kara is meant to do).

In the new series, Starbuck only achieves a small measure of closeness through an illusion taking her back to a time before her mother's death. The situation isn't real—Kara's mother is long dead—and Starbuck herself rapidly approaches death before she gains this measure of peace regarding her relationship with her mother.

The scenes between Kara and her mother seem all too realistic; the physical (as well as career) resemblance between blonde mother and child increases the audience's awareness that, despite her protests, Kara may rightly fear growing up to be just like her mother. Although 1970s Starbuck's reunion with his father provides plenty of warm fuzzies and suggests that father and son may develop a closer relationship in the future, the 2000s Starbuck's "reunion" with her mother offers only a belated band-aid for a gaping emotional wound. Both Starbucks are products of their upbringing; both rely on Commander Adama as a father figure—but the similarities stop there. Charming rogue Starbuck merely inherits his father's tendency toward blarney; swaggering Starbuck fears she inherits her mother's dark side and tendency to drive away those who would love her.

Another difference between original and reimagined Starbucks involves their reasons for military service. Benedict's Starbuck is an ace pilot with "familial" ties to Commander Adama, Apollo, and Athena, as an unofficially adopted son, best buddy, and sometimes suitor, respectively. Nevertheless, he confides to Boomer during a trip to casino planet Carillon in the pilot episode/movie that he'd like to manage an alien "girl group"; with such a hit client, he could retire from the military. Although Starbuck does seem loyal to his friends, he lacks the "do or die" military bearing of Sackhoff's Starbuck—of course, the original series makes the Cylon peril less life threatening on a daily basis. Benedict's Starbuck isn't afraid of combat, in fact, quite the opposite—he knows he's an excellent pilot and would do just about anything to keep his friends safe. The military, however, isn't as appealing a life plan as, say, traveling across the galaxy with beautiful women and watching them perform at interstellar casinos.

Sackhoff's Starbuck loves military life, even if she bemoans its neverending level of fear and danger in the long months following the initial exodus. She doesn't quite know what to do with herself in civilian life, not only before her captivity with Leoben on New Caprica but after the second exodus and subsequent return to *Galactica*. Her identity relies on her status as a pilot. Only when she returns to *Galactica* and agrees to rejoin Adama's family (and not rebel against military decisions post–New Caprica) can she regain her true family (Apollo and Adama) and her self-esteem.

Finally, although both Starbucks have healthy sex lives, their escapades are portrayed differently and, more important, the way they perceive love greatly differs. Starbuck in 1978, not surprisingly for a primetime program broadcast on Sunday nights at 8:00 Eastern, became more of a tease than a flamboyant lover. His relationship with Cassiopeia hinted at a greater intimacy than the cameras would ever show. His primary love interest in the pilot episode wore thigh-slit clothing and showed some cleavage, as appropriate for a "socialator," a woman sanctioned for legitimate paid sexual activity, similar to *Firefly*'s Inara (a certified Companion) years later. Between the pilot and the first regular episode, however, ABC changed its mind and had Cassiopeia change into something far less revealing. Spang remembers that "Suddenly I went from having skirts up to the top of my thigh and wearing high-heel shoes to wearing a dress that went to mid-calf in tan/khaki colors. I was disappointed that there wasn't an easier transition. I didn't mind toning her down ... but I wish they had just let me be a normal woman."[22] Even if Starbuck saw a lot of action, in and out of his Viper, only a few lingering looks, hugs, and kisses indicated what else might be going on off screen.

Starbuck's sex drive survived the gender switch in 2003, but the female incarnation, like most characters in the new series, showed a great deal more flesh in much more explicit sex scenes. Wondering at her estranged husband Sam's rapid arrival on the *Galactica* after her request for a quickie, she reminds him that she has been less than a faithful wife, even as she indicates her pleasure with their recent encounter. This Starbuck has a doomed affair with Apollo: She doesn't mind adultery but won't divorce her husband, which she believes is a sin against the gods; Apollo believes a divorce would be the honest solution but doesn't want to cheat on his wife any longer. This stalemate drives them apart for a while, but eventually they again form strange love triangles. Will Kara/Starbuck ultimately choose Lee/Apollo or Sam? Will Lee stay with Dualla or return to Kara for good?

Although the 1978–79 series also features a love triangle among Athena, Starbuck, and Cassiopeia, the women mostly act jealously toward each other while Starbuck can't make up his mind which one he wants. The Sam-Kara-Lee triangle is much more graphic and realistic, although even its portrayal leaves some viewers, and Katee (Starbuck) Sackhoff, wishing that Kara would just choose one man or the other and get on with her life. During a *SciFi World* interview early in 2007, the actress said, "I actually hate the triangle. I think it's ridiculous. I wish she would just be with one of them and call it a day,"[23] adding that such a choice wouldn't be as dramatic as the way the story has played out.

Starbuck's final episode in *Galactica 1980* did little to resolve his love triangle on *Galactica*; of course, now stuck on a distant planet with little to no hope of a reunion with either Cassiopeia or Athena, his final comments indicate that he loves them both. He briefly settles down with a "wife" and "son," however unconventional the situation, but apparently ends up alone. Perhaps with the end of the new series looming in the not-so-distant future, Kara will more successfully decide if she wants to settle down into a more conventional, monogamous marriage or play the field a while longer.

Changes in Mythology

Changes to the Starbuck character provided a titillating hook to lure viewers to the new series to see what else had been changed. Although new fans could watch the reimagined series with an open mind, fans of the original series had some difficulty accepting the reimagined premise. Initially a more troubling change, especially to die-hard fans, was to the original series' mythology. Old-series fans first viewing the new miniseries soon realized that the difference in the Cylon race was more than skin deep. The reimagined series created a new backstory for the Cylons, one which provides plenty of room for dramatic confrontations as well as cautionary tales about the rise of technology. After a forty-year absence from interaction with humanity, the new Cylons emerge looking exactly like humans, especially drop-dead gorgeous women. Humanity finds itself in the precarious position of having "played god" by developing a race that later turned on them. But the creation myth wasn't the only change to the series' bible. The new Cylons govern themselves in a new hierarchy of command and, as explained later (see *Jump*: In the Name of Gods: Monotheism and Polytheism in *Battlestar Galactica*), have a well-developed monotheism in opposition to the humans' polytheistic religion. A full understanding of the scope of changes to the core story and the reimagined series' ever-developing mythology requires a look back to Larson's original concept for the 1970s series.

The Initial Mythology

The original story, in brief, is this: After "yarons" of warfare, the humans and Cylons plan to sign an armistice, one brokered by Baltar, a human from Picon who has worked closely with the Cylons. Baltar, however, has been promised his home world will be spared, paving the way for him to become ruler of the remnants of humanity after the Cylons wipe out everyone else.

Long ago, the Cylons changed their appearance in response to interactions with humanity. They first were a warlike reptilian species who, upon encountering fierce resistance from humans during early Cylon invasions, found something worthwhile to imitate in their enemy. The Cylons took robotic form to appear more human and, perhaps, also to gain strength against humanity for future warfare. The *Encyclopedia Galactica: From the Fleet Library Aboard the Battlestar Galactica* describes the original species as a "technologically advanced reptilian race from a far corner of the Galaxy. ... The key to the success of the early Cylons' conquests was their development, first of sophisticated robots, and then of fully intelligent androids. ... But ultimately, the machines became the superiors of their creators, and the Cylons themselves were destroyed by their own machines."[24]

The most common robot models are the Centurions, almost mindless soldiers with one scanning red eye, and the more advanced I-L series. Centurions fly Raiders and engage *Galactica*'s pilots in space battles; they also invade planets and are on the front lines of land-bound confrontations with humans. Some I-L series models cleverly plot political strategy in the background. The aptly named Lucifer is a devilishly "exceptional Cylon I-L computer of the I-L series that rules the Cylon Empire. His particular villainous duty is to aid the treacherous Baltar."[25] The highest level of Cylon development, and thus the ruler of all, is the Imperious Leader. A Leader showing weakness or erring in judgment, especially in the war to eradicate humanity, might be assassinated by another I-L series Cylon, who then becomes the next Imperious Leader. Baltar deals with both the I-L series and the command-obeying Centurions.

The original story explained that the Cylons and humans long fought each other; dominance of the universe (Cylon objective) and protection of humans and other species being invaded (human objective) providing the interplanetary friction for warfare. Baltar is clearly a traitor to his race who plots with Cylons for his own political ambitions; his brief appearances after the pilot movie only further his depiction as a shifty villain.

The humans' ruling council, which includes Adama, unites representatives from the twelve home worlds; Adar is the elected president. Just exactly what the council can do, other than attempt to overrule military commander Adama during the first stages of the Cylons' attack, never is revealed. Council members wear white toga-like garments, perhaps a way to invoke a link with the Greeks on Earth. After all, characters such as Apollo and Athena share names with Greek gods.

Larson also linked the Colonials' shared history with us on Earth through a suggestion that early Earth inhabitants, including the Egyptians, Aztecs, Mayans, and Toltecs, may have come from "out there," and *Galactica*'s pilots wear helmets suggesting an Egyptian, or possibly Mayan or Aztec, design. The Colonials find the pyramid-like tombs of Kobol, play Pyramid with triangle-shaped cards, and enjoy a rousing game of Triad, resembling a combination of basketball or a less deadly form of Mayan ball game. (The new series switches the names: Pyramid is the basketball-type contact sport, and Triad is the card game.) During the reimagining, these ways to make the Colonials similar to humans while remaining in the realm of science fiction were toned down or eliminated. Whereas the new series retains names like Apollo or Starbuck, they are the pilots' call signs, not their real names.

Of course, the original mythology introduced problems that limited storylines. A review of the about-to-be-canceled 1978–79 series (which had been axed by the time the article was published in September 1979) provided an in-depth consensus of fan criticisms about *Battlestar*:

> First, the humans were forced into forever running away from the Cylons ... meeting a new Cylon menace every week and just barely managing to escape. ... The *Galactica* also seems limited as to the kind of action in which it can become involved. As protector to the Colonial fleet, it cannot stray too far from the rag-tag collection of ships in its wake. It serves more as a mascot than as an explorer. ... Each character was given several facets, but there was no depth to them. They were never really hurt by their adventures; they seemed like Greek demi-gods who just ran from adventure to adventure with no problems or concerns.[26]

Not only did Moore and Eick, as well as director Michael Rymer, seek to address these flaws, but they also tried to find more ways to open the plot for what would become a multiple-season series. Character development, emphasis on modern concerns to expand the storytelling, and writing in response to viewers' real fears after a recent attack on U.S. soil necessitated making sometimes significant changes to the original characters and storylines.

Beyond the basic annihilation-of-home-worlds-exodus-to-Earth premise, the original and reimagined series do share some plot points: When Adama is injured and unable to command, Tigh steps in and realizes just how difficult command really is; the *Pegasus*, guided by Cain, joins forces with the *Galactica*, but Cain is "lost" (disappearance during battle versus death); Starbuck is lost during a mission, Adama and Apollo openly grieve Starbuck's loss, and, several episodes later, the missing pilot's whereabouts are revealed. Along the way episodes introduce the Colonials' recreational activities, including sports and card games, and legal systems as evidenced through laws and trials. The 1978 version, however, provides romance and romantic visions of life on the run; the 2003 version gets down and dirty far more often.

SPIRITUAL LEADERSHIP

The reimagined series provides far more insights into and development of the humans' religious expressions, whether they are as devout as the Gemonese (also originally portrayed as extremely conservative through their vehement opposition to socialator Cassiopeia) or as cynical but politically astute as Adama. Nevertheless, in addition to the passing mention of the gods in the original, many fans have found links between Larson's Mormon faith and other spiritual elements in *Galactica*'s mythology.

Several fans and authors have written essays linking parts of *The Book of Mormon* to *Battlestar Galactica* episodes,[27] in particular "Lost Planet of the Gods" and the novelization *Battlestar Galactica 3: Tombs of Kobol*. In name, Kobol is similar to the star Kolob in Mormon theology. Other noted similarities include the importance of free will, the role of Satan/Mephistopheles in humanity's development, and the doctrine of eternal progression, illustrated most clearly in a later episode, "War of the Gods":

> The angelic beings appear to warn the Battlestar *Galactica* crew about Count Iblis although they refuse

> to interfere in the crew's exercise of free agency. The angels also make it clear that they are simply an advanced form of humanity that all humans can aspire to. One of the angels said, "As you are now, we once were; as we are now, you may become." This is a rewording of a quote from former Mormon President Lorenzo Snow who said, "As man is, God once was; as God is, man may become."[28]

In this story arc, Count Iblis may be a demon (a form briefly illustrated when he shows the true nature of his power), a savior, or simply an alien with powers of telekinesis and telepathy, as well as a charismatic personality that helps him get others to do his bidding. Perhaps he is all these, but his presence on *Galactica* makes him a highly formidable potential leader of humanity.

As the *Encyclopedia Galactica: From the Fleet Library Aboard the Battlestar Galactica* notes, before Count Iblis (which it spells Ibley) mysteriously disappears, he has a violent confrontation with Apollo, apparently leading to Apollo's death and resurrection after another alien's intervention. In the aftermath of the confrontation, Starbuck and Sheba are transported to an unexplained location, where their uniforms are transformed from khaki to white, the color of this ethereal setting. Upon seeing Apollo's body laid upon a bier, Starbuck vows to whatever alien being can help them that he would gladly give his life for Apollo's. Perhaps this willingness to sacrifice himself for his friend moves the unknown aliens not only to restore Apollo but to help the humans on their way. Apollo, Starbuck, and Sheba return to *Galactica* "with a memory of explicit time/space coordinates that they claimed were those of the mythical planet Earth. None of the three could explain the source of these coordinates; in fact, they felt as though they were blurting them out without conscious control, as though another was speaking through them."[29]

Both the original and the reimagined series suggest divine

guidance in humanity's search for Earth, whether from a supernatural alien encounter or a magic arrow opening a hidden tomb that reveals a star map. The new series, however, moves far away from any links with the Church of Jesus Christ of Latter-Day Saints but imbues more of its own mythology with spiritual elements.

Entertainment or Art?

During a sci-fi convention in summer 2007, fans broke out in a heated argument about the value of Moore's and Eick's *Battlestar Galactica*. Several fans apparently resented this GINO version and bitterly complained that the new series, unlike the old, is not science fiction. Although its setting technically is outer space, either onboard spaceships or landside unfamiliar planets, the personal dramas take precedence over anything uniquely "sci fi." Some fans argued that if they wanted to watch a traditional drama, they'd watch shows like *The West Wing*. They want space exploration, strange aliens, out-of-this-world technology, or at least something more than they can find on Earth. They added that the new *Battlestar* is not entertaining so much as a "relevant" war or political drama.[30] In the 2000s, should *Battlestar Galactica* be more *Star Trek* or *West Wing*?

The West Wing, oddly enough, comes up frequently in discussions of what *Battlestar* now is or should be. Jamie (Apollo) Bamber described the series as "more akin to *The West Wing* or *24* than it is to *Stargate* or *Star Trek*," a fact for which he's grateful. Bamber isn't a big sci-fi fan because it often doesn't make sense to him; he doesn't "relate" to it.[31] Eick contends that having a hand-held camera or morally ambiguous characters are simply techniques of effective storytelling. "Maybe if you do that in *The West Wing* it's just great storytelling. But if you do it in a science-fiction show with a goofy title like *Battlestar Galactica*, then people will start using the term 'groundbreaking.'"[32]

Although the producers have long said that their series is

more than science fiction, it also has the opportunity to move beyond traditional dramas because its assigned genre is perceived as otherworldly. Moore admitted in 2006 that "we get a lot more freedom to play around with things than we would if we were just telling it as a straight drama. ... Even though the show has a lot of allegorical elements and metaphors and what have you, it's not a straight analogy."[33] (See "Under the DRADIS" for further discussion of *Battlestar Galactica*'s political overtones.)

Moore likes the possibilities presented by dramatic and thematically rich parallels with current sociopolitical crises. Because the *Galactica*'s situation is tough enough, Moore saw "no need to run into bumpy-headed aliens who are threatening you with lasers every week."[34] Likewise, miniseries' director Michael Rymer envisioned the series differently from most science fiction. *Battlestar Galactica* is "a very fresh and compelling human drama, which I hope transcends the sci-fi genre. We've made a very conscious attempt to open up the show to a larger audience who may be a little impatient with aliens with bumpy heads and the more fantasy-driven approach shows like *Farscape* and *Babylon 5* have taken."[35]

Even *Battlestar*'s "aliens"—the Cylons—are now human creations instead of an alien reptilian race. In many ways the new series owes more to Ridley Scott's *Blade Runner* (1982), Steven Spielberg's *AI* (2001), or Isaac Asimov's 1950 book-turned-movie *I, Robot* (2004, directed by Alex Proyas) than *Star Wars* or *Star Trek*, although the "artificial" and "robot" labels for Cylons seem racist as the series goes on. Number Six badgers Baltar to stand up for the Cylons when his human colleagues onboard *Galactica* discuss their hatred of "toasters." "Your child will be a 'toaster,'" she reminds him, a fact which both intrigues and horrifies the scientist. How strange that in this reimagined version the Cylons, once perceived as the alien enemy deserving death for their attack on Lorne Greene's people, now are the sympathetic bastard human children of very flawed parents. The enemy not only looks like us and walks among us undetected but might be us without our even knowing.

The new series certainly takes its premise from a post-9/11 world but, ironically, the 1970s version is more similar to the government's and much of the U.S. public's early response, pre–Iraq War, to the attacks. The War on Terror draws as clear a line between "them" and "us" as Greene's Adama does between the Cylons and humans. As the Iraq War loses support among the public and the War on Terror loses focus, the new *Battlestar Galactica* reflects changes in U.S. public opinion toward very real social issues—genocide, occupation, infiltration by "aliens" into a culture, terrorism, battle fatigue, and an uncertain future for humanity. As Moore reiterated, "There's plenty of drama and scary things and you just don't need to go off to the casino planet!'"[36]

The reimagined *BSG*'s determination to be socially relevant art as well as entertainment brought it lots of critical praise. Its promising pilot episode set the standards high, and the following seasons lived up to early expectations for *Battlestar*. By the beginning of Season Three, which would be a turning point in many respects for the story, the series had won "a prestigious Peabody Award and an American Film Institute Award, [had been] ranked number one on *Time* magazine's list [of] Best TV Shows of 2005 and received consistent critical gushing from publications like *Rolling Stone* and *Entertainment Weekly*."[37] According to Melanie MacFarlane, TV critic for the *Seattle Post-Intelligencer* and a member of the Peabody Award committee, "Science fiction doesn't get taken seriously because people think of it as aliens and space suits. Really great television shows comment on their times, and *Battlestar* does that."[38]

The crucial third season pushed the plot forward a year, showing the failure of the human settlement on New Caprica and the Cylon occupation of it. True to Moore's idea that *Battlestar* has to be different from other sci-fi shows but also keep evolving, Season Three storylines took a turn reminiscent of *Lost*'s Season Three examination of The Others (*Battlestar* looked more closely at the

Cylons) and *Lost*'s tendency to use flashbacks and flashforwards to bump up the stories' intensity. Whereas *Lost* chose the Season Three finale to reveal its "game changer" for its just-announced three remaining seasons, *Battlestar* leaped a year into the future at the beginning of Season Three and, later that season, the series creators announced an end to their story with Season Four. All good stories must come to an end and, like *Lost*'s creators' interviews stating that, whether characters ever get off the island, they will ultimately find themselves by the end of the series, Eick promised that the characters and their relationships will come to a decisive end point. "The show has always been about the search for Earth, and … to end the series without getting to Earth or a version of Earth or something we call Earth or having at least somebody say 'Earth' … would be unsatisfying."[39] For a "sci fi" series to be more easily compared with *The West Wing* or *Lost* doesn't seem strange to *Battlestar*'s reimaginers, who set out to tell a different kind of sci-fi story with their reimagined pilot.

From the beginning, Moore and Eick wanted to tell an "honest" story, because they prefer that type of television. If people want to call their series "groundbreaking" because it embodies certain elements, such as "morally ambiguous protagonists who don't have all the answers and aren't always right and are not there to function as role models,"[40] that's fine with them. Eick thinks that it's simply good storytelling, the type that his *Battlestar Galactica* began telling in its pilot miniseries in 2003 and finished in 2008.

* * *

Since 1978 there has been at least some print or televised version of *Battlestar Galactica* available for eagerly awaiting fans. Whether Starbuck and Apollo undertake their adventures on first-run or syndicated TV episodes or pages of novels or comic books, whether the mythologies of old and new mesh, they and the rest of the *Galactica* crew have found a lasting home in popular culture.

Chapter Two

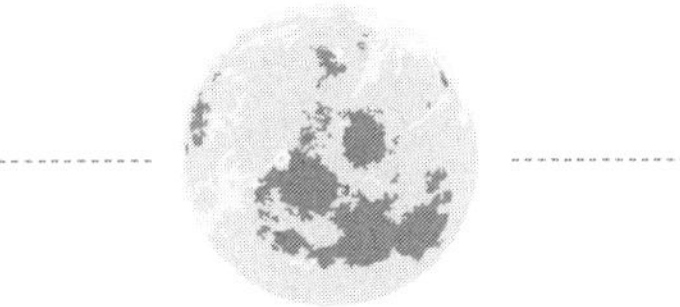

THE NEXT GENERATION: *BATTLESTAR GALACTICA* CREATOR RON MOORE REIMAGINES DEEP SPACE

—Heather E. Ash

The following, originally published in the summer of 2007 in a publication of the Writers Guild of America, offers a close encounter with the reimagined BSG's co-creator. We present it here as it originally appeared.

If you're not already watching, you've heard of it. Your friends have told you about this great show, but you can't get past the title: *Battlestar Galactica*. "That cheesy '70s show?" you ask. "Fur collars? Robotic dogs? Casino planets?"

Try suicide bombers, prisoner torture, and hot sex. This new *BSG* has an epic storyline worthy of *Hill Street Blues*, as much political intrigue as *The West Wing*, morally questionable characters like *The Sopranos*, and more nuclear explosions than *24*. It's also a critical favorite, twice selected for the American Film Institute's TV Programs of the Year, nominated for a Writers Guild Award, and winner of a Peabody.

Intrigued? Season Three comes out on DVD in August, or you can find all fifty-five episodes on iTunes. Start now and you'll catch up in time for Season Four's premiere in January without the agonizing eight-month wait for the new season that the rest of the fans will endure following Season Three's *Sixth Sense*–like finale twist.

Two days after that end, I approach series creator Ronald D. Moore's office at Universal with one thought: *I will not be a fanboy*. Never mind that Moore is responsible for a significant chunk of the *Star Trek* oeuvre, the reason I began writing for television. Never mind that we share friends and colleagues. Never mind that I'm here as a journalist. It would be inappropriate to begin an interview with, "Cylons? Are you KIDDING ME?!"

Moore's assistant, Maril, meets me at the door and hustles me into the next building. Suddenly I'm standing in the Inner Sanctum: the *BSG* writers room. Fans will understand when I say it's more like the *Galactica* CIC than the bridge of the *USS Enterprise*: Old school, baby. No table, just two couches and two armchairs shoved against the walls of a standard-size office barely large enough to hold the eight writers. No whiteboards either—index cards cover three large bulletin boards.

Moore interrupts himself mid-pitch to introduce me to the staff and then resumes the discussion. Pacing the small space, he pitches a character arc for Episode 8 that thematically, metaphorically, and visually references events in this and past episodes, including the pilot, all off the top of his head. It's impressive, but I'm distracted as I realize the bulletin boards hold the secrets of next season within their Sharpie scribbles. All my questions answered—except I don't have my glasses. I feel like Burgess Meredith in *The Twilight Zone*.

CREATED BY MAN

Science fiction writers usually can point to a singular image or passage as the genesis of their passion. For Moore, it's the *Enterprise* "cruising across the television screen" of his childhood home in Chowchilla, California. "*Star Trek* painted a noble, heroic vision of the future, and that vision became my lodestar," he wrote in a 2006 *New York Times* editorial. It wasn't until discovery of Stephen Whitfield's *The Making of Star Trek* at a school book fair that Moore's future career coordinates were set. "Reading that book was a revelatory experience for me in that it laid out the entire process by which Gene Roddenberry had pitched, sold, and created the series," says Moore. "In my fondest dreams, I hoped that when I grew up, Gene would bring *Trek* back to TV and I'd get to write for the show."

When *Star Trek: The Next Generation* premiered in 1987, Moore had flunked out of college and was crashing on a buddy's floor. His screenwriting aspirations involved little writing, until a friend arranged for him to visit the *Star Trek* set. Moore arrived on the Paramount lot with a finished *Next Generation* script and promptly handed it to the studio tour guide.

Improbably, the spec led to a pitch, which led to a staff job, and Moore spent the next decade living out his boyhood dream. After *The Next Generation* ended, he worked his way up the ranks of *Star Trek: Deep Space Nine*, co-writing two *Trek* features in the meantime. Joining *Star Trek: Voyager* as a co-executive producer was the logical continuation of his career, but Moore soon became frustrated with both the creative and professional directions of the show. He left.

He was outside *Trek* for the first time. He was also outside the creative limitations imposed by Roddenberry's heroic future, which left little room for true dramatic conflict. "I had these thoughts like, *Why can't you shoot a sci-fi show documentary style? Why can't the characters be more deeply flawed?*"

THEY EVOLVED

"*Star Trek* the franchise essentially set the gold standard for science fiction television, and everybody was trying to do the same thing," says Moore. Weird aliens, a bridge with a viewscreen, lots of technobabble; the original *Battlestar Galactica* had them all, so when exec producer David Eick approached Moore about a remake, it wasn't an obvious candidate for overhauling the genre. But Moore watched the original *Battlestar* pilot and found the basic premise resonated strongly with the recent events of 9/11. A remake would have to embrace the core conflict of humanity's fight for survival. Viewers would embrace it only if they recognized it "as if they had accidentally surfed onto a *60 Minutes* documentary piece about life aboard an aircraft carrier" instead of another spotless starship deck.

Moore outlined his vision in *Battlestar Galactica: Naturalistic Science Fiction*, what in the sci-fi community is known as Ron's Manifesto. Depending on who you ask, it's either a revolutionary call to arms or Moore biting the genre hand that fed him. The true origin is disappointingly mundane. "It was a sales document," Moore explains, written to get the network executives into a proper frame of mind for reading the pilot. Without his knowledge, the document became appended to the final script distribution, so when Edward James Olmos kept praising the first pages of the script, Moore thought he liked the teaser.

Eschewing space opera conventions means more creative freedom for the show's writers, many of them *Trek* veterans. "We can do entire shows that are about our characters where we don't feel enslaved to having the space battle of the week," says Mark Verheiden, a co-executive producer who joined the show in 2005. At the same time, the science fiction element gives them unprecedented freedom to explore the same grand, even controversial themes that routinely appear in mainstream dramas, "but because we're one step removed we can explore them even further," Verheiden says. So while an episode about abortion on network television pretty much guarantees protest calls to the FCC, the same topic on *Battlestar* might spark a flame war on the fan boards.

This does not mean that *Battlestar* is issue-driven, which was a hallmark of *Trek* storylines. Everything here stems from character, and unlike *Trek*'s shining examples of tolerant humanity, the denizens of *Battlestar Galactica* routinely violate the network maxim that all main characters must be likeable. When *Battlestar*'s President Roslin orders a prisoner's summary execution, the writers don't care that our hero just acted despicably … just that it's logical for the character. "Good people can make bad, even horrific decisions, just as bad people can make noble, even righteous ones," Moore writes in his online blog.

Such decisions can be shocking to the regular viewer, but even *Battlestar*'s writers are also routinely surprised by the sudden detours a story can take. In fact, it's a mandate, as Jane Espenson learned during her first freelance assignment: "The episode was already broken when I got here, but they said, 'Feel free to change things. Surprise Ron.'"

"So much of series television is expected," says Moore. "What I say to them is, 'I want you to tell me something about these characters I didn't know.'" Yes, it's hard to write your episode when the previous episode's writer decides to assassinate a major character (it did happen), but the willingness to go down unexpected paths is a key ingredient to the show's success … and some kick-ass season cliffhangers.

THEY REBELLED

Yes, the show is successful. DVD and iTunes sales are strong, but the Third Season audience is "soft," according to Moore, blaming it on time-shifting. Even then, he says, "the audience is not huge. It's still a cult audience when you get right down to it."

Cult audience. Raise your hand if that produces an image of a 98-pound weakling living in his parents' basement. If Hollywood really is "high school with money," then network drama sits at the cool table and God forbid it should acknowledge the science fiction kids in the corner, much less give them an Emmy.

Espenson sees this lack of respect for the genre as a problem of perception. After all, the most beloved films of all time—*E.T.*, *Wizard of Oz*, *Star Wars*—are science fiction. "What they mean when they say they don't like sci-fi is space opera, something very specific that doesn't exist anymore," she says.

Those who write for science fiction also know that these fans hold the writer in equal or higher esteem than the actors. Where else will you find complete strangers who can list your credits—by episode title—quote specific lines to you and know that you wrote those lines, not the producer who rewrote you? Maybe more writers would sit at Table Nerd if they realized how much these fans genuinely respect the craft and the power of those who practice it. And few are shut-ins; witness the fan Moore encountered in New York City. "I approached this cop and he looks at me [suspiciously] and says, 'Do I know you?' I immediately said, 'No, I don't think so,'" Moore recounts. Then Moore's wife asked the officer if he'd ever seen *Battlestar Galactica*. "The guy immediately said, 'Ron Moore, no fuckin' way!'

"I remember getting invited to conventions, and it was the only place I could imagine that a writer could stand on stage and be applauded and have people know their work," he says. He pauses. "It's one thing to go to a *Star Trek* convention—it's another thing to be stopped on the street by a cop."

Moore is remarkably free with his information. Letting journalists into the writers' room is one example. In some deep corner of the University of Southern California is an archive that contains every script, memo, production schedule, and random note Moore has amassed since he began writing for *Star Trek*. These files contain everything from *Battlestar Galactica* and every show in between—*The Making of Television by Ron Moore* writ large. The amateur historian in Moore thinks someone, somewhere, will one day find this collection as useful as he found Whitfield's book. "I can see a point where your show's website contains dailies and drafts of specs, recordings of art department meetings," he imagines. "You can see as much as you want because all this stuff is stored digitally."

An AOL folder he maintained while on *Trek* in which he answered fans' questions has evolved into a blog on the Sci Fi Channel's official *Battlestar* website. His answers to fan's questions are deeply personal, introspective descriptions of life events and his thoughts on matters private and public. He seeks to reward the fans' wonderment as his was rewarded. So when the Sci Fi Channel approached Moore about creating podcasts for the website, Moore took it beyond DVD-like commentary (recorded for every episode and meant to be listened to as the episode plays in real time)—he took the digital recorder into the writers' room. "It's one of my favorite parts of the job, and that's where so much of the show is done," he says. "I just thought it would be interesting to hear what the process is on this show."

Now anyone in the world has a front-row seat to the creative process for at least one *Battlestar* episode, a rare glimpse into the decisions, detours, and dead-ends that lead to a finished episode. Moore also takes listeners behind the scenes of production meetings, editing sessions, and "frak parties," where members of the cast and crew gather to answer fans' questions (and drink rare scotch).

So when the Sci Fi Channel approached Moore about also doing webisodes, Moore didn't hesitate to say yes. Supervising producers Bradley Thompson and David Weddle wrote ten two-minute episodes that bridged the gap between Seasons Two and Three, using regular series characters. They shot guerilla-style on standing sets because of a minuscule budget, but Thompson and Weddle found the process exhilarating. "Creatively it was so exciting to participate because you felt like it's a whole new genre and here we are on the ground floor," says Weddle.

The webisodes were in postproduction when Moore learned that NBC/Universal considered them "promotional content" and had no intention of listing credits. "I was adamant on the point: You pay people, you had to credit them." The Writers Guild stepped in on behalf of *Battlestar* and other NBC/Universal shows, but no resolution was reached. The studio took possession of the nearly finished webisodes and posted them on the website. But there were credits: Moore used his Sci Fi Channel blog to list every member of the webisode crew on his September 6, 2006, entry, "Who Did What on the Webisodes."

Moore calls me a few days after the interview. He's worried that a comment he made about first season rewrites would be misconstrued as denigrating the talents of the first season's writing staff. The rewriting was a result of him needing to figure out what *Battlestar* was going to be, not a reflection on the writers' skills. In fact, he's done little rewriting this season because the writers are doing so much "heavy lifting."

"Ron would never change a script that was really good just to have his fingerprints on it," says co-executive producer Michael Angeli. "If he has issues with what was written, he'll go off and they'll settle it together." Angeli has seen many bad things happen in rooms, with showrunners who did not respect their staffs. Not here. "You don't know how much that liberates a writer in a room when you know that even if you fail as a writer on the show, as a human being you haven't."

Moore credits his showrunning style to two men: Michael Piller and Ira Steven Behr. Piller, with whom Moore worked on *ST:TNG* and refers to as his "first father-figure in the business," passed away in 2005. Moore describes their often-contentious relationship in a moving tribute on his blog. "As much as you hated [Michael] for what he was doing to your script," Moore writes, "you could never accuse him of being a political gamesman or screwing you over, because he was so fundamentally decent." Piller's ultimate concern was making the best show possible and critiques of the material, while often blunt and abrasive, were always in service to that goal. "That imprinted on me, that trusting the integrity of the showrunner even as you were battling him," writes Moore.

He saw this again at *Deep Space Nine*, where the writers would passionately argue about a story, then go to lunch and have a great time. Moore wistfully describes it as "the tightest writing staff I've ever been on." And Behr, *DS9*'s executive producer, saw the showrunner's position as "first among equals," a quality Moore actively strives to replicate on *Battlestar*.

"You never have the sense that you can sit back, that he will ultimately step in and take care of it," says Espenson. Thompson describes him as "an Olympic coach in asking more than you think you can deliver." But the writers are eager to deliver it, because, as Weddle puts it, "you want more than anything not to disappoint Ron Moore. You just want to be able to come up to the level he's asking you to come up to."

The writers all come back to one word: *humanity*. According to Angeli, showrunners like Moore make the industry better because "they get such creative juice out of their writers, not because they intimidate them or don't give them praise. It's because they're great human beings."

They Have a Plan

When we talk, no formal announcement has been made about the show's end, but Moore says, "I'm thinking it's going to happen sooner rather than later." *Sooner* arrived May 31, with news that Season Four would be *BSG*'s last.

Moore firmly believes that *Star Trek: The Next Generation* went one season too long, and he's determined not to repeat that with *Battlestar*. As for life beyond this show, "*Battlestar Galactica* will be hard to top in many ways. The trick is to continue to do better work, to keep struggling to improve my craft." And he will continue to do so within genre bounds. He's completing the sequel to *I, Robot* and beginning a new version of the 1950s sci-fi classic *The Thing*. "In science fiction, I create all the rules," he says. "I can play around with the parameters of my drama in ways that other writers cannot."

Will *Battlestar* change the future of science fiction television, as he set out in the manifesto? Moore contemplates this. "I hope it opens up the possibilities to make things that aren't so escapist and silly and that you can use the genre for what it was initially intended to do, to make you think of those possibilities while commenting on the human condition from a different point of view. It was a challenging genre. It made you think, grapple with different concepts like contemporary fiction does. I hope we get back to that."

I thank him for letting me inside the writers' room. He gives a small nod. "I hope I don't see any of it crop up on the Internet tonight," he says, obviously not worried. We fanboys don't do that.

Chapter Three

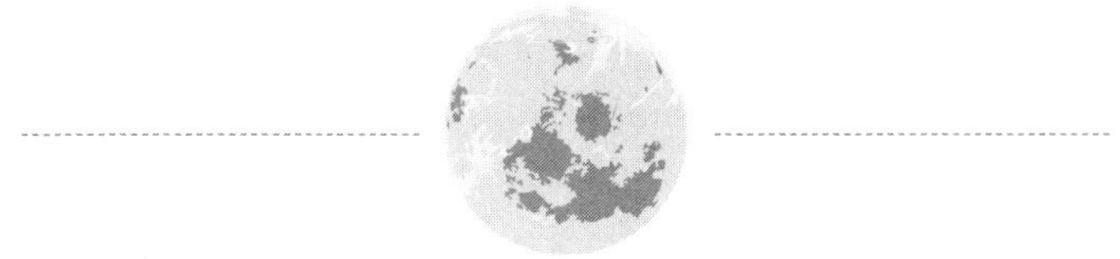

PILOTING A SERIES

Most new TV series begin with a clean slate—an idea developed into a TV pilot movie or episode that everyone involved with hopes will be picked up by a network and lead to numerous additional episodes. Even "reimagined" series often are so far removed from their original version that, even without a clean slate, much of the original has been erased from the audience's collective memory. *Battlestar Galactica* presented more of a challenge; its "pilot" episode from the original series had undergone numerous changes—and long-time fans keeping the franchise alive for more than twenty years clearly remembered each version. For anyone to create a successful pilot for the reimagined series meant not only dealing with multiple well-known variations of a beloved story but also distancing it enough to be recognized as a new entity, not merely a recycled script. A closer look at the changes and challenges from Glen Larson's pilot(s) to Ronald D. Moore's and David Eick's provides some insights into each generation's vision of what *Battlestar Galactica* should be and the unique evolution of the *BSG* saga. The differences between Larson's pilot(s) and Moore's and Eick's point to more than personal interpretations of the story; they also hint at differing ideas about what television should offer its audience and how a series reflects (U.S.) culture during its broadcast life.

Larson's original story of *Battlestar Galactica* has been slightly modified many times during its long journey from 1978 to the present. It has been a theatrical movie, an ABC-TV pilot, and multiple edited versions for syndication and DVD sales. Each slightly altered storyline renders some characters more important than others: Baltar, for example, dies or lives; Serina remains a powerful journalist or becomes a more passive mother-wife. Nevertheless, the major themes of good versus evil and the importance of family and friendship stand out in each version.

Moore and Eick's 2003 miniseries, which in effect became the pilot of the reimagined series, immediately illustrates more significant shifts in theme and tone from Glen Larson's pilot(s). These shifts not only indicate a different initial purpose for each series (beyond winning audience rating share and thus more revenue), but, as noted in Chapter 1, suggest different places for each series within the history of sci-fi or television in general.

In any epic, or a series striving to maintain enough mythology to become epic sci-fi television, battles between good and evil, whether between warring species or within a character, become a crucial part of the story. Larson's pilot emphasizes great outer space battles between a cold, reptilian-turned-metallic race imitating humans and the warm-blooded, freedom-loving, romantic but fallible remnants of humanity. Moore and Eick's does not; it focuses on characters far more often than battles and presents a less unified front. Their conflicted characters deal with crises far differently than the original *Galactica* crew. Larson's pilot clearly establishes the distinction between aliens and humans, as well as the line between evil and good; Moore and Eick's lets audiences grapple with those issues.

Although the 1970s might be better remembered for disco, *Star Wars*, and fluffier ABC-TV series like *Happy Days*, this era also echoed the Cold War, the aftermath of Vietnam, and Watergate. Nevertheless, the emphasis in U.S. television in the late 1970s was less on global warfare and dirty politics than family-friendly fantasy entertainment, with only a peripheral awareness of global changes, including increased U.S. relations with China and a tentative peace agreement between Israel and Egypt. The 2003 Moore-Eick miniseries could more easily harken to a pivotal world event: the 9/11 attacks in the U.S. Subsequent terrorist activities in other Western countries heightened viewer preoccupation with changing world events, and constant media attention on a seemingly permanent "War on Terror" filtered into every aspect of entertainment. Whereas the premise offered in 1978 was only the backdrop for an epic fiction, by 2003 that fiction had immediate parallels to the real world. The *Battlestar Galactica* pilots emphasize conceptual differences between Larson's and Moore/Eick's visions of the universe and, especially, humanity's very nature and values in very different political times.[41]

Something seemingly as insignificant as a change in the role of one character—Baltar—not only reimagines him but takes the series on a different route toward Earth. Changes in his character, revealing greater complexity and shifting audience sympathy between Baltar as an ambiguous villain or hero, begin in the beginning; Baltar 1978 is a very different man from Baltar 2003. The pilot of each series sets the tone for what follows, and Baltar becomes a barometer of just what kind of stories each series would tell in later episodes.

The Battle Between Good and Evil

The first twenty to twenty-five uninterrupted viewing minutes of each pilot firmly indicate the characters who will receive the most emphasis, the storytellers' philosophy or point of view, and the type of stories that will be told—as well as introducing viewers to the series' premise and providing some necessary mythology-building backstory. Even the opening credits and theme music preface the series' differing approaches to basically the same premise: the Cylons attempt, and nearly succeed, in wiping out humanity during surprise attacks.

IN THE BEGINNING

The "tags"—voiceovers or text providing context to the story—alert audiences to each pilot's viewpoint. Larson's "Saga of a Star World" begins with a brief overview of the series' mythology and concludes with Adama's pronouncement that the humans in the "rag-tag fleet fleeing the Cylon tyranny" are clearly the victims. No one mentions the possibility of the humans ever being tyrants; they are the hapless victims whose greatest flaw is to believe their enemy wants to make peace. In sharp contrast, the Moore-Eick miniseries calls Cylons the children of men who come home for an unholy reunion with their parents.

Unlike the human-centric first pilot that emphasizes space battles and sets up a traditional TV conflict between good and evil, the 2003 Cylon-centric miniseries immediately presents the story in more ambiguous terms. Just who are the heroes in this saga? The opening text, presented within the silence of space, offers an eerie and unsettling backstory:

> The Cylons were created by man. They were created to make life easier on the Twelve Colonies. And then the day came when the Cylons decided to kill their masters. After a long and bloody struggle, an armistice was declared.

This text uses passive-voice verbs to show just what had been done to the Cylons, the result of humanity playing gods and turning their "children" into slaves—not an enticing portrait of humanity. The Cylons are the victims who rise up to free themselves. The music, not a typical movie or TV series theme, haunts the credits; its sound may be otherworldly, and it doesn't resemble "ordinary" Western-style music audiences are used to hearing over opening credits.

The contrast from the original is immediate and startling. *Battlestar Galactica*'s original fanfare, played by the Los Angeles Symphonic Orchestra, heralded the arrival of the first pilot. Its opening narration intones, "There are those who believe that life here began out there, far across the universe, with tribes of humans who may have been the forefathers of the Egyptians or the Toltecs or the Mayans ... There may yet be brothers of men who even now fight to survive far, far away amongst the stars." Playing on *Star Wars*' story in a galaxy far, far away, the voiceover emphasizes humanity's link across the stars with those just like the audience; the new pilot places humanity's importance, and perhaps its crimes, in a very different universe.

The Opening Scenes

The organization of the first few scenes (roughly the first half hour, give or take commercial interruptions), making that all-important first impression, tips off the direction each series would take; Table 3 highlights the opening moves that either prompt audiences to switch channels or to stick around not only through the rest of the pilot but to return for the next episode.

Table 3. The Opening Scenes of *Battlestar Galactica*'s Pilot Episodes

Glen Larson's U.S. Theatrical Movie-turned-U.S. TV Pilot	Ronald Moore & David Eick's TV Miniseries
Credits and Theme Music	Opening text with backstory—introduction of the mythology

Backstory narration—introduction of the mythology	Human-Cylon meeting on a space station created for annual meetings after the armistice—first look at Cylons
Self-congratulatory meeting of the Quorum of Twelve at armistice between Cylons and Humans—introduction of Baltar	Credits and Music
Discussion among Zac, Starbuck, and Apollo of an upcoming patrol—introduction of Starbuck and Apollo	Bustling Galactica on the brink of decommissioning—introduction of Starbuck and Adama
Viper launch of Apollo & Zac's patrol	Unveiling of Adama's restored Viper
Adama's suspicions about Cylons—introduction of Adama	Starbuck's card game
Apollo & Zac's discovery of hidden Cylon vessels and the subsequent Cylon attack on the Vipers—first look at Cylons	Tigh and Adama's discussion of Starbuck
Baltar's vs. Adama's advice to President Adar	On Caprica, Laura Roslin's cancer diagnosis
Starbuck's card game	On Caprica, Six's murder of a human baby
Cylon attack begins—Zac killed, Atlantia blown up (with the Quorum inside), Tigh's discovery of Cylon base ships, Caprica strafed	Baltar's TV interview—introduction of Baltar and of Baltar's relationship with Six
Cylons' Imperious Leader's command to annihilate humanity	Apollo's arrival on Galactica—introduction of Apollo
	News of Cylon attack filtering through various scenes and locations: on shuttles, *Galactica*, Caprica

The original pilot focuses immediately on the people on *Galactica* who will become an integral part of the story: Adama, Starbuck, and Apollo. During the Quorum's meeting on the *Atlantia*, Baltar is praised during the President's toast to "the most significant event for mankind" approved by the "greatest leaders ever assembled." Adama, however, soon raises his objections about the armistice with a patriotic speech that illustrates the series' "us" and "them" mentality: "[The Cylons] hate us, with every fiber of their existence. We love freedom; we love independence to feel, to question, to resist oppression." Humanity's old enemy doesn't understand this love of freedom and independence; they are fundamentally different from humans. Within the first few minutes, the key players and their feelings toward the Cylons are obvious.

Unlike the second series' pilot, the Cylon attack in the first series (and plenty of *Star Wars*–style space flights and battles) arrives early in the story. The battles don't last long, the destruction most graphically depicted through a series of fire stunts on *Atlantia*. Anything with a roving red eye is clearly out to get humanity, and the Imperious Leader announces "the first annihilation of the life form known as man—let the attack begin." Within a few minutes, the good guys and bad guys are easily separated, and the Cylons won't be portrayed as anything but evil until *Galactica 1980*'s final episode, which allows Starbuck's retooled Cylon "buddy" Cy to give his life for his friend. It takes some rewiring and isolated quality time with a human before one Cylon can become socialized as a friend. Even so, the series questions whether even Cy is trustworthy when other Cylons show up. The pilot movie doesn't allow this ambiguity; Cylons are always the bad guys (not a misnomer—they all have masculine robotic voices).

Through Starbuck's first scenes, the original series' lighthearted tone (and Starbuck's character) are also set. A shirtless Starbuck unconvincingly fakes illness so Zac can take his place on a space patrol with Apollo. Of course, Apollo plays along with the deception, and he and Starbuck share some buddy-buddy camaraderie. Starbuck also becomes the focus of a friendly card game, which he wins, scooping coins into his trousers just as *Galactica* goes into alert mode. His is one of the featured faces shown in close-up during the Viper fight scenes, his dialogue indicating his prowess as a pilot. In these first few scenes, family and friendship are paramount, and Adama's family and Apollo's and Starbuck's friendship, two key elements throughout the series, already have been established.

Although the 2003 miniseries also quickly introduces Adama and Starbuck, Baltar receives a longer introduction and much more to do, and Apollo only comes aboard the story when his Viper makes a symbolic rough landing on *Galactica*. His displeasure with his father and the *Galactica* quickly become known, setting up further tensions for the pilot episode and the later series.

The new pilot creates plenty of tension in a variety of settings; the conflict between Cylons and humans is only one untapped source of drama. The Cylons seem both monsters and freedom fighters, murderers and lovers of humanity. Number Six marvels at the newborn she holds, only to snap his neck when his mother turns away for a moment. Is she purely a monster, or is this death a mercy killing because she knows of the more painful attack soon to come? Does she hate Baltar for being oh so willing to be seduced while mistakenly thinking he seduces her, or does she love her human lover? Indeed, the Cylons do seem to have been created in humankind's image, and the similarities, rather than the differences, make the new battle between good and evil so difficult to understand, much less fight. No character is inherently good or bad. The new pilot insinuates that people may never know who they really are; they are defined and redefined by what they do. Peace may never be possible; war may be the new daily reality. Enemies may not only live among us, as our friends, colleagues, even family members, but we may someday find ourselves one of "them."

Family Values

The 2003 pilot also undermines the original's traditional values, a not-so-surprising shift.

Larson's "conservative" pilot promotes an us-versus-them world in which the ideals of family are highly prized. The 1978 pilot sometimes stalls for a family moment. The best illustration is Captain Apollo's visit to the freighter *Gemini* in search of supplies. The widowed Serina and her young son, Boxey, are among the passengers. Acting like the journalist she is in the novelization and theatrical films (her scenes as a reporter are cut from the TV version), Serina asks a lot of questions but also lets Apollo know what's happening onboard; Count Yuri has been hoarding food and wine (not to mention beautiful women) instead of sharing the wealth. She also shares her worries about her young son, who seems more depressed about his lost daggit (dog) than his late father. Apollo immediately stops what he's doing to visit Boxey. He promises him the first daggit found on the journey and pins his flight insignia on the boy. When Serina thanks Apollo for his help in cheering up her son, she mentions that he seems good with children, and Apollo explains that he grew up with a younger brother. Apollo's sorrow over Zac's death and his need to "win a few of the small ones" endears him further to Serina.

A later scene onboard *Galactica* shows Boxey meeting a mechanical daggit. At first Boxey balks because the daggit isn't real, but the scientist who created the mechanical version assures Boxey that his role in training this prototype is most important. The adults, including Apollo and Serina, gather around to smile at the boy and his daggit playfully getting to know each other.

The presence of Boxey, with or without Muffitt (adorably nicknamed Muffey), became an irritant to some fans when the action in regular series episodes also slowed to provide "cute" moments. As one contemporary article commented on the series' ups and downs, the later episodes improved once the cute kid and fake dog appeared less frequently and the focus shifted back to the grown-ups: "Fortunately, the character of Boxey and the robot Muffey have been reduced in importance. There were times when whole episodes collapsed because of these two! Would you believe that the kid and his robot could sneak aboard a shuttle during the dangerous expedition to stop the giant laser cannon?"[42]

Larson's pilot showcased variations on the importance of family at the expense of realism. Ever-vigilant Apollo, the epitome of responsibility and exhibiting a grim demeanor in many scenes, first abandons his supply search mission—and holds off a confrontation with Count Yuri—to spend time with a child he doesn't know. A scientist onboard *Galactica* takes time away from other duties—and presumably there would be many pressing issues while the remnants of humanity flee the Cylons and head uncertainly toward Earth—to build a robot dog for the soon-favored child. Apollo even takes Serina and Boxey on a little joyride to Carillon, the planet from which the *Galactica* crew hopes to gain fuel, where they find more than they anticipated: the planet hosts a wildly popular casino filled with humans and aliens who have no idea the Colonies were attacked. Of course, Muffey runs off shortly after Apollo's shuttle lands, and Boxey runs after Muffey. The child conveniently stumbles into the subplot of a Cylon-run, Ovion-assisted human death factory and helps Apollo uncover what's really happening on the planet.[43]

Serina often looks adoringly at Apollo after these adventures, and Boxey wonders if he would make a good daddy, both surprising events considering that Boxey's father was killed during the recent Cylon attack on Caprica; Serina obviously gets over her grief quickly enough to have a near-miss kiss with Apollo by the end of the pilot episode. (Indeed, Serina and Apollo wed early in the series, but Serina soon dies, leaving Apollo to become a single father and Adama to dote on his new grandson.) The importance of family, especially the creation of an extended one based on love more than blood, takes precedence over the "battle" aspects of *Battlestar Galactica*.

Adama's marriage is only briefly depicted in the pilot episode, but he clearly loves his now-deceased wife. She is at home on Caprica during the attack, and Adama wants to take a shuttlecraft to the decimated surface to find her. Instead, Apollo flies his father in his Viper to search the remains of what turns out to be their burned-out home. Adama finds only a photograph of his family, but he knows his wife is dead. Apollo suggests that maybe she wasn't at home, but Adama knows her routine of taking an afternoon nap at the time of the Cylon attack. Because Ila had difficulty hearing, she wouldn't have been aware of the attack until it was too late to escape. That a battlestar commander would take time (and a fighter Viper) to search for his wife is a moving family moment, but it defies military logic or the demands of command. The grieving Adama acts more like a loving husband than a military leader in this scene.

Larson's novelization also supplies details about Ila and Adama's marriage that provide backstory for Adama's obvious grief in the visit-to-Caprica scene. Although separated sometimes for years because of his military duties during the long war with the Cylons, the couple lived the ideal of "absence makes the heart grow fonder." Larson described the couple:

> If it had not been for the war, they could have had the kind of balanced, happy life that now came only at well-spaced intervals, although, as Ila often argued, perhaps their love was intensified by the long disruptions. Without them, she said, she and Adama might have become dull old married folks … Instead, they remained bedazzled, youthful lovers who still appreciated each other's virtues.[44]

A happy marriage, whether as long as Adama's or as short-lived as Apollo's, is as aspirational as it is inspirational. By the end of the first season, Cassiopeia and Sheba have set their marriage-minded sights on Starbuck and Apollo, and romance leading to a happy ending seems a good possibility. The importance of marriage and family is well established in the pilot episode, and these scenes lead to the further development of romantic couples throughout the rest of the series.

Father-son relationships also are happy more often than argumentative. Although Apollo confronts his father in scenes edited from the TV pilot (and which also appear briefly in the novelization), he only admires Adama in the televised version. At one point Apollo says, "You've been more than a father to me. You've been someone I can trust and respect. My ideals rise and fall on your standards." As the music crescendos, strings emphasize familial emotions. For his part, upon learning that Apollo has discovered Cylons lurking in unexpected places on Armistice Day and something bad might soon happen, Adama confidently tells Tigh, "If I can't trust my first-born son, who can I trust?"

The Moore-Eick miniseries emphasizes military duty and job responsibilities far more than family needs. Setting the tone for many episodes throughout the series, Apollo confronts his father, and the two seem to have a long history of disagreement. As Jamie Bamber commented in an early interview, in the pilot, Apollo

> isn't necessarily happy in his own skin ... stranded in the *Galactica*—a ship he would least like to be aboard because he has a problematic relationship with his father—but he has nowhere else to go. ... He's good at his job—the military life is something he was born into—but because of his falling-out with his Dad and the death of his brother, he questions everything the military stands for.[45]

Not only does the Moore-Eick Adama have problems with his son, but he certainly doesn't seem the type to rush home to check on his (ex)wife; he only grudgingly asks Apollo about his mother, learning in the process that she is about to be remarried. Duty, especially in the aftermath of a devastating Cylon attack, becomes paramount, and personal considerations have a much lower priority in the face of the survival of humanity.

This theme is borne out in later episodes, when young families such as Galen and Cally Tyrol and Karl and Sharon Agathon must leave their babies in daycare while they go to their jobs. Marriages often suffer under the stress of the continuing exodus and frequent life-or-death crises. Apollo's marriage to Dualla seems fragile at best. Despite Sam Anders' determination to make his marriage succeed, Kara openly commits adultery. Tyrol bitterly drinks a toast to bars, made necessary by the institution of marriage. Tigh's troubled marriage ends in his (justified?) killing of his wife. Adama's marriage, shown through his memories, seems doomed to failure from the start. The tone of TV family life has shifted greatly since the 1978 pilot; the "happy family" ideal seems an unlikely possibility in the new miniseries and its later episodes.

Baltar as Common Opportunist or Misled Narcissist?

The Baltar revealed within the first few minutes of the 1978 pilot is a smooth-talking but sneaky villain who, by the end of the theatrical version at least, is killed and thus pays for his overt treachery toward humanity. The *Encyclopedia Galactica* succinctly sums up his part in the Cylon attack and indicates viewers' understanding of this one-dimensional character:

> His greed and lust for power led him to deceive his fellow Councilors into relaxing their defenses, opening the door to the massive Cylon offensive in which at least seventy billion humans perished. The Cylon Imperious Leader promised Baltar safety for his own

> Colony, Picon, and personal rulership over the rest of humankind. Baltar, in turn, persuaded the Quorum of the Twelve that the Cylons were sincerely interested in peace, and that they had already shut down most of their attack forces in a gesture of friendship. The humans then disabled most of their weapons.[46]

Although Baltar's role in setting up humanity (and thus the series) is important, his actual on-screen role was initially very small. As John Colicos, the original Baltar, recalled in a 1989 interview, he was only supposed to be a character in the pilot, but Larson "decided he liked the character and the work that I was doing, so he [kept] Baltar as a running character. He re-directed the pilot's final scene himself, so that when the sword came down to cut my head off, he stopped at the last second and I was spared if I would betray the human race."[47] A later (syndicated and DVD) version shows Baltar's meeting with the Cylons' Imperious Leader, who simply orders the human's beheading when Baltar asks for his reward after betraying humanity. Strangely, Baltar is shrewd enough to trick the Quorum of Twelve but naïve enough to believe the Cylons will spare his home world and make him a leader on Picon after they've wiped out the rest of humanity.

Once Baltar was established as a series regular, appearing in fourteen episodes, his character underwent considerable change, sometimes simply because different writers maintained different visions of who Baltar should be. Baltar's changing personality reflected the series' early struggle whether to be a children's show or sci-fi romantic drama for an older audience. Colicos remembered that the writers "hadn't come to grips with the storyline. They hadn't quite decided what audience they were trying to reach, whether it was cutesy kid audiences … college-level science-fiction fans, or the general populace. By not … having a bible to follow … Baltar kept flipping back and forth"[48] between a pure villain and something less sinister. Fans developed their own theories about Baltar's true nature, which they shared with Colicos, whose earlier work in sci-fi such as *Star Trek* (memorably playing the first on-screen Klingon) endeared him to the sci-fi crowd.

One theory held that Baltar was framed, which seems unlikely from his calculated manipulation of President Adar and sudden disappearance, shown in the first few minutes of the pilot, just as the Cylons attack. Another theory is that Baltar might be Adama's spy, secretly working to eliminate the Cylons once and for all. In the pilot as well as later episodes, Baltar infiltrates Cylon society and has access to the Imperious Leader. Baltar's actions, however, never seem nuanced enough to imply he is a double agent. Colicos strove to play Baltar somewhat ambiguously, a smart actor's choice to keep his character alive, whichever direction the series writers eventually decided to take him. "Because the writers never decided who and what he was, we never found out. 'I've played villains,' I thought. 'I've played monsters. We'll do a fine line and make it enigmatic.' When in doubt, be enigmatic."[49]

David Bassom, a frequent author of books and articles about the new series, explained the difference between Baltar's first and second incarnations. John Colicos' Baltar is "a treacherous villain who purposely betrayed humanity to the Cylons," whereas James Callis' Baltar is a "self-serving scientific genius who unwittingly becomes a pawn" by divulging secrets to the Cylons via Number Six, Baltar's lover.[50] In the miniseries Baltar comes across as a narcissist who can easily believe in Six's adoration—after all, he believes he is worthy of worship—but becomes horrified when her true identity is revealed. Baltar successfully deludes himself about his life, work, and personal choices; although he wants to survive, he really has no idea how to do so if he can't think his way out of an immediate problem.

Audiences first see him trying to buy time out of an uncomfortable dilemma when, in the throes of passion, Six plaintively asks, "Do you love me, Gaius?" He briefly freezes before asking what she means and instantly is relieved when she gives him a knowing smile to suggest she was only kidding and could never be a needy female. Baltar once again focuses on his pleasure; he doesn't have to deal with her emotions or "love" during sex. She placates him by throwing him on the bed and taking charge of their encounter, which seems fine to Baltar. His response to sex with Six symbolizes his relationship with Cylons and authority; he doesn't have to be in charge or on top as long as he survives (and preferably enjoys) the encounter. Baltar may always be "screwed" by the Cylons, but frequently he enjoys it. Later, when he begins mentally channeling Six in all her audiovisual glory, audiences and Baltar himself wonder if he's become so good at rationalizing his actions that he can't discern reality from his self-aggrandizing fiction.

Callis agrees with Bassom's assessment of the Baltars. Unlike the original, his character isn't a villain. He thinks the new Baltar is only out to protect himself; he is weak and surprisingly naïve at times, for all his scientific knowledge.[51] Baltar thus becomes a sympathetic character—a strange twist considering that the fall of humanity comes about because of his very human flaws. Baltar at first wants to keep his part in the Cylon attack a secret, although the other survivors on *Galactica* initially believe his presence is beneficial and don't look to make him a scapegoat for their plight; having a renowned scientist aboard ship to advise the military commander and newly installed president should be helpful. Because Baltar is first introduced by a TV reporter as a specialist in AI and friend of President Adar, not to mention a Ministry of Defense consultant, he seems an effective potential mediator between Adama's hardline military authority and Roslin's fledgling civilian president. Not only does Baltar's potential for both good and evil complicate the plot, but it reflects civilians' modern concerns about who is advising the government in wartime and just how trustworthy are well-known celebrities, including scientists, politicians, and military commanders.

The Baltar of the 2003 miniseries only hints at the many layers to be tantalizingly uncovered through the first three seasons. By the end of Season Three Callis updated his analysis of Baltar: He "has made an art out of sidestepping the blame that's coming his way ... This is a man who believes, really, that he's only partially responsible, if at all, for the near total genocide of his own race."[52] Baltar feels tricked by the Cylons and, in some ways, is just another victim. By the third season, however, Callis says that Baltar is "all cried out."[53] He becomes grimmer and more dissident and definitely is not hero material, although he also isn't a one-dimensional villain. The actor finds it interesting that fans like the character, but he hopes that "no one out there ... wants to emulate Baltar! If not wanting to follow in his footsteps is what draws people to him then I guess that's a good thing."[54]

* * *

The first pilot is pure entertainment that reflected the popular culture, rather than the politics, of its decade. It is fun and exciting and not all that scary, providing escapist fantasy in an appealing form to viewers in the late 1970s. The 2003 pilot perhaps had to meet loftier expectations; it established itself as "art," a well-made story that invites audiences to think as well as enjoy. In fact, at times the heavy drama and brutal battles make the pilot and following episodes difficult to watch as "entertainment" and thus instigate more of a recurring debate among sci-fi fans whether *Battlestar Galactica* even *is* true science fiction or merely another drama set superficially against the backdrop of space.

What will be remembered about Larson's pilot? Dirk Benedict fans can easily answer that: Starbuck. This now long-beloved character has won his place in sci-fi fandom. What was groundbreaking and novel in 1978 is kitschy in the 2000s, but Starbuck is forever.

Moore's and Eick's pilot miniseries likely will be evaluated long term by very different criteria. After all, the resulting series has been better received by TV critics who applaud the quality of the storytelling (for the most part) and the intriguing ambiguity of characters. If anything, the way the story has been told will make this *Battlestar Galactica* a memorable entry in the annals of TV history.

The 2003 version will be remembered for another notable distinction: reimagining. Although borrowing or copying from other series or simply remaking a classic is a staple of modern TV storytelling, Moore and Eick succeeded in totally revamping the concept and characters. "Reimagining" is now a viable means of translating a complete concept from another era of storytelling into a format more appropriate for the current sociopolitical environment. In 2007 Eick applied this technique to another 1970s cult show, *The Bionic Woman*, which didn't fare nearly as well as *Battlestar Galactica*. *Galactica*'s Katee (Starbuck) Sackhoff took on the role of a psychologically damaged early bionic model, but even her fun-to-watch "villain" couldn't sustain a basically bland series. To date, *BSG* remains the best reimagined series on the air.

Part II

REIMAGINATION AT WORK

Battlestar Galactica was, famously, reimagined from a 1970s series, and in this section we consider that process in two chapters—David Kociemba's "From the Buffyverse to the *Battlestar*: Jane Espenson Comes Onboard" and "R & D: Ronald D. Moore and David Eick as Collaborators"—which consider, respectively, a writer who came to the series after working on Joss Whedon's three TV shows and with *BSG*'s two co-creators/reimaginers; and three "jumps"—"Cutting Corners: Keeping Science Fiction Real," Sean Hockett's "Michael Rymer: More Than a Go-To Guy" and "Under the DRADIS: *Battlestar* and the Critics"—commentaries, in turn, on *BSG*'s "naturalistic science fiction," the series' most prolific and important director, and the critical response to its reimagining.

CUTTING CORNERS: KEEPING SCIENCE FICTION REAL

"Every time you start to get all starry-eyed and latch onto Roslin as the second coming of Josiah Bartlet, the show reminds you that it's a whole lot tougher—on its characters and its viewers—than* The West Wing *was.* Battlestar Galactica *may be set in outer space, with robots, in the far distant past, but* it reminds us every week that the other TV shows are the fantasies. *'This,' as Roslin tells her stricken assistant in a recent episode, 'this is life.'"

—Laura Miller, "Space Balls" (Salon.com)

"The illusion I wished to create was that of reality."

—Henrik Ibsen

Ronald D. Moore's podcasts, various DVD commentaries, and David Bassom's official companion books—all confirm that the decision made in the reimagined *Battlestar* miniseries to cut off all the corners of books and papers visible in the frame came back to haunt the show's makers when it went to series. Intended to be a kind of idiosyncratic mark of distinction in a series otherwise "naturalistic," the need to "cut corners," its makers admit, soon became a bit of nuisance, but continuity required nothing less.

Yet the new *Battlestar* has done anything but cut corners in its commitment to realism. When *BSG* was reimagined, the Ibsen principle was invoked. The Norwegian playwright (1828–1906), you may recall, was the father of realistic drama: in one of his plays (*Hedda Gabler*), a woman came onstage smoking a cigarette; in another (*A Doll House*), a woman walks out on her creep of a husband (the slamming door that ended the play could be heard all over the world). In yet another (*Ghosts*), a man succumbs to the ravages of inherited syphilis. Yet many miss the subtle implications of Ibsen's famous statement: reality is an "illusion": it is the product of a certain artifice; it must be created.

On *Battlestar* the "illusion" of realism was conveyed in a variety of ways, already identified in detail in books and websites and in the remainder of this book. The characters are believable individuals with real flaws and real problems. The spaceships which they inhabit seem inhabitable by actual human beings; *Galactica* is no *Enterprise*. *Galactica*'s CIC (Command Information Center) is more like something we find on a submarine than a starship (no viewing screen, no captain's chair). The technology is low tech. These and other *BSG* elements contribute mightily to its illusion of reality.

Battlestar, we should note, was not the only sci-fi series that aspired toward the realistic. Joss Whedon's short-lived *Firefly* (2002), which likewise eschewed the use of aliens, banned latex from the set, and even made use of the same effects house (Zoic) as *BSG*, also aspired toward realism as it spliced sci-fi with the Western, but the adventures of Captain Tight Pants and the crew and passengers of the *Serenity* had barely gotten up a head of steam when it met an untimely death at the hands of FOX.

Moore's choice of words in his *BSG* bible to describe the illusion he wished to create is revealing. He calls not for realistic science fiction, but "*naturalistic* science fiction" (my italics). As anyone who has taken an American literature course knows, realism and naturalism are definitely related—part of the same *fin de siècle* (end of the century) movement in the U.S. and abroad. But they were not the same. Your basic realism held a mirror up to ordinary life or (depending on your choice of metaphor) sought to capture a "slice of life": to leave a record of its time and its world, how it looked, how people behaved in it. Naturalism, which came chronologically later, had a not-so-secret agenda. Pessimistic, naturalism took determinism, the philosophical stance that denies human free will and argues that human beings are forever manipulated by both nature and nurture, to be its default setting. In the great works of naturalistic literature, men and women are pushed and buffeted by forces beyond their control.

We can't be certain that Ronald D. Moore was paying attention in his American lit classes two decades ago or that he was familiar with this distinction, but followers of *Battlestar* will agree that its prime mover's verbal and artistic choices are seldom without clear purpose, and naturalism is not such a bad choice anyway. Though *Battlestar* cannot be categorized as pessimistic—at least not yet—it remains a dark and deep narrative grappling with themes of human freedom and destiny. In its philosophical profundity, it can never be accused of cutting corners.

Chapter Four

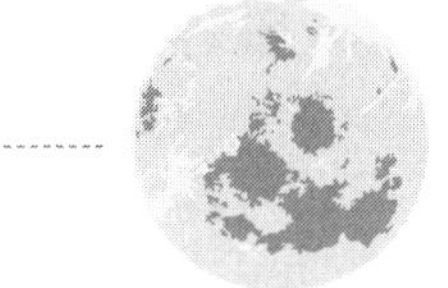

FROM THE BUFFYVERSE TO THE *BATTLESTAR*: JANE ESPENSON COMES ONBOARD

—David Kociemba

Any fan of Joss Whedon's television creations—*Buffy the Vampire Slayer*, *Angel*, *Firefly*—is likely to recognize the name of Jane Espenson, well known as the scribe of some of the Whedonverse's most clever and hilarious episodes.

In one sense, Espenson is a craftswoman, not an artist. A TV screenwriter often isn't considered a real author until he or she creates an original series. There can be as many as nine different realizations of the original idea for the story, and writers like Espenson—best known as a key contributor to *Buffy the Vampire Slayer* (The WB, 1997–2001; UPN, 2001–2003)—don't write the shooting draft version of the script. She doesn't control the final edit of the episode. Nor has she directed an episode. From this perspective, examining the two episodes of *Battlestar Galactica* written by Espenson through the lens of her past work may seem trivial.

Fans, however, recognize that certain writers express a personal, consistent vision, even if they work in other creators' narratives and under other producers' power structures.[55] Television Without Pity's *BSG* recappers explicitly draw parallels between Espenson's two *BSG* episodes and her prior work. Moreover, the creators of *Battlestar* reached out to hire her as a freelance writer for "The Passage," brought her back to co-write "Dirty Hands" with Anne Cofell-Saunders, and then hired her full-time for their final season.[56] The series creators evidently saw Espenson as having a unique approach they could use to complicate their story. The real question is what Espenson's artistic values, writing techniques, and worldview bring to the series.

The most prominent Espenson signature is the use of rituals that involve food to reveal character. This should come as no surprise from a writer who ends every entry of her blog on writing spec TV scripts, "Jane in Progress," with a description of what she had for lunch. Her writing on series ranging from *Buffy the Vampire Slayer* to *Gilmore Girls* to *Andy Barker, PI* has featured magical band candy, an episode best described as "*Soylent Green* meets *Fast Food Nation*," Andrew's soft-core cereal ad, a fourth grader's story about "The Happiest Doughnut," and a shot of an obese man running while waving a sub with "three kinds of ham" just before his fatal heart attack.

So *Battlestar*'s "The Passage" (3.10) is Espenson's kind of episode. Contaminated food forces the fleet to fly through a radioactive star cluster to a planet with sufficient algae to reprocess into food. The pilots gather and share the last protein bars they have. When Kat protests that she gave away her last protein bar to Cottle, Starbuck intimates that her former protégée and current rival is lying, saying, "Right. Right after I gave him head." Apollo, of course, makes peace by stating that the lack of food is making everyone paranoid and orders them all to eat—the most delicious meal of crackers, pretzel bits, and crumbs you ever did see. They gasp, gulp, and grunt in ecstasy; even Starbuck eats—off the edge of her Butterfly military knife.

One of Espenson's best-known traits is her facility with writing secondary characters such as Jonathan, Andrew, Anya, and Spike on *BtVS*, or Kaylee on *Firefly*. So for Espenson's first episode on the series, *BSG*'s creators brought her in to kill off exactly that kind of character, maximizing the death's emotional impact on its very media-literate audience. "The Passage" centers on the heroic death of the pilot Kat, an important but secondary character who grew from a cadet to CAG over eighteen of the series' fifty-three episodes, and who saves a transport ship at the cost of her own life.

Espenson's second episode, "Dirty Hands," helps *BSG* become even more ensemble oriented. Here, she focuses on the hardships faced by the "knuckle-draggers" on the *Battlestar* flight deck and the fuel refinery ship, leading to their fight for recognition of their sacrifices and a more just society. Espenson describes it as

> one of those stories—always my faves—that looks at the underpinnings of the series, at the supporting players in the fleet. The way my *Buffy* episodes 'Storyteller' and 'Superstar' both moved a tertiary character to center stage, this episode does that with a whole slice of the surviving human population. I'm very pleased about that.[57]

Espenson had investigated class conflict before with "Doublemeat Palace" on *BtVS* (6.12) and "Accession" for *Star Trek: Deep Space 9*.

In addition to showing kids and nigh-elderly workers on the fuel-processing line, Espenson and Cofell-Saunders write life into a middle-class youth, Danny Noon, as he resists being drafted into maintenance duty:

> Danny: Sir, I worked on a farm for a summer, 'cause I was saving up to go to college—architecture—but then the Cylons attacked, and … Now I'm a farmer? How is that fair? How is that in any way fair?

The idiosyncratic use of "in any way" in the last line is what makes Danny particular and affecting rather than generic, tendentious, and manipulative. As he's dragged off, this boy's faith in the system is still intact enough for him to be asking whom he needs to talk to clear this up. Later, on the line, Danny gets maimed volunteering for a dangerous job Chief Petty Officer Galen Tyrol can't accomplish, perhaps still believing in individual accomplishment as a solution to the predicament posed by his new class position.

Espenson has been drawn to these stories of characters on the margin:

> I feel that even in real life, a lot of people see certain people in their lives as fringe characters, as people who don't live lives as real and complex as their own. I personally enjoy those moments of reveal that show there's a person there. I wish I had the power to do it in real life as well as in a script.[58]

Made flesh and blood through just a few lines by the writers and the acting of Bryce Hogson, Danny has the effect of motivating the Chief's decision to risk death by instituting a strike, but that's not the purpose of this character. Espenson and Cofell-Saunders use Danny's loss of innocence to persuade the middle-class *BSG* audience that class matters as much as sexier topics like fighting Cylons or power politics.

Espenson is, of course, also known for her sense of humor. As she noted in a TV Squad interview, "I know people expect humor from me. I hope they understand why, given a story about Kat's redemptive and unglamorous death, I kept the funny knob turned down." While neither "The Passage" nor "Dirty Hands" is remotely lighthearted, there are some comic moments.

In "The Passage," Baltar observes that D'Anna's hair has resurrection goo in it from her many visits to the Cylon resurrection chambers, which is a funny bit of blasphemy. Starbuck's use of the very contemporary term "bitch slap" in "The Passage" is funny due to the anachronism. "Dirty Hands" features another anachronism which Espenson and Cofell-Saunders emphasize with "crickets"—jokes that use the character's delayed or absent response as the punch line.[59] Admiral William Adama tells the temporarily displaced President Laura Roslin, "Well, if the quarters become cramped, you're always welcome in one of my beds," which leads to a long pause before he says, "... in a manner of speaking." The anachronism is a part of the humor, but the real laugh is in the delayed (and mutual) recognition of the ancient come-on line. Both scripts, however, are consistent with Espenson's past use of wordplay, put-downs, and comic scenes within dramatic narratives.

Espenson previously studied linguistics at UC-Berkeley's graduate program, so it makes sense that her characters reveal themselves through their wordplay. In "Dirty Hands," Baltar admits that his accent is designed to manipulate and conceal his true nature. Yet, that decision is also insightful, as he understands how class is embedded not just in the language but also in how we speak it.

Espenson prefers not to mock her characters, and yet Starbuck mocks Kat twice in "The Passage." In addition to the protein bar spat between them, there's another squabble later. Kat, who formerly abused stims, objects to Apollo's suggestion that the starving pilots use of them will cause erratic flying. Starbuck jibes, "You used to like the stims, Kat." Rather than just revealing something about the butt of the put-down, Espenson argues, "almost all of them are flashlights trained on the character that says them" too—namely, that Starbuck deals with her anxiety through joking aggression.[60] Nor is this bitter sarcasm intended to be particularly funny. Espenson tries to use put-downs to foster understanding, not gall or hate.

"The Passage" uses a comic release to intensify the tension. Colonel Saul Tigh is briefing Admiral Adama on the effects of severe food rationing on the colonists:

> Adama: I hear they're still eating paper. Is that true?
> Tigh: No. Paper shortage.
> Short pause.
> Slight smile forms involuntarily on Tigh first.
> Angle on Adama, who laughs. Long helpless laugh from them both.
> Adama: Not a good sign. (Breathlessly laughing)

Over time, their shared laugh is heartening, silly, crazy, worrying, and even thrilling as the actors stretch this moment out. In a TV Squad interview, Espenson explained her use of humor in this scene, saying, "There is a way in which some humans react to dire circumstances with humor. Or even a sort of giddiness verging on hysteria. And there are situations, even dark ones, that come with their own absurdities. I'm not above exploiting these."

Espenson is not afraid to relieve the episode's tension with a joke; she can build the suspense back up again. She knows from her time on *BtVS* that reminding the audience of the essential humanity of tough protagonists only raises the stakes in the long run. As on *BtVS*, the comic and the deadly serious build off one another. That causes the distinctions between comedic and dramatic characters to begin to collapse. That's an important step towards creating characters who evolve into being more than fictions even as they remain fictional.

Characters avoid saying exactly what they feel or precisely conveying information in Espenson's scripts. To craft sympathetically flawed characters, she'll have them hesitate or trail off, anticipate other characters, and interrupt themselves. In her blog, she writes, "I love this trick. It's easy and efficient. It reveals character without a bunch of words. …"[61] This technique often sets up a blurt of true feeling in Espenson's scripts. She observes "one natural reaction to suddenly finding oneself inarticulate is to push too hard to get through it. And then you get the blurt. Also effective, and also all wrapped up with the truth. You don't blurt a lie."[62]

Espenson saves this technique for the sick bay bedside conversation between the dying Kat and Starbuck in "The Passage." Starbuck enters the scene not knowing exactly why she's been called. Actress Katee Sackoff uses stiff body language and a stance with her hands clasped behind her back to indicate that Starbuck's bracing herself. Kat could want absolution from Starbuck. Or Starbuck's protégée could force her guilt out into the open. Far from protecting her nugget, Starbuck's threat to reveal Kat's past as a drug-runner essentially drove Kat to heroic suicide to avoid the public dishonor. Having to face either kind of emotional vulnerability would be agonizing for Starbuck. Espenson economically conveys Starbuck's uncertainty through her carefully neutral opening salvo: "They said you wanted to see me."

Kat's response, however, is delicate and undemanding. She says, "Yeah. … I don't think we should end the way we ended." Kat doesn't ask for forgiveness or an apology from Starbuck for herself. To do so would use the power of her martyrdom to force Starbuck into an emotionally vulnerable position of responsibility and place Starbuck back in control of their relationship. (In short, Starbuck would be thrust unwillingly back into the role of surrogate parent, a role in which she's struggled mightily.) By stating her opinion about the state of their relationship, Kat talks to Starbuck as an equal. For the first time, Kat steps beyond the roles of Starbuck's subordinate, rival, or antagonist.

The onus is now firmly back on Starbuck. Here's how Starbuck responds, "Listen, um … everybody is … everybody is stuck with the things that they're not proud of. That, uh … that thing about good people, I …Um, I didn't mean that." The opening of her line uses two verbal stalls for time, then a use of repetition to gain yet more of it. Espenson wants the viewers to know Starbuck's thinking out loud in a way that's not prepared or calculated, which is so rare in a show filled with manipulation and ulterior motives. Starbuck's not acting in the received roles of gruff sergeant or maverick. Espenson's use of the word "everybody" indicates Starbuck's discomfort and inexperience with this aspect of herself, because the general term denies the particularities of their relationship.

But then Espenson writes the blurt that reveals the truth that Starbuck's inarticulateness indicated she was trying to find. Everybody is stuck. Kat's stuck dying. Starbuck's stuck living. Everybody in this fugitive fleet is stuck doing things they're not proud of. Even the Cylons are stuck trying to live their way out of their monstrous innocence. Sackoff makes a good decision here by emphasizing the word in her delivery of the line with a short pause before and a longer pause after, but this moment is not solely hers. Espenson has a long history of writing important speeches in exactly this manner. A notable example would be when Spike reveals his survivor's guilt to Buffy in "Afterlife" (B6003), confessing, "Every night I save you" (in his dreams) to the woman he crucially failed.

Espenson uses the same technique to set up the apology that Starbuck can struggle to give because she wasn't forced to make it. But, since she's writing Starbuck, Espenson has the character retreat back into her tough shell. Starbuck brought sleeping pills. Espenson signals the emotional skittishness of Starbuck at this unplanned intimacy by having her slip into the imperative form, saying "Here. Take these." It's what a veteran soldier should do for a mortally wounded rookie. But the single word of explanation, "enough"—and all that it means—calls her back to more authentic forms of communication. Starbuck explicitly acknowledges Kat as an equal capable of ending her life on her own terms.

Kat can "take 'em if you want." Later, we'll see her pin Kat's photo on the memorial wall. As Espenson had with Spike, she allows a tough character to display vulnerability while remaining true to the character's nature.

That kind of expression of vulnerability gives characters power in Espenson's scripts. In "Dirty Hands," Chief Petty Officer Galen Tyrol can effectively negotiate for his union with President Laura Roslin only after he helplessly asks her if his son can expect nothing more than his class-limited lifestyle.

Finally, Espenson's track record may explain why she was assigned "The Passage." Facing denied, repressed, or emergent aspects of the self is a common theme in her *BtVS* episodes, which are populated by evil twins, robot replicas, past selves, impersonators, and fan-fiction-inspired alternative representations of characters.[63] "The Passage" is her first return to this device, interestingly enough.

As Starbuck confronts Kat about her past as Sasha, a drug-running trucker, Starbuck says, "You're not smart enough to accept who you are." In the next scene, suffering from radiation sickness, Kat stares at her pallid face in the mirror, pulling out clumps of her hair. Her current identity—so constructed by how others see her and thus aptly expressed through reflection—is literally and metaphorically crumbling. As a bridge to her next scene with Kat's former smuggling comrade Enzo, a flashback transforms Starbuck's condemnation into psychological guidance: "Accept who you are." It's voiced three times, like an incantation. Actress Luciana Carro expresses Kat's profound ambivalence physically. Kat's head shakes diagonally between a "no" and a "yes." Eyes half-lidded, Kat steps forward towards Enzo, stops, steps again. An exceedingly fleeting and perfunctory smile never reaches her eyes. They speak:

> Enzo: Yeah. Remember me?
> Kat: Yeah. I remember you. Thieving bastard, ruin everything I've got. Come here.

And they have sex, because it's not love and Kat doesn't have time for sleep. Why?

The important thing to notice here is that Enzo's question doesn't make sense on the surface. Espenson previously established the pair's relationship over several scenes. Enzo is the expression of Kat's past self, Sasha. And this works because Enzo's unimportant except to the extent that he reveals Kat's character. In Jungian psychology, one must come to terms with one's shadow self without giving in to its demands. Kat has to unify her past and her present to get the kind of wholeness and authenticity to be at peace with what she has to do. The sex is a physical representation of that psychological process. Adama describes Kat's rescue of the civilians as "harder than facing a bullet. And you did it without putting one other soul in harm's way." That description also stands for the psychological work that made that heroism possible. I like to think that Espenson was thinking of how Spike served as Buffy's shadow self while writing this *BSG* scene. Remember how difficult that was?

Like her favorite characters, Espenson's career might be similarly described as hidden and extraordinary, with no offense intended to the creators that overshadow her. A real challenge for TV studies in the digital era is to uncover those writers like Jane Espenson who function as authors without the "created by" credit. I suspect scholars will find many more out there once they let go of the heavily promoted cult of the TV auteur. We just have to find some way to recognize them, hidden amongst the army of humanity that creates modern TV series.

MICHAEL RYMER: MORE THAN A GO-TO GUY

—Sean Hockett

"Producers want intelligent directors who use the camera to tell the story, and understand editing as a tool."

—Marita Grabiak

During the first three seasons of *Battlestar Galactica*, Michael Rymer has directed nearly three times as many episodes as any other (a total of seventeen, in addition to the entire miniseries) and in Season Three became a credited producer for the entire run. Like Michael Vejar for *Babylon 5* or Kim Manners and Rob Bowman for *The X-Files*, Rymer's directorial contributions cannot be overlooked. It is a testament to his abilities that time and again Ronald D. Moore and David Eick have been more than happy to leave him in charge of pivotal episodes throughout the *BSG* seasons. From helping to create the look and feel of the show during production of the miniseries, to helming season openers and finales (as well as important mid-season episodes), Rymer is certainly more than just a "go-to guy."

Starting as an independent filmmaker in his native Australia, Rymer garnered home-grown critical acclaim—Best Film, Best

Director, and Best Screenplay awards from the Australian Film Institute—for his first feature length film, *Angel Baby* (1995). From a well-received debut independent feature to a Hollywood sequel, he has certainly experienced all sides of filmmaking. A critic for the *Sydney Morning Herald* would go as far as to describe these polar extremes as being a "low-budget drama about the marginalized" to a "big-budget vampire frightener for teens"—*Queen of the Damned* (2002). Rymer has also given us two improvised pieces—*Allie and Me* (1997) and *Perfume* (2001)—and a conventionally made feature—*In Too Deep* (1999). His first foray into the world of television was with the pilot episode of *Haunted*.[64] It was Rymer's experience of working on *Queen of the Damned* that drove him to seek a "back to basics" approach:[65] his post-"*Queen*" desire to move away from an effects-heavy narrative and return to the more familiar waters of human-based storytelling. One can only imagine his reaction when being given the script to this reimagined *Battlestar* by his agent—perhaps along the lines of "*what the frak?!*";

What we have come to see, though, is exactly the kind of storytelling at which Rymer excels. On *Battlestar Galactica*, he has been able to capture the small moments of intimacy that are sometimes lost in this battle for survival. "I think the most important thing [about directing]," Rymer tells Nuytens, "is to be present and really 'see' what's going on around you—that's where all the best ideas come from." Re-watching Rymer's episodes and listening to commentaries by Rymer, Eick, and Moore, it becomes clear how much fluidity there is in *Battlestar*'s production process and how it lies at the heart of the series' humanity. Moore's desire that *Battlestar* be the antithesis of the *Star Trek* universe with which he was too, too familiar seems to have captured Rymer's interest, enabling him to embellish upon the scripts to give us what we have seen for three seasons. Here we also have an indication of Rymer's position within the show hierarchy—not just one of director, but as a collaborator, one who has helped set the standard for the series' "naturalistic science fiction."

Battlestar Galactica's realism is apparent in nearly every frame—in its use of handheld camera work (or shaky-cam for want of a better description), whip-pans, in-shot focus-pulls, ill-framed shots, or any other multi-hyphenated technique that lends itself to a viewer's feeling of "being there"—and Rymer set the precedent for this house style in his direction of the miniseries. As such, *BSG* invites comparison to both cinéma-vérité and direct cinema, new forms of documentary filmmaking, which came to the fore in the early 1960s. Kolker describes cinéma-vérité as being "marked by the absence of voice-over narration and striv[ing] to achieve a perfect illusion of ongoing life, casually observed by the camera."[66] In a similar vein, direct cinema "sought to study individuals, to reveal the moment-by-moment development of a situation, to search for instants of drama or psychological revelation."[67] Under Rymer and other *BSG* directors—notably veteran documentary filmmaker Robert M. Young ("Six Degrees of Separation" [1.7], "Final Cut" [2.8], "Unfinished Business" [3.9], "The Son Also Rises [3.18])—these new cinematic styles become televisual.

Rymer's direction is also intertextual (see the Jump on *BSG*'s intertextuality later in this volume). A three-minute fifteen-second continuous steadicam shot beginning with Starbuck running through the hallways of the *Galactica* pays homage to the infamous steadicam shot used in Martin Scorsese's *GoodFellas* (1990), as Henry escorts Karen through the bowels of the Copacabana to their front row table. Here we see it used as a device to introduce the viewer to many of the principal cast members of the show.[68]

Yet another intertextual directorial flourish can be observed in the miniseries scene among Baltar, Doral, and the imagined Number Six in *Galactica*'s CIC after the dead Leoben is brought onboard following his demise at the hands of Commander Adama on Ragnar Anchorage. Once again Scorsese is the inspiration—this time *Taxi Driver* (1976). In that movie, as Travis Bickle pulls into the taxi garage with the camera to the right of the shot, the camera pans right and ends on the left side of the shot as the taxi pulls into a parking space. A similar kind of rotational shot can be seen as Baltar and Doral finish their exchange. The camera pans around as we follow Doral across the CIC to take up his position next to Dualla, then continues its rotation to finish back with Baltar, but this time with Number Six sitting on his lap.

Or consider one of the closing scenes of act three in "Resurrection Ship, Part 2" (2.12). The use of metaphorical imagery to convey a sense of drifting towards the unknown that Lee Adama is experiencing after ejecting from the Blackbird is shown in a more literal sense by Richard Gere's adulterous character in *Intersection* (1994). As the last of Lee's oxygen expels from his flight suit, we see him sinking into the depths of the water he feels he is floating in as he drifts in space. While he is more fortunate insofar as being rescued by a Raptor and resuscitated, Gere's character continues his plunge to the depths, his fate sealed.

"Resurrection Ship, Part 2" also earned Rymer his first writing credit of the series.[69] His continuing desire to tell a human story is never more apparent than in the scene among Baltar, Gina, and Number Six—the complexity of which cannot be overlooked, considering that the only "human" element of the triumvirate is Baltar. The intimacy shown among these characters, a sense of realism in the connection that is made between Six and Baltar, and Baltar reaching out to this real manifestation of his dream partner, elevate *Battlestar* to the realms of high drama, not just your usual sci-fi. This is what Rymer brings to the table, a directorial style which, by focusing on acting and character, works in perfect accord with Moore's "naturalistic science fiction" mission, and this is why he has been such a key figure in this ongoing series.

Chapter Five

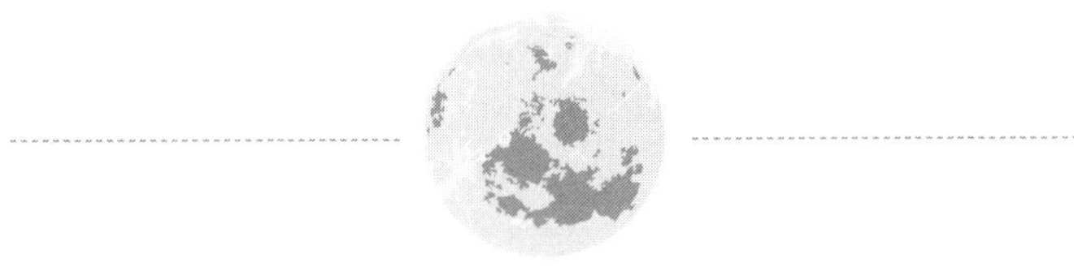

R & D: Ronald D. Moore and David Eick as Collaborators

"Genius is not having enough talent to do it the way it has been done before."

—James Broughton, *Seeing the Light*

The contributions of writers like Jane Espenson and directors like Michael Rymer notwithstanding, the prime movers of *Battlestar* remain Ronald D. Moore and David Eick.

In an interview in *Psychology Today*, the late scholar of creativity Howard Gruber (1922–2005) observed that the nature of collaboration may be the final frontier in the study of creative individuals. Anyone seeking to explore that threshold would do well to investigate the making of film and television, where collaboration, of necessity, reigns supreme. Thinkers about the movies from the historian Erwin Panofsky to the Swedish auteur Ingmar Bergman have compared the creation of films to the conception and execution of the largely anonymous medieval cathedrals.

The televisual cathedral known as *Battlestar Galactica* has been the work of hundreds, given transient identity only in the rapidly scrolling small print at the end of each episode, or on the IMDB, or (more fully) in the official companion books. The names above the title—those of Ronald D. Moore and David Eick, *BSG*'s two prime reimaginers—are, of course, better known. In cartoon incarnations, the pair, R & D, do horrible, horrible things to each other in the grand guignol closing moment of each regular season episode: slicing, dicing, decapitating, eviscerating their better halves. (See Appendix B for a catalog of these.) Is this how collaboration works? Does each member of a creative pair secretly dream a nightmarish demise for the other?

One of the authors of this book, David Lavery, is currently at work on a book on television creativity, which will offer in-depth case studies of some of the ingenious minds now at work making series for the small screen. Readers of this book will, alas, have to wait for that volume in order to get to the bottom of the Moore-Eick collaboration, which will merit a lengthy chapter. The aforementioned Howard Gruber once noted that creative individuals "wittingly or not, create the conditions under which we can study their development."[70] He was thinking of the notebooks, letters, and journals of individuals like Charles Darwin, but the observation is true of Moore and Eick as well—particularly of Moore and Eick.

In fact, no individuals making television have ever given us more. Moore's podcasts—for almost every episode of *Battlestar* to date—offer unprecedented, blow-by-blow accounts of the thinking that went into each installment of the narrative. Perhaps more importantly, Moore has deposited in an archive at the University of Southern California a complete record of his creative process: to quote Heather Ash in this volume, "every script, memo, production schedule, and random note Moore has amassed since he began writing for *Star Trek*. These files contain everything from *Battlestar Galactica* and every show in between—*The Making of Television by Ron Moore* writ large." And it doesn't stop there. At Moore's bidding, we have been given a podcast that takes us behind the scenes of the *Battlestar* "room" as they wrestle with problems in the episode "Scar" (2.15). (See, too, Adam Rogers' discerning essay on the podcast.[71]) Eick, too, has contributed to our knowledge of the show, creating a series of wry but observant video diaries (available on the Season Two DVDs).

A preliminary investigation, which is all this Jump purports to be, can trace the broad outlines of the Moore-Eick collaboration:

1. Moore and Eick (especially Moore) have, without hesitation, stood up against the very different agenda of their network (Sci Fi) in order to stay true to their vision. On the Miniseries DVD commentary, Moore acknowledges dumbing down the scripts sent up the chain of command for approval and then, committed to a dominant "less is more" approach to narrative, paring away superfluous fat in the shooting script.
2. A frequent complaint from the network, we learn, has been that *Battlestar* is "too dark." Moore and Eick feel comfortable in the darkness.
3. R & D are quick to acknowledge the contributions of everyone from editor Dany Arnold to cinematographer Steven McNutt to go-to director Michael Rymer to production designer Richard Hudolin to visual effects supervisor Gary Hutzel. On one DVD commentary (for "Home, Part 1"), Eick goes out of his way to compliment Moore on his openness to interpretation of his writing.
4. They often abandoned best-laid plans to follow on-the-set inventions and suggestions from cast and crew. They especially love working with improvisational performers like James Callis (Baltar).
5. Empowering directors—allowing them atypical freedom—was a prime directive.

6. Like many ingenious television creators, they have been surprised if not amazed at what they have been able to "get away with."
7. Other movies and TV shows constantly inform their conception of scenes and stories. (See the "The Swirl" Jump later in this volume.)
8. The positive response of fans and critics to the show convinced them that they had done the right thing by "setting the bar high" and inspired a redoubled effort to make their creation special.
9. As we discuss later (in "Frakking Up: When *Battlestar* Goes Awry"), Moore, in particular, is quick to acknowledge episodes that, for a variety of reasons, didn't quite work and to offer speculations about the causes.
10. The success of *Battlestar*, its "genius" if you will, confirms again underground filmmaker and poet James Broughton's insight (see the epigraph above). The genius of Eick and, in particular, Moore, who had come to *BSG* bored to death with the Star Trek franchise's way of doing sci-fi, was the result of total rejection of the expected, of the status quo.

One day, then, the collaboration of Moore and Eick may well provide a key to the riddles of television creativity, helping us to understand how a great series like *Battlestar Galactica* became unforgettable when so many others crash and burn—shows like *Bionic Woman* (NBC, 2007–), another reimagining of a 1970s show that did not work and that was created by D (Eick) without the help of R (Moore).

UNDER THE DRADIS: *BATTLESTAR* AND THE CRITICS[72]

In 2006, *Salon*, the online arts, culture, and politics magazine, awarded *Battlestar Galactica* its "Buffy," an "annual token" named after Joss Whedon's "under the radar" masterpiece (WB, 1997–2001; UPN 2001–2003), "of our deep and abiding love for a relatively underappreciated TV show." Praising its "elaborate yet intuitive mythos," extolling "its satisfyingly complex conflicts and characters" ("We're not sure there has ever been a show with a stronger array of fascinating female characters"), acknowledging its avoidance of "the genre's lazy kitsch" ("there's not one damn Wookie or Ewok or any other variety of Furry in sight"), Kerry Lauerman dares his readers—even Republicans—to watch *Battlestar*.

By general consensus, *Buffy*, foreordained to be underappreciated thanks to its low-status genre and its broadcast niche on a netlet, benefited from its below-the-radarness, which may have enabled it to get away, as it nearly always did, with controversial themes, language, and imagery that would have drawn harsh criticism on a more mainstream show. Has *Battlestar*, a reimagining of a failed 1970s series, airing far down the cable spectrum (57 on the local Comcast lineup) on a genre-specific, basic cable channel, similarly benefited from being under the DRADIS (if you will)?

Like *Buffy*, "a great show with a goofy title" (Rogers), Moore admits that the title alone "means a swath of [its] potential audience doesn't tune in" (Rogers); *Battlestar* will never win an Emmy Award (neither did *Buffy*),[73] and has been occasionally derided.

Writing in *Slate*, Troy Patterson half-praises the look of the series—its "doggedly sober" palette "of gun-metal grays, military greens, matte blacks, dull whites, and deep blues" and its design of the Cylon Centurion ("RoboCop as reinterpreted by H.R. Giger")—but characterizes Number Six as "a dime-novel femme fatale as Joe Eszterhas might have written one," dismisses its narrative as a "comic-strip story (Humans vs. Robots, Round 15) not especially eager to make any sense" and lacking "complete confidence in its goals." He also finds this "slip of entertainment" heavy-handed: "The show also tries terribly hard to be heavy, piling on allusions to the war on terror and sluggish existential hoo-ha in a way that may get you wondering what's in the fridge."

Of course, we must note, Patterson admits to unfamiliarity with the show (he acknowledges needing to make use of his press kit to make sense of the story). Unaccountably, he insists, as part of his emphasis on *Battlestar*'s noirish tendencies, the show he is so certain about "is not science fiction—or 'speculative fiction' or 'SF,' or whatever you're supposed to call it these days." Moore, as we have seen, wanted to reimagine science fiction, wanted to take it in a "naturalistic" direction, wanted his series to be "character-driven," but he was not trying to disavow or disparage the genre, as Patterson, highly critical of *BSG*'s ambition and content with having it remain a "space-age mood piece," seems to be.

For the most part, however, the critics have loved the new *Battlestar Galactica*. Based on fourteen reviews collated on the metacritic.com website, Season Three of *Battlestar* garnered a rating of 94 out of a possible "metascore" of 100, earning it the categorization of "universal acclaim." (One hundred twenty-three site users ranked it only slightly lower at 93.)

For *TV Guide*'s Matt Roush, for example, *BSG* is "one of TV's boldest and best dramas." The *San Jose Mercury News*' Charlie McCollum insists that *BSG* "transcends its genre" to become "one of TV's most invigorating and intellectually stimulating series. …" The *Detroit Free Press*' Mike Duffy finds the series "filled with strong writing, a colorful gallery of vivid characters and a rocking good mix of cool dialogue and explosive action." "*Galactica* is so beautifully designed, shot, edited and acted," writes *Newsday*'s Diane Werts, "that you can practically smell and taste its emotional validity." The *Pittsburgh Post-Gazette*'s Rob Owen judges *BSG* to be "one of the most politically relevant and necessarily bleak series on television today." *San Francisco Chronicle*'s Tim Goodman notes that *Battlestar* "should be considered straight up as one of television's most appealing dramas, no matter the genre." Alan Sepinwall of the *Newark Star-Ledger* calls the acting, writing, and directing "superb." *Entertainment Weekly*'s Ken Tucker, admittedly no devotee of science fiction, nevertheless concludes, "Any show that can accommodate decadent cruelty, tragic bravery, and political divisiveness is one you ought to be watching, frakkin' spaceships or not."

Let's take a more in-depth look at several reviews of *Battlestar*.

Unlike the sci-fi-ignorant Patterson, *New Republic* author Forrest Ackerman (writing as well in Slate) acknowledges that "Like many science-fiction shows before it, *BSG* concerns itself with the porous membrane between humanity and barbarism." And yet *Battlestar* has a unique context: "Unlike most of its predecessors … it has the benefit of an open-ended, real-life war as its backdrop, making its lessons about barbarism unavoidably resonant."

Conceding that "it often seems as if the whole motive of the creative talent behind *BSG* is to make you feel uncomfortable about being an American during the occupation of Iraq,"[74] Ackerman remains impressed by the audacity, the "praiseworthy" bravery of its Bush-era politics:

> The American public may be anti-war, but now *BSG* is going *way* beyond public sentiment. In unmistakable terms, *Battlestar Galactica* is telling viewers that insurgency (like, say, the one in Iraq) might have some moral flaws, such as the whole suicide bombing thing, but is ultimately virtuous and worthy of support. Wow.

Writing at the beginning of Season Three, Ackerman—in sharp contrast to the dismissive Patterson who reduces *BSG* to allegory and slights its art—ends his piece by worrying that the series is "charting a course far out into space ... its viewers may not be able to follow."

But other critics, most notably Laura Miller in *Salon*, seem more than ready to embark. In two essays, "Where No TV Show Has Gone Before," which appeared just before Season Two began, and "Space Balls," which went online six episodes into Season Three, she unequivocally praises *BSG*. Though slow to come to a series mired on "the wasteland of Friday night basic cable programming, on a channel otherwise devoted to no-budget thrillers about killer centipedes" ("Space Balls"), she now finds it to be TGIF "appointment viewing" and, with the possible exception of HBO's "not TV" masterpiece *The Wire*, "the most thrilling and trenchant dramatic series on TV at the moment" ("Space Balls").

Well aware, like Ackerman, of *BSG*'s politics, the more observant Miller finds it anything but a simple allegory:

> The parallels to current events are obvious, but *Battlestar Galactica* has always kept more than one historical touchstone in play. The early scenes, when Secretary of Education Laura Roslin was sworn in as president because everyone above her in the civilian line of command had been massacred, cited the swearing in of LBJ after the Kennedy assassination.

> The scene of the shiny, terrifying Cylon centurions (a servant class of robots that actually look like robots) marching down the main road of New Caprica while the devastated colonists looked on was the Nazis marching into Paris. ("Space Balls")

Miller finds two characters especially fascinating: Starbuck (obsession with the character, she notes, inspired her to read Marjorie Garber's *Vested Interests: Cross-Dressing and Cultural Anxiety* "in search of the key to her appeal" ["Where"]) and Laura Roslin.

Joanna Wiess, who readily acknowledges "proselytizing" for a series that surpasses nearly everything else on television, would agree with Patterson and Tucker that the secret of appreciating it may be to set aside its SFness. In the *Boston Globe*, she suggests that

> The secret to *Battlestar*, as one of my colleagues keeps saying, is not to think of it as science fiction. This is a show about religion, politics, parent-child relationships, and the moral dilemmas of insurgency. Consider it a workplace drama where the business is armed resistance.

In a sense, then, *Battlestar* is not unlike other contemporary dramas such as *24*: "Most come as wish-fulfillment: unassailable heroes, embodied by the likes of Kiefer Sutherland and Dennis Haysbert, conquering black-hearted enemies. These shows can make you cheer if you need escape, but they won't make you think." *Battlestar*, Wiess concludes, has a different agenda: it "aims to unsettle us."

In *the Seattle Post-Intelligencer*, Melanie McFarland observes that, unlike many "ambitious series people aren't avidly watching" in "our so-called golden age of drama," *Battlestar*'s "fan base is devoted, obsessive even, but relatively small: the second season averaged 2.3 million viewers." Writing at the beginning of Season

Three, she too is fascinated with the parallels between the series and events in Iraq.

She reports being told by David Eick in an interview that the use of the word "insurgency" was quite conscious.[75] "Asking such a question out loud and on the record in 2003," McFarland observes, "would have invited accusations of terrorist appeasement, even treason on the most extreme end of the political spectrum. In *Galactica*'s corner of the universe, it's a natural evolution of an epic survivor's tale."

McFarland is especially good at pinpointing *BSG*'s profound ambiguities. Consider, for example, the case of Laura Roslin: "When she was president, Roslin banned abortion, claimed a mandate from the gods and tried to steal an election. Sound familiar? Except ... her decisions were correct."

Miller's fellow *Salon* writer, TV critic Heather Havrilesky, was, for a time at least, an equally strong admirer of *BSG*'s "intoxicating darkness," which she identifies in engaging prose as the inextricable "calling card" of its high art "from those opening shots of mushroom clouds and lonely ships, wandering off to find Earth, to the show's haunting, melancholy theme music, to the claustrophobic interiors of *Galactica* and the stifled rage and sadness of its occupants." *Battlestar*'s greatness lies not so much in its politics (although she praises *BSG* for "turning the current political climate on its head" in its depiction of the Cylons as monotheists) as in its interrogation of human character *in extremis*. "What better environment," she asks, "in which to examine the boundaries of personality and group dynamics than a fantastical scenario where the survival of humankind is at stake?"

For Havrilesky, *Battlestar*'s look and character are of a piece: "Like those lonely spaceships in the opening credits, floating off into the abyss of space, the souls onboard remain indefinitely lost and uncertain of their true calling." Key to its genius is that *BSG* offers no easy answers: "There are temporary victories, epiphanies, discoveries and moments of grace, but the colonists, for the most part, muddle through the darkness just like the rest of us, unsure of where it all leads, yet determined to find out at any cost."

Havrilesky, we should note here, was one of many severely displeased with the Season Three finale. (See the Jump "Frakking Up: When *Battlestar* Goes Awry" later in this book.)

* * *

In one of *Battlestar*'s primal scenes, those gathered in the CIC, including Adama, Col. Tigh, and Gaeta, look on with grave attention to see what shows up on the DRADIS. Are Cylon Raiders incoming? Are Basestars within range (as they both are in the cliffhanging final scene of Season Three ["Crossroads, Part 2" 3.20])? Did the rest of the Colonial Fleet succeed in making the jump (as it did not in "Scattered" [2.1])? The metaphor, whether based on Earthly or Colonial technology, suggests stealth, the arrival of something not seen coming.

No doubt about it: no one saw *Battlestar Galactica* coming. Except, of course, those making it, reimagining it as quality television in nearly every aspect, those who saw in a failed old series a possible renaissance in a new era of television. And those critics who, in singing its merits, spreading the word, would not allow *BSG* to remain below public consciousness for long.

Part III

THE BATTLESTARVERSE

In four chapters and six "jumps," this section, the book's core, goes deep inside the *'verse* of *Battlestar Galactica* to investigate a variety of topics: love ("What's Love Got to Do with It? or Love is a *Battlestar*"), sex ("Red Spines and Hot Sex: *Battlestar* Erotics"), gender (Ewan Kirkland's "Starbuck and the Gender Dynamics of *Battlestar Galactica*" and "Women on Top"), religion and mythology ("In the Name of Gods: Monotheism and Polytheism in *Battlestar Galactica*" and "Gods & Stars: Mythology and Astrology in *BSG*"), humor ("In Space, No One Can Hear You Laugh: *Battlestar* Does the Funny"), blood as a signifier ("Blood Will Tell"), the face of the series ("The Face of Edward James Olmos: Reflections on Television and Physiognomy"), and intertextuality ("The Swirl, or the Intertextual *Battlestar*").

IN THE NAME OF GOD(S): MONOTHEISM AND POLYTHEISM IN *BATTLESTAR*

"Polytheistic psychology has room for the preferential enactment of any particular myth in a style of life. One may be Protestant, or Herculean, or Dionysian, or a melancholic child of Saturn, according to the archetypal core governing one's dominant complex, and thus one's fate. And even the myths may change in a life, and the soul serve in its time many Gods."

—James Hillman, "Psychology: Monotheistic or Polytheistic"

Even if the reimagined *Battlestar Galactica* had not been a product of an era in American history presided over by a born-again Christian President of the United States who once called Jesus Christ the most important political philosopher of all time and took the U.S. to war in Iraq secure that he was fulfilling his god's will, Ronald D. Moore's ingenious decision to make his Cylons militaristic, zealous monotheists would have attracted attention.

While the original Glen A. Larson's *Battlestar* was infused with its creator's monotheistic Mormonism, the Moore version converts the species to a polytheistic faith, complete with evocation of

Greek deities and appropriate oaths. In "Flight of the Phoenix," to pick a sample at random, we find Starbuck asking "My gods! What are they doing?" and her nemesis Colonel Tigh proclaiming, "We are looking at a godsdamn bloodbath." (For more on *Battlestar*'s incorporation of Greek myth, see the Jump entitled "Gods and Stars: Mythology and Astrology in *BSG*" later in this volume.)

It may well be, however, that *Battlestar*'s most intriguing use of the monotheistic/polytheistic clash is psychological rather than theological. In books like *Re-Visioning Psychology*, archetypal psychologist James Hillman has sought to formulate anew the science of the soul in a way not unlike Moore and Eick's reimagining of *Battlestar*. According to Hillman, the Western world, including the relatively new "science" of psychology, is "ruled by a bias toward the one. Unity, integration, and individuation seem an advance over multiplicity and diversity."[76] "*E pluribus unum* [the motto of the United States of America] is only a tiny manifestation of the ubiquity of singleness whose ultimate magnifico is the Western Ego."[77]

For Hillman, the pre-Roman soul was by contrast "polytheistic," not just believing in multiple gods but able to embrace multiple perspectives and multiple personalities—prepared, consequently, to believe in the truth of the imagination. But the monotheistic soul, born out of a fusion of "Roman ego" and Christian dogma, instead seeks, in the words of a medieval church father, to "take captive every thought for Christ"—to eliminate the many voices of the psyche and bring them into line behind a single conception of the self. For Hillman, Freud's early 20th-century advocacy of the formula "Where Id is, there let Ego be" is a modern version of the same monotheistic tendency: the overcoming of the unbridled, irrational, animal aspect of the psyche (id) with the civilized character-driven face with which we meet, and accept, the "reality principle" (ego).

According to Hillman, monotheism's reign has led to a smug sense of superiority and religious intolerance,[78] whereas "polytheistic psychology favors differentiating, elaborating, particularizing, complicating, affirming and preserving."[79] From monotheism's point of view, the polytheistic can only equate to fragmentation and splintering, but, in the words of Hillman collaborator Thomas Moore, "In a polytheistic view of the psyche, conflicts no longer seem so decisive. From the start, the motive in polytheism is to honor all sides. The idea is not to conquer or be conquered. There is no one hierarchical, unified head." It recognizes that "The soul's complexes ... are not to be simply ironed out, because they are the stuff of human complexity" and "would accept the multiplicity of voices ... without insisting upon unifying them into one figure." For Hillman, polytheism makes possible a kind of creative tension in which "all parties concerned find a way to co-exist."[80]

If Cylon and human fit the standard monotheism and polytheism templates, they match up even better with Hillman's distinction between the two mindsets. Convinced of their status as their god's chosen "people" and that sinful humanity has betrayed the divine being (being in the singular) and rebuffed his love, the Cylons feel justified in replacing their creators and becoming humankind 2.0. Certain of the truth of their god, they are equally positive the multiple deities worshipped by their parents—parents they set out to exterminate—are complete illusions (even though they claim to know more about human beliefs that their adherents). They have a concept of sin; for example, both Six, who warns Baltar not to kill himself in "Tigh Me Up, Tigh Me Down" (1.9) and Gina (also a Six), who will not take her own life despite undergoing horrible torture, believe suicide to be sinful, but evidently do not find speciescide damnable. They hold reproduction by biological means (not downloading) sacred and have gone to great lengths to try to replicate a process wholly natural for their rejected parents.

Having failed at outright extermination and now committed to a human reclamation project, "skin job" Cylons find themselves tainted by their brush with human flesh: Boomer is changed by her affair with the Chief; Caprica Sharon's love for Helo alters her forever; Six, and later Three/D'Anna Biers, can't shake themselves free from Baltar. Even Brother Cavil seems to have a trace of Ellen Tigh's lusty humanness—at least until that moment in "Occupation" (3.1) when he insists that "Fear is a key article of faith, as I understand it, so perhaps it's time to instill a little more fear in the people's hearts and minds." Spoken like a true monotheist (according to Hillman).[81]

Moore and Eick's deeply flawed humans, on the other hand, are exemplary polytheists in Hillman's sense: though certainly capable of great folly, they remain idiosyncratic, recalcitrant, complicated, resilient, and often brave, more concerned with the development of their own souls than adherence to some abstract notion of divine perfection. "[U]nshackled by dogma," Hillman writes, "we may assume as many souls as necessary"[82]—as many souls, indeed, as there are on *Battlestar Galactica*.

We return to the subject of monotheism and polytheism in Chapter 11, "Cylon-Vérité: Monotheistic and Polytheistic Stories in 'Final Cut.'"

THE FACE OF EDWARD JAMES OLMOS

"Garbo still belongs to that moment in cinema when capturing the human face still plunged audiences into the deepest ecstasy, when one literally lost oneself in a human image. ... when the face represented a kind of absolute state of the flesh, which could be neither reached nor renounced."

—Roland Barthes, "The Face of Garbo"

"Alas after a certain age, every man is responsible for his own face."

—Albert Camus, *The Myth of Sisyphus*

Casting in film and television would seem to be governed by a rule of inevitability. When we learn that at one point in its development Morpheus in *The Matrix* (Larry and Andy Wachowski, 1999) was to have been played by Val Kilmer, not Laurence Fishburne, we shudder at the thought. The possibility, once contemplated by *Sopranos*' creator David Chase, that Tony Soprano's shoes might have been filled by Steven Van Zandt, not James Galdolfini, seems, on the face of it, ludicrous (even though Little Steven was a great Silvio Dante). Sarah Michelle Gellar as

Cordelia Chase and not Buffy Summers would have been just wrong. In these and many other cases the just-right match of actor/actress and role was made; those movies and series that made the wrong decision—well, we don't talk about them because they have, for the most part, been forgotten.

We learn in an official *Battlestar Galactica* companion book that the part of Commander William Adama did not always belong to Edward James Olmos. Before Olmos ever intoned his first "So say we all," for over two decades in pop culture memory, the face of Adama was the quintessentially white, patriarchal, virtually infallible countenance of Lorne Greene, best known as Pa Cartwright from *Bonanza* (NBC, 1959–1973). (Watching the original *Battlestar*, Heather Havrilesky recalls, "I felt very strongly that Lorne Greene belonged on a ranch with Little Joe, not in outer space."[83]) In the first official *BSG* companion, David Bassom can't even spell his name right, omitting the final "e."[84]

Though Moore and Eick admit on the DVD commentary to the miniseries that Olmos was the first actor for the reimagined role (he was initially reluctant), others were considered: the indelibly gruff Brian Cox, the ever-boyishly handsome Tom Skerritt, the innately laconic Sam Elliott, the congenitally sinister Powers Boothe. It is hard to imagine the new series with any of them commanding *Galactica*. In a series constellated with great faces, often captured in discerning close-ups—Katee Sackhoff's Starbuck, Michael Hogan's Colonel Tigh, Mary McDonnell's Laura Roslin, James Callis's Gaius Baltar—the face of the "old man," Edward James Olmos, though no Garbo, remains the face of the franchise.

An Hispanic-American activist and actor, prior to *Battlestar* Olmos was best known for his roles as Gaff in *Blade Runner* (1982), Crockett and Tubbs' superior, Lt. Martin Costillo, in the TV series *Miami Vice* (NBC, 1984–1989), inspiring math teacher Jamie Escalante in *Stand and Deliver* (1988) (a performance that garnered him a Best Actor Oscar nomination), mobster Montoya Santana in *American Me* (1992), Paco in *My Family* (1995), and the singer's father in the biopic *Selena* (1997).

Writing in *Salon*, Laura Miller observes that

> Olmos' Adama is in most ways your basic fictional military hero, what we imagine we want our leaders to be in the dream world of American popular entertainment: a tough, decisive straight-shooter, the proverbial man who does what has to be done. But, as tradition dictates, Adama's emotions are never entirely submerged and are sometimes allowed to overwhelm his judgment … because, as in our real lives, we want to be shown that our leaders are both better than us *and* the same as us. ("Where")

The face of Edward James Olmos succeeds, however, in communicating so much more.

In an important early work of film criticism first published in the 1940s, the Hungarian cineaste Béla Balázs suggested that one of the unique capabilities of film art was to transform the medium's seemingly inherent superficiality (literally "on the face of things") into a profound kind of "physiognomy." (Balázs was thinking of the once common but now discredited ancient "science" that assessed character and personality on the basis of a person's outward appearances, particularly the face.) Film may be limited to capturing the surface of things, but, thanks to the powers of the close-up, which renders "[t]his most subjective and individual of human manifestations … objective in the close-up," and the revelatory performance of the actor, we find ourselves able to "read" *beneath* the skin, to intuit, if you will, the character of a character.

In some of *BSG*'s most memorable moments, Steven McNutt's camera lingers on Olmos' expressive, deeply weathered, responsible (in Camus' sense—see the epigraph) face:

- With powerfully suppressed, stoic, and finally dismissive rage he listens as his pride-and-joy Starbuck confesses her role in Zak Adama's death ("Act of Contrition," 1.4).
- At the end of "The Farm," (2.5), he visits the morgue to view the corpse of Sharon Valerii, the sleeper Cylon whose attempted assassination he has barely survived, and though he speaks only one word—"Why?"—his tears at the full realization of her betrayal and his own mortality speak volumes.
- In another indelible moment, this time completely nonverbal, in "Exodus, Part 2" (3.4), he removes the "pornstache" (as "Television without Pity" deems it) grown while most of the surviving human race suffered in Cylon internment on New Caprica. For almost a full minute of reflection we watch him shave—and watch him watch, sans his signature glasses, himself in the mirror, Adama doing a self-physiognomy of Adama—before he leaves his quarters and, the

slightest of smiles apparent on his now bespectacled face, joins the traffic of a busy *Galactica* corridor, returning to the CIC, the camera lingering for a moment on his back before he turns down another hallway and disappears.

- In "Hero" (3.8), an episode in which he learns that he may have been involved, while following the Admiralty's orders, in provoking the Cylons' attempted genocide, he acquiesces, after President Roslin refuses to accept his resignation, to her insistence that he receive a "frakkin' medal." ("It's not for you; it's for them. That will be your penance—even if it kills you," she explains.) In a memorable shot near the end, the camera lingers again on the wonderfully real face of Adama, showing new scars from the beating he has just taken from Bulldog, as he does reparation, in full dress regalia, his shiny medal commemorating "forty-five years of courageous service" around his neck.
- In "Unfinished Business" it is Adama's blood-covered face (the result of a battering in the ring by Chief Tyrol) on which the camera dwells, and this time the power of the scene is not merely nonverbal, for he has a message to deliver to his now reunited crew:

When you stand on this deck, you be ready to fight, or you dishonor the reason why we're here. Now remember this: when you fight a man, he's not your friend. Same goes when you lead men. I forgot that once. I let you get too close. All of you. I dropped my guard. I gave some of you breaks, let some of you go, before the fight was really over. I let this crew and this family disband. And we paid the price in lives. That can't happen again.

- A final, definitive example, once more from the end of an episode, once more involves the daughter he never had, Kara Thrace. In "Maelstrom" (3.17), Starbuck has died, her demise witnessed by Apollo. Later, alone in his quarters, the

> Admiral works patiently, as he has throughout the series, on his scale model of a tall ship. Only the figurehead remains, and as Adama patiently affixes it to the prow, he suddenly explodes, destroying his project in a paroxysm of grief, anger, and, finally, tears.

We do not yet know what the finale of Season Four of *Battlestar* holds in store for us: a final showdown with the Cylons? The discovery, at last, of Earth? Whatever transpires in the episodes that air after this book has gone to press, whatever mankind's fate, we can safely predict that we will find it written not just in the stars but in the face of Edward James Olmos.

RED SPINES AND HOT SEX: *BATTLESTAR* EROTICS

"I think we inadvertently created this idea that we were trying to be the show that was going to have lots of sex in it."

—David Eick (Bassom 1: 31)

Twenty minutes into the *BSG* miniseries a tall, blond, beautiful woman, looking for all the world like a supermodel, wearing a see-through, open at the navel dress, enters the front door of the spectacular, lakefront home of Dr. Gaius Baltar (we know who he is because we have just seen him identified on television). The blonde, who we will later come to know as "Number Six" (or, more precisely, "Caprica Six"), we also recognize: a Cylon, she destroyed the Armistice Station (after seducing the aged human ambassador) in the pre-credit sequence moments before. Instantly, Baltar and Six begin stripping off each others' clothes and begin to copulate, the "woman" on top, asking—pleading?—for a profession of love, her naked back radiating red all along the spine as she emotes "I'm so hot! I'm so hot!" This is definitely "not your parents' *Battlestar Galactica*!" (Bassom 1: 28).[85]

Director Michael Rymer explains the context of the scene:

> I think science fiction tends to be a little antiseptic in its depiction of sexuality. … It's clearly aimed at teenage boys and usually consists of just a babe in a tight outfit, so I wanted to do something that had more of relationship to reality and shows that sexuality is a huge part of life. (Bassom 1: 30)

On the DVD commentary, Rymer adds that the scene helps to establish that human sexuality is, in fact, our "Achilles' heel," for Six's seduction of Baltar was an essential phase in the Cylons' successful scheme to crack the human defense shield.

Ronald D. Moore expands on the subject, identifying the "babe" Rymer spoke of as none other than Carrie Fisher as bikini-clad Jabba-the-Hut captive Princess Leia in *Return of the Jedi* (Richard Marquand, 1983), criticizing the tendency in much science fiction toward "fetishism" and "objectification" of women. He wonders if some in the sci-fi audience know how to respond to the depiction of actual sex, and he insists that the sex on *BSG*—the subject of a great deal of early fan buzz about the new series—was no more prominent than that on *NYPD Blue* or *ER*.

Rymer and Moore's characterization of the puerile nature of sci-fi movies and TV sex is for the most part accurate. To read Peter Nicholls' seven-column, in-depth discussion in the definitive *Encyclopedia of Science Fiction*, however, or even the quite good survey in Wikipedia is to appreciate, by contrast, how rich, diverse, and provocative literary SF's investigation of the subject has been.[86] The multiplicity of sexual subjects so common on the page—bisexuality as normal, hermaphrodism, human-alien sex, human-robot sex—are not, except, of course, for the latter, Moore and company's major concern. There are, after all, no aliens on *Battlestar*, and the sexual robots are "skin-jobs," human in appearance (but for those scarlet backbones).

BSG is, nevertheless, a very erotic show, punctuated with a variety of sex scenes. Many involve Starbuck. In "Kobol's Last Gleaming," Part 1 (1.12), an earlier flirtation leads to sex between Baltar and Kara. In "The Farm" (2.5), we are privy to the post-coitus dialogue, and continuing sex play, of Anders and Kara. In "Unfinished Business" (3.9) Kara and Lee have drunken, flash-back sex under the stars on New Caprica—just before she sneaks away to marry Anders.

Starbuck is not, however, the only one on *BSG* who is sexually active: Chief Tyrol and Sharon Valerii are involved in a furtive (Cylon on Cylon, as it turns out) affair until Tigh orders it to end. Later, Sharon (or rather Caprica Sharon) will have sex with, and get pregnant by, Helo. The late Ellen Tigh is rumored to have slept with everyone in the fleet, and in the series itself has relations with her husband and Brother Cavil (on her husband's behalf—see "The Swirl" elsewhere in this book). Lee sees a prostitute ("Black Market," 2.14) and, of course, has sex with Dualla, his wife.

Throughout the first three seasons of *BSG*, Six, often provocatively dressed, continues to radiate her sexuality and to serve as the red-hot spine of *Battlestar*'s sexual nervous system. Straddling a chair, naked, in "Home, Part 2" (2.7) might be the series' most indelible image.

But for the most part the erotics of *Battlestar* are very much in keeping with Moore's original bible, naturalistic, real, and very human.

Chapter Six

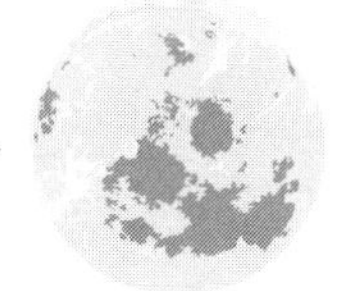

WHAT'S LOVE GOT TO DO WITH IT?, OR, LOVE IS A BATTLESTAR

"Believe me, believe me, I can't tell you why / But I'm trapped by your love, and I'm chained to your side."

—"Love Is a Battlefield," M. Chapman, H. Wright

First impressions can be deceiving: in the initial *Battlestar Galactica* miniseries, the Cylon we will later know as "Six" is introduced as a beguiling, svelte blonde with a heartbreaking penchant for Gaius Baltar as they desperately embrace in his house on Caprica. As he fumbles with her clothes, she plaintively inquires if he missed her, and when he replies in the affirmative (and with an enthusiastic kiss), she asks a far more pointed question: "I know your body missed me, Gaius, but did your soul?" Baltar noncommittally answers yes, but this doesn't placate his partner, and the inevitable question, the one he dreads to hear, follows: "Do you love me, Gaius?"

He freezes as she gazes intently into his eyes. "Are you serious?" he asks, unsure whether to laugh or bolt. She smiles—that long, slow, deceptive grin we will soon recognize as a trademark self-protective measure for this particular Cylon. She fools him into thinking she's only after sex, not love, as he hikes up her skirt. The camera pulls back to reveal that this Six is radiating heat—literally—from her blood-red spine as she claws at his skin and moans that she's *hot*.

Indeed. Baltar's response to Six gives us pause about the nature of love on *Battlestar Galactica*. That first scene welcomes the audience into the sex, lies, and love that permeate the mythos of *Battlestar*. Within the first few hours of the miniseries we are introduced to a host of characters who will complicate their lives (and storylines) with torrid love triangles, forbidden attachments, and soul-consuming love. On *Battlestar* love is not a sugar-coated confection: it's tart or bittersweet, far more complicated, dark, and more deceptive than the stuff of romance novels and typical network dramas. Love is a battlefield: a danger zone where hearts are trampled and torn, alliances betrayed, morality bent.

Battlestar's concept of love is murky, especially to the Cylons who both crave and revile it. To the "enlightened" Cylons—Caprica Six, the Six inside Baltar's head, Boomer, and to an extent, D'Anna—"love" is all consuming and transformative, the ultimate reflection of goodness. Love, whether of other Cylons, humans, or god, should be a religious experience. All their god asks of his followers is love—to know him is to love him, and through love, anything is possible. Cylons understand at a philosophical level that love has the power to get the Cylon Sharon pregnant with Karl's baby, as well as create peace between man and machine. Some Cylons, however, become ensnared in love once they've experienced the emotion. There's no greater Cylon advocate of love than Six, who loves Baltar to the point of her own destruction, and romance complicates as well the relationships between Chief Tyrol and Boomer and Caprica Sharon and Karl.

For humans, love seldom seems a precious gift from god. Love is a weakness that produces devastating results. Kara Thrace's love for Zak Adama resulted in her giving him a license to fly that proved fatal ("Act of Contrition," 1.4; "You Can't Go Home Again," 1.5). The *Galactica* XO's love for wife Ellen resulted in years of alcoholism and self-depreciation; her love for Saul eventually costs her own life ("Tigh Me Up, Tigh me Down," 1.9; "Exodus," 3.3). Bill Adama's often negative, angry love for his wife and deep-seated regret for spending so much time away from his family result in his inability to show potential love interest Laura Roslin the extent of his feelings for her ("Scattered" 2.1). Lee Adama, paralyzed by fear of love, runs away from a woman on Caprica who carried his child ("Black Market," 2.14) and rushes into the arms of wife-to-be Dualla, in large part because she is available when Kara is not. In retaliation, Kara marries another man (Samuel Anders), resulting in a self-destructive spiral and the formation of love triangles among Dualla-Lee-Kara and Lee-Kara-Sam. For both human and Cylon on *Battlestar*, love's transformative powers usually result in heartbreak, disappointment, and pain.

Gaius Baltar and Six

Battlestar's most complicated love relationship involves Gaius Baltar and his doting, devoted Number Six. Gaius, a womanizing fool, undoubtedly thought the extent of his union with Six on Caprica was immediate sexual gratification, nothing more. When Six reveals the Cylons' plan to destroy the human race—a conversation that follows Gaius' realization that he allowed Six to access the defense mainframe in payment for her intellectual assistance—she tells him she didn't help him for profit. She did it for *love*. Well, that and because god told her to do it, a revelation with which Gaius is visibly uncomfortable. Thus begins the first arc of the Gaius/Six drama, a relationship partially theological (the love for, and belief in, the one god Six venerates), and partially emotional (Gaius's return of affection for Six). Six is a complicated woman/Cylon, and as the audience learns she is not human, it still cannot help but identify with her desperate hope that Gaius will love her unconditionally. Like many human women trying to get what they need, Six pouts when Gaius shuts her out, manipulates him by granting or withholding sex, and, in short, performing every stereotypical "trick" on *Cosmopolitan*'s How Not to Keep a Boyfriend list.

In the Miniseries, when Six catches Gaius in bed with a "friend," he offers petty excuses ("It's me, I'm screwed up … always have been. It's a flaw in my character that I've always hated and tried to overcome, but …" Six coldly tells him to spare her "your feigned self-awareness and remorse. I came here because I have something to tell you." This scene is important for two reasons. First, she's bluffing—she's deeply hurt by Gaius' betrayal, and we later learn that she hopes she can change him from a womanizing sex addict to a repentant, devoted lover. Second, the scene proves that she's *real*: on Caprica other people can see her; she's got a physical form and function. This revelation complicates matters later when, near the close of the epic miniseries, Six later takes spectral form, existing for a time only in Baltar's head.

What Six has come to tell him, of course, is that it's the end of the world as he knows it, and—surprise—she's a Cylon/machine, a fact that she's sure he's already aware of on some level. As he tries to process all she's telling him, he never asks her why she is there. Six's return to Baltar and explanation of what is to come lets us know that her love for him is genuine: she really does care enough to save this man—a womanizer, a flake, a fake—we might think is hardly worth saving.

Baltar survives the holocaust only because Six protects him with her body; her physical form "dies" during the blast, and Gaius assumes she is gone forever. Soon, however, he realizes that Six lives on in his mind—with all her dangerous, jealous, manipulative ways intact. Living with Six is both a blessing and a curse. Most of their Season One conversations take place in Baltar's lab on *Galactica* or inside his mind during flashbacks to his Caprica apartment. In these heated arguments they debate love and the nature of affection. More than once the argument results in a sexual tryst, much to the confusion of Baltar's shipmates, who think of him as a peculiar genius. They're never sure what's going on in his mind, but they are glad that he's on their side.

It's not until the third season that we learn Cylons' consciousness is determined by their surroundings, causing Baltar to wonder if he, too, is Cylon, given that he can so easily dissolve into the mental landscapes of a seashore or a long-destroyed home ("A Measure of Salvation," 3.7). Baltar's ability to "think" like a Cylon suggests that Cylons and humans are not so far removed from one another, and perhaps everything is a matter of perception. The ability to alter the way one views and experiences the world may be a universal trait, albeit one achieved more easily by Cylons after years of practice. We get a better understanding of the Cylon concept of "projection" in the episode "Torn" (3.6): The Cylons are able to envision any reality they choose, a unique perception that blurs reality into fantasy. It's what helps Baltar overcome the painful torture enacted by D'Anna as he projects himself into lovemaking with Six.

One great area of difference between humans and Cylons continues to be religion, and this difference again is exacerbated in the Six-Baltar relationship. Six spends the majority of Season One attempting to convert Gaius to monotheism. (Although Baltar resists religious conversion, when he learns of Six's deception and the Cylon doomsday plan, ironically he utters "My god," instead of the series' more commonly used plural form.) Most of the time, Baltar picks at Six's faith, demoralizing and demeaning it, suggesting she's insane. Even when he claims to have accepted her god and faith, it takes him some time to be a true believer—a task aided by Six's disappearance from their little mental fireside chats when he tells her she's little more than a toaster ("Six Degrees of Separation," 1.7). Her departure coincides with a witch hunt as Baltar is fingered for being a Cylon collaborator, thanks to Miss Godfrey, a tangible form of Six bearing evidence of Baltar's betrayal.

The appearance of Miss Godfrey and Six's conspicuous absence send Baltar into a paranoid frenzy. He fears he will lose his freedom (and life) for aiding the Cylons (however inadvertently). During this stressful time, he first confesses his love for Six, yelling his declaration because he assumes that is what she wants to hear. Six, however, is waiting for something more transcendent. Gaius totally surrenders his will to god: "I now acknowledge that you are the one true god. Deliver me from this evil and I will ... I will devote the rest of what is left of my wretched life to doing good, and ... uh ... to carrying out your divine will is what I want to do." Immediately after his confession, Six returns, Baltar is venerated, and Shelly Godfrey disappears. God's will has been done.

Despite her righteous indignation when Baltar refuses to understand god's will, Six rather humanly strays from the straight and narrow herself. Her love for Baltar isn't simply the product of god's love or plan. Her jealousy and possessive nature often lead to "discussions" with Baltar and make her wonder if he can even grasp the concept of monogamous, unconditional love. For his part, Baltar often guesses at what Cylon women really want and alternately placates or provokes Six's jealous streak. In "Colonial Day" (1.11), Baltar and Six share a rather eye-opening conversation about her capacity for jealousy and vengeance. She informs him that the Picon *Star Tribune* columnist Playa Palacious lacks certain undergarments and tells him he can have any woman he wants—as long as he knows that she has his heart. He noncommittally replies, "Of course you do." Her eyes narrow as she reminds him, "I can always rip it out of your chest if I need to."

Despite Six's threats (with many others to follow), her Cylon model cannot help but be drawn to Gaius Baltar. Whether (as Shelley Godfrey) trying to destroy him or (as god's "angel" Six) redeem him, Baltar and the Sixes seem destined to be together. While the audience may doubt Baltar's pledge of love to Six, we see, time and time again, that his affections are real. As prophesied,

"All this has happened, and will happen again." Such is the history and continuing development of their relationship.

A more human adage is also appropriate: "Can't live with him/her, can't live without him/her." There's no denying that there's a true (and very real) connection between Baltar and Six. Caprica Six has her very own Gaius living in her mind ("Downloaded," 2.18); she struggles over the missing physical form of her lover, and when the two are reunited on New Caprica, they enter into a physical relationship ("Occupation," 3.1). Baltar confuses the two Sixes and admits his love for "her," and their relationship results in Caprica Six rescuing him from New Caprica by taking him with the Cylons ("Exodus" 3.3–3.4). She tries to leave him many times (just as the figment Six tries to leave Gaius), without success. Despite every tribulation, Gaius and Six become the quintessential representation of Us and Them.

STARBUCK AND APOLLO

Audiences love a star-crossed romance, and that certainly describes Kara (Starbuck) Thrace and Lee (Apollo) Adama. Their very first scene together in the miniseries hints at a familiarity deeper than friendship, as Lee and Kara trade smiles across a room. Later, the audience learns that she had loved, been engaged to, and lost Lee's younger brother, Zak, who died in a crash two years prior. In the intervening time, Kara became Commander Adama's pseudo-adopted daughter, and Lee and Kara shared a bond over a mutual love for Zak. It's hard to say when that emotion became muddied—some fans felt the sexual tension from day one, whereas others saw Lee's concern for Kara's propensity for drink and self-abuse as a brotherly like concern ("33," 1.2; "Water," 1.3). No one, however, can dispute that something is there, beneath the surface, when Apollo appreciatively looks Starbuck (in a dress!) up and down at the Colonial Day celebration and the two share a dance ("Colonial Day," 1.11) All bets are off when the audience is treated to

Starbuck's private fantasy: making love to her CAG, Lee Adama—if only in her mind. She unfortunately cries out "Lee" while in the throes of drunken passion with Gaius Baltar ("Kobol's Last Gleaming," 1.12).

This cry reverberates throughout the battlestar. Lee beats himself up over his lust for Starbuck after learning of her one-night fling with Baltar. Gaius' vast ego is wounded, and Starbuck feels humiliated about vocalizing feelings she does not fully understand. When Lee and Kara later literally duke it out, he asks her "why she did it." Attempting to punch him, she replies, "Because I'm a screw up" (Kobol's Last Gleaming," 1.12).

There's more to the story than Kara's fragile emotional state: she seems to feel guilt at her affections toward the Adama brother who survives. Lee outranks her, knows how to fly (nearly) as well as she does, and is the only person she trusts as a confidante. In flashbacks, we see that Kara and Zak had an open, affectionate relationship; she had been a softer, kinder woman, despite her abusive childhood. In the two years following his death, however, Starbuck becomes a randy drunk, entering into alcohol-fueled trysts with any man willing to fall in her bunk. Baltar is hardly the first, and far from the last to be caught in Kara's web.

Starbuck and Apollo share a love-hate relationship: even after their boxing match in "Kobol's Last Gleaming," they deal with their mutual attraction as the elephant in the room. Kara's brief (and somewhat puzzling) love affair with Samuel Anders results in her rather self-absorbed depression and avoidance of Lee. This response lasts until three-fourths of the way through "Scar" (2.15) when Lee and Kara revisit their mutual interest in one another. After a night of drinking, they kiss, and Kara undresses her CAG but tells him she just wants a quick frak. For her, there is no relationship, no "us." Lee, understandably hurt, tells her that her problem isn't being hung up over dead guys (including Zak and the missing and presumed deceased Sam); she just doesn't know what to do with the living ones.

His words hit home. She slaps but then passionately kisses him, showing her conflicting emotions—only Apollo provokes such a wide range. Starbuck is most vulnerable with him and exposes her softer, gentler side while (most often successfully) keeping her emotions at bay. The audience cannot help but wonder why Starbuck is so resistant: Perhaps it's the failed relationship with her mother that has left her feeling scared, vulnerable, and emotionally available; perhaps it's knowing that her love for Zak made her do things for which she still feels guilt.

Although some fans recoiled at Kara's attachment—and eventual marriage—to Sam Anders, the relationship is understandable. The circumstances of their meeting and attraction in some ways allowed Kara to be whoever she wanted to be—and she is allowed to take on a far more feminine role in her marriage than with Lee. Anders is not a superior or even an equal in the ranks; he's subordinate and submissive in many respects, though only to his wife. He risks his life to save her from the Cylons that hold her captive (and steal her eggs) ("The Farm," 2.5), and she genuinely respects him. When she returns to Caprica to save him, the two are instantly reunited, resulting in Lee's jealousy and eventual union with future wife Dualla.

Kara may crave a companion different from her in some ways (after all, Anders can't compete with her flight skills or her hard-as-nails attitude, even though after her supposed death he begins flight training). Lee craves a woman he can control. Ironically, Dualla is Kara's opposite, and Anders is Lee's. In essence, the two are almost more substitutes—or placeholders, if you will—for the "real" thing, acting as surrogate companions and bedmates, as neither fulfill Kara and Lee's need for one another, both physically and emotionally. Perhaps the most compelling theme that exists in the complicated human relationship between Apollo and Starbuck is that of sacrifice. To rescue Starbuck, Lee willingly sacrifices his own wife to save his lover ("The Eye of Jupiter," 3.11), which is hardly Apollo's first crazed attempt to rescue the woman he loves. Earlier, when Apollo was Kara's CAG on *Pegasus*, he didn't hesitate to sign her up to sacrifice her life on the Cylon transport ship when a detonator wouldn't work, resulting in Kara's request to leave *Pegasus*, since he "keeps trying to kill her" (*Razor*). While Lee appears flippant, her departure initiates a spiral of increasingly difficult events that further complicate their relationship.

This problematic relationship is based on a nearly violent denial of the way the two truly feel for one another. The level of tension between the two frequently results in violence, perhaps most notably expressed in the episode "Unfinished Business" (3.9), in which the audience learns of the beginning of Apollo and Starbuck's physical relationship. It also discloses the conversation that the two have about her future plans, where she tells him she doesn't plan to marry Anders, prompting Lee's "The rest of your life, Kara. Is this how you want to spend it? Is this who you want to spend it with?" His thorny questions result in a kiss that leads to a scene of impassioned lovemaking and, later, to both confessing they love one another.

This shared scene between them—a giggling, adorable couple in a cabin in the woods—is one of the most innocent moments we see between Kara and Lee. Although the audience knows that somehow Lee and Kara do not end up together, they see the vulnerability that each expresses to one another. They also witness the destructive force of Kara's own insecurities. Perhaps her childhood conviction of being undeserving of love and affection prompts her to leave and marry Sam Anders the next morning. It's certainly Lee's stubborn pride that makes him marry Anastasia Dualla as a retaliatory response. In the months that follow, the two characters go through more transformative changes not due to their separation: Kara is held hostage by Leoben, who brainwashes her into believing she is a mother; Lee becomes Commander of the *Pegasus*, and even after her eventual rescue from New Caprica, their relationship is tense. It's not until the bloody boxing match in "Unfinished Business" that they get to the heart of the matter: that they had missed one another.

Honesty never proves a positive factor in this beyond-complicated relationship, as the two again begin a sexual affair. Lee suggests divorce ("The Eye of Jupiter" 3.11), Kara denies him, telling him marriage is "a sacrament. ... I made a vow in the sight of the gods, and I'm not gonna break that." Lee says he won't cheat, and the two revisit the issue in "Taking a Break From All Your Worries" (3.13), where he explains their situation as "trapped." Anders confronts his wife, asking if she loves Lee. Kara, visibly upset and near tears, tells him that she doesn't know, and then answers "maybe." He tells her she has to go to him. In this same episode, Dualla tells Lee that she knows he is going to see Kara and that she'd married him because she loved him. She tells him, "It's not a marriage, Lee. It's a lie. You want to be with Kara, Lee? Go ahead. I won't stand in your way."

When the two meet, Kara asks if she should leave Sam if he'd leave Dualla, and, based on her previous actions, he expresses his distrust. Lee hits the bottle and loses his wedding ring, and he later meets up with his wife in their prearranged dinner, where he tells her he once loved Kara but now loves his wife and wants to be with her, and that she's good for him. Kara watches with Anders from a distance, and as the two drink, the audience realizes that it's over between Lee and Starbuck, again. Their bittersweet relationship is about sacrifice: Lee can't bear to hurt Dualla when he knows how much she loves him, and as soon as Kara realizes she'll sacrifice her faith for Lee and go against the sacrament of marriage, she realizes that she's already lost him.

Perhaps this would be the end of the saga between the two star-crossed lovers, but we see that Lee's love for Kara is far from dead: when he witnesses her death in "Maelstrom" (3.17), he is visibly depressed and loses his initiative to fly. His role as counsel in Baltar's treason case results in his permanent removal as CAG. His new allegiances and emotional distance prove more than

Dualla can take: she leaves him after standing by his side during his first depression on *Pegasus*, where his eighteen-month separation from Kara results in his ballooning weight and intense bitterness. After Dualla leaves him, and as soon as Lee starts to recover from his loss, the conclusion of Season Three's "Crossroads" reflects his return as "Apollo." He becomes CAG and a Viper pilot once more. As *Galactica* suffers a power surge and encounters a massive Cylon fleet, Lee hops into the cockpit, ready to fight. What he finds during his mission surprises him as much as the rest of the audience: Starbuck, back from the dead, ready to lead the entire human race to Earth.

Lee and Kara's relationship, volatile at best, plays with the role reversal so prominently begun with Starbuck's gender switch from the original series. Apollo is far more romantic than Kara (he is first to declare his love and harbors romantic sentiments that their love will result in marriage). Whereas Kara hopes for just an affair (playing a more socially accepted masculine role), Lee takes on the stereotypical feminine role of the marriage-minded; he is the one who suffers emotional burdens from Kara's betrayal. Their love-to-hate relationship, and mutual need for one another, is similar to the one between Gaius and Six.

As the series draws to an end, it's understandable that fans want to see Apollo and Starbuck end up together in an "happily ever after" tableau of romantic bliss. Now that we know her husband and his new love Tory are Cylons, and Dualla has left her husband because of his obsession with Gaius Baltar's criminal case (and the ghost of Kara Thrace), the possibility of a happy union seems all the more unlikely. But that's the stuff of fairy tales, and the ever-realistic *Battlestar* is far from a fairy tale. On *Battlestar Galactica*, love is a battlefield: a place where love carries the ultimate risk of self-sacrifice, and emotion as always exhibits a capacity for destruction.

In some ways, we can expect that the series' most prominent lovers will meet dissatisfying ends. Gaius and Six will continue in an unrequited imaginal relationship that may never be fully real or tangible. When the woman you love exists only in your mind, that can be an obstacle in the route to happily ever after. Starbuck and Apollo may be living, breathing "real" people, but their stubbornness about the myriad issues keeping them separate could well keep them apart as a matter of course. All the same, we keep watching—and hoping—for some resolution, however slight, to love on a *Battlestar*.

CHAPTER SEVEN

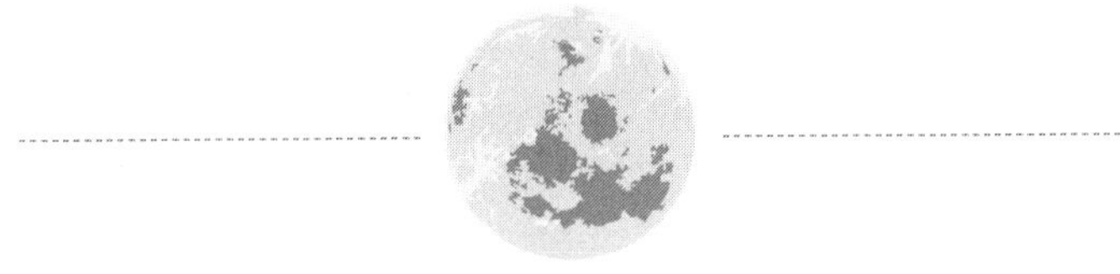

STARBUCK AND THE GENDER DYNAMICS OF *BATTLESTAR GALACTICA*

—Ewan Kirkland

SITUATING STARBUCK

Starbuck, aka Lieutenant Kara Thrace, represents the most recent in a long line of film and TV action heroines. And she stands in good company. Starbuck's lineage incorporates the heroines of the silent movie serials, post-war women's pictures, blaxploitation cinema, and rape-revenge exploitation thrillers, alongside the police dramas, action adventures and espionage series of *The Avengers*, *The Bionic Woman*, and *Cagney and Lacey*. But Starbuck's most contemporary point of reference is undoubtedly Ripley of the *Alien* series.

Ripley's transformation from crew member to alien slayer, military leader, alien mother, and genetic hybrid has been the subject of countless essays, books, PhD theses, and film student debates. Other sci-fi and fantasy heroines of film and television follow in Ripley's wake, including *Terminator 2*'s Sarah Connor, Tank Girl, Aeon Flux, Buffy, Xena, *Relic Hunter*'s Sidney Fox,

Alias' Sydney Bristow, *Dark Angel*'s Max Guevera, Kim Possible, and Lara Croft.

As with all these women, it is hard not to interpret Starbuck's current incarnation as a reflection of contemporary gender politics. The cigar-smoking, tough-talking action hero of 1970s *Battlestar Galactica* has been transformed—or transgendered—into the cigar-smoking, tough-talking action heroine of *Battlestar Galactica* the next millennium. The character's gender reassignment is undoubtedly a sign of the times, testimony to three decades of feminist sexual politics, the many tough girl heroines of fantasy film and television whose presence has become an accepted—even expected—addition to any futuristic ensemble, and the increased presence of women in the workplace, the media, and the military.

Nevertheless, despite their growing visibility, deep ambivalences circulate images of active, violent, powerful women. Our culture continues to associate femininity with passivity, pacifism, domesticity, and maternity. It is men who have historically—so we are repeatedly told—gone out and got things done. The film and TV industries stand charged with innumerable instances of perpetuating that mythical history, from the Western to the sci-fi space opera. Activity in film and television, as many feminist authors have asserted, is an almost exclusively male preserve. Men direct the narrative, the camera, and the gaze, while women exist as window dressing staged for the heterosexual male eye. Consequently, whenever a woman steps into the active role traditionally occupied by a male she embodies a challenge to such assumptions, although the extent of such a challenge remains debatable.

Often films and TV shows that appear to contradict this structure are seen as surreptitiously supporting old-fashioned assumptions about gender difference. How progressive is it for a woman to occupy the traditionally male position if ultimately all she wants to do is hang up her helmet, grow her hair long, and settle down with a pyramid ball player on New Caprica? Frequently fictional women's activity is constructed as an abnormality, the symptom of childhood trauma or dysfunctional parents, like a violent and overcritical mother whose admonishing words continue to ring in her daughter's ears. Time and again active women are ultimately controlled and contained by male mentors, father figures, lovers, Watchers, Cylon stalkers, battlestar commanders, and so on.

Characters like Kara Thrace represent attempts, in fictional form, to engage with a range of pertinent issues: the gendered grammar and iconography of action heroism, the increasing visibility of women in the armed forces, dreams of a utopian/dystopian future where gender becomes irrelevant, sexual difference and its impact on human desire, interpersonal relationships, and the workplace. *Battlestar Galactica* provides an often ambiguous, frequently contradictory engagement with such themes. The series employs traditional conventions of gendered representation, while conspicuously mobilizing them for thematic ends. Starbuck is permitted a considerable degree of agency and authority, but equally *BSG* works to contain her transgressive potential. Focusing on the ace fighter pilot, counterterrorist expert, super fistfighter, sharp cardplayer, alcoholic, suicidal "world-class frak up" ("Maelstrom," 3.17) Starbuck throws light on broader representations and constructions of gender within *Battlestar Galactica* and the media. What emerges is a complex and contradictory picture of men and women, gender and sexuality, humans and Cylons.

HUMAN MASCULINITY AND CYLON FEMININITY

Despite *Battlestar Galactica*'s apparently gender-free regime, Starbuck's character exists within a highly polarized universe divided between a masculinized humanity and a feminized Cylon race.

Mankind—a term used here quite deliberately—lives under the benevolent protection of Admiral Adama, the consummate patriarch. Military leader, joint head of humanity, firm-but-fair father figure, Adama's gravelly voice is complemented by an equally gravelly complexion. At the helm Adama exhibits qualities associated with being a man: tough, stoic, level-headed, professional, ruthlessly unemotional when necessary, whether destroying a potentially Cylon-infiltrated civilian vessel ("33," 1.1) or nuking a planet's surface to avoid irreplaceable artifacts from falling into enemy hands ("The Eye of Jupiter," 3.11). When off duty, Adama is no less the man. Scenes of Adama shaving with traditional soap and razor, drinking neat spirits, or building model ships underline the commander's masculinity. His dark quarters, their walls hung with battle scenes, leather-bound books, and weaponry, similarly reflect Adama's stalwart maleness.

The frequently drunken, perpetually henpecked Colonel Tigh represents a figure of masculine weakness, which contributes to enhancing Adama's male authority. President Roslin, a leader prepared to shed a tear over civilian losses, who falters over her inauguration speech ("Miniseries"), presents a more emotional, feminine response to the situation of wartime governance. Yet the series resists feminizing Roslin too much. The eagerness with which Roslin orders Cylons be flung out of airlocks ("Home, Part 1," 2.6), her Machiavellian political machinations, recruiting Baltar for purely tactical reasons ("Colonial Day," 1.11), going so far as to compromise democratic processes ("Lay Down Your Burdens, Part 2," 2.20), and Roslin's maternal promise of protection to Leoben immediately followed by his evacuation into space ("Flesh and Bone," 1.8), suggests a ruthlessness associated with masculinity not femininity.

This is because throughout the series femininity—or more specifically, film and TV representations and constructions of femininity—is most clearly aligned with the Cylons. Masculinity in the Cylon scenes is deflected onto the older models,

Terminator-style creations, with their hard steel bodies and hands of phallic whirling blades. The three main models—Numbers Three (D'Anna), Six (Caprica), and Eight (Sharon)—are all women, and conventionally attractive women at that. As introduced in the miniseries, Caprica Six is a *femme fatal* figure, using her sexuality as a weapon to disable and manipulate men. Her infiltration of the human defense mainframe, as depicted in her cold confession to a whimpering Baltar, becomes not only a wrathful vengeance visited upon an unfaithful sexual partner, but also the virtual rape of a male military establishment by a duplicitous sexually captivating woman.

Like Adama's stoic quarters, the Cylons' surroundings extenuate their gender. Our first glimpse of Cylon architecture ("Kobol's Last Gleaming, Part 2," 1.13), clearly inspired by H. I. Geiger's designs for *Alien*, represents a no less gynecological investigation of the Cylon Basestar, complete with primal scene where Boomer discovers her true self/s in the belly of the mothership. Similar imagery informs the resurrection ship ("Resurrection Ship, Part 2," 2. 12), its gothic structures housing row after row of womb-like chambers. The Cylon baseship of Season Three, whose dark metallic corridors resemble those of *Galactica*, is distinguished by the blinding bright lights lining its walls, variously suggestive of a disco, a fashion shoot, a red-light district, a sex stage, all associated with erotic displays of female bodies and female sexuality.

The piercing spot lighting of the Cylon ship, the frequent nudity of Cylon females—the only models seen regenerating—and the phantasmagorical dream-like style in which Cylons are often depicted, serve to locate the entire race in structures of visual representation associated with women. This contrasts with the *Galactica* females: Cally with her grime-smeared overalls, Dualla in her unflattering unisex uniform, Kat's brash bravado and challenge to Starbuck's hard-bodied toughness. While these women struggle within their respective professions, getting dirty, sweaty, and physically drained, the Cylon women never appear with a hair out of place, either in their roles as midwives to newly downloaded sisters or coolly controlling Cylon technologies through a device resembling a manicurist's nail bath.

The spectacularly conspicuous camera trickery whereby numerous naked Sharons crowd the screen differs from the understated special-effect sequences depicting dogfights in space. Here wobbly virtual cameras, simulated lens flare, and hasty refocusing imply a documentary realism and authenticity more associated with masculine genres and texts. Further testimony to the distinction between Cylon space and human space are Baltar's frequent hallucinations of Number Six. When she appears on *Galactica*, draped across his shoulder, her red dress introduces a primary color rarely featured in the battlestar's somber palette. In deeper reveries, Baltar is transported back to his lakeside home on Caprica in scenes where bright colors, deliberate static framing, natural lighting, and soft-core content contrast rudely with the gloomy sets and grainy documentary aesthetic the doctor finds upon awakening.

At the core of the reimagined *Battlestar*'s exploration of gender, of course, is the character of Starbuck, and it is to her that we now turn.

GENDERING STARBUCK

Understanding the gendered structure of *Battlestar Galactica* allows greater appreciation of Starbuck's location within the series, and her relationship with action heroines of the recent past.

One consistent criticism of the action heroine is her masculinization. In her transition from lowly crew member to alien scourge, it is claimed Ripley loses any signs of femininity. Proving herself more man than any marine in *Aliens*, appearing entirely bald and dressed in unflattering prison overalls in *Alien 3*, Ripley is divested of all terrestrial maternal obligations, and appears barely human by *Alien Resurrection*.

Sarah Connor undergoes a similar transformation between *The Terminator* and *Terminator 2: Judgment Day*, becoming like her cyborg adversary: hard emotionally and physically. *Thelma & Louise*'s female leads, as noted by many commentators, jettison all signifiers of femininity—jewelry, cosmetics, women's clothing—on the road, becoming increasingly masculine in appearance while gaining greater affinity with male-coded technologies, such as the gun and the car. While challenging and exhilarating, such aspects are considered to communicate reactionary or pessimistic messages. At best: in order to survive in a male world, women must adopt male attitudes and sensibilities. At worst: activity is inherently masculine, reserved only for masculine men or masculine women.

Conversely, action heroines who appear too feminine are understood as equally problematic. Much discussed is *Alien*'s final scene where Ripley undresses for the camera. Is this reminding audiences of the character's femininity in order to emphasize the political challenge posed by the action heroine, or is it reframing the female body once more for comfortable male visual pleasure? Charlie's Angels, Buffy, Xena, Max, and Lara are seen as compromised by their conventional femininity, their impractical clothing and hairstyles, their objectification and sexualization, implying a re-establishment of traditionally gendered ways of seeing that militate the political challenges they pose. Even Ripley and Connor are regarded as recuperated by their maternity, the former rescuing Jones the cat and Newt, while Connor's actions are motivated by a fervent desire to protect her son.

Starbuck, at first glance, belongs in the masculine brand of action heroine. With her short hair, tomboyish features, and stocky frame, the pilot can be understood as evoking iconography of the masculinized woman as hero. As well as being a hotshot pilot, Starbuck smokes cigars, drinks from the bottle, and excels at fist fighting, shooting, and playing pyramid ball. Also, according to Lee, Starbuck smells, a particularly unfeminine quality.

But Starbuck's masculinity, according to the structure outlined above, also signifies her humanity. Despite her phenomenal proficiency, Starbuck functions as an everyman character. Not part of the political or military elite, the impression is that Starbuck's rank has been earned solely through ability. Starbuck is, in many respects, superhuman. Hers is the first human body we see to survive, post credits, jogging purposefully along the battlestar corridor, warning the gaggle of curious tourists blocking her path to "make a hole" ("Miniseries"). Immediately an opposition is established between the active heroine's body—laboring, sweaty, clad in gray—and the scarlet-draped platinum blonde Cylon Number Six who marches coolly on stilettos and reacts unflinchingly to her impending pre-credit destruction. One woman moves the camera along, while the other occupies a space already configured by the frame, visual representation traditionally marked as masculine and feminine respectively.

Having invested in the gendered dichotomy described above, *Battlestar Galactica* cannot subsequently feminize Starbuck's body without undermining her humanity. At the same time, depicting Starbuck as too masculine would suggest an unnatural lack of gender-appropriate qualities.

In part, the show's location on *Galactica* helps negotiate this problem. Like *Aliens*, *Starship Troopers*, *Space: Above and Beyond*, and *Farscape*, *BSG* presents a futuristic image of society at total war, where traditional gender distinctions have become irrelevant or untenable. Men and women are equally conscripted into the service of fighting a relentless enemy seeking mankind's total destruction. Against a backdrop of communal bathroom facilities, unisex sleeping quarters, and the virtual absence of domestic or civilian life, a normalized and unquestioned masculinity embraces everyone. Whether post-apocalyptic dystopia or post-gender utopia, sexism and sexual discrimination are absent from this world. At no point must Starbuck argue her equality or superiority to men, an absence that undoubtedly limits her potential as an explicit feminist figure.

Nevertheless, Starbuck's femininity is emphasized in ways that negotiate the synonymity between maleness and humanity represented by Adama's regime. Notably these instances take place outside *Galactica*'s physical confines. On pleasure dome *Cloud Nine*, we see Starbuck for the first and only time wearing a dress ("Colonial Day"). On New Caprica Starbuck grows her hair long and becomes nurse to new husband Sam. This is of course indicative of a wider malignant feminization resulting from the absence of war's masculine discipline: Sam gets sick, Lee gets fat, while the Presidency is occupied by a man who, despite the concubines lolling around a grounded Colonial One, appears fey and unmanly ("Lay Down Your Burdens, Part 2," 2.20).

Cylon interest in Starbuck places a premium on her maternal potential. In "The Farm" (2.5), Starbuck finds herself incapacitated in a military hospital. A suspicious doctor—eventually revealed to be the Cylon named Simon—discusses her post-war duty to bear children while conducting secret invasive medical procedures on her reproductive organs. Before escaping the hospital, unaided by Sam's pyramid ball freedom fighters, Starbuck destroys a ward of human women wired to grotesque contraptions designed to harvest their breeding capabilities. Her actions constitute a rare moment of female solidarity and defiance at the Cylon's planned exploitation of her own child-bearing abilities.

THE CYLON GAZE

Like much science fiction, *BSG* expresses a fascination with the possibility of human/mechanical hybridization. As indicated by the coupling narratives of Sharon/Helo, Caprica Six/Baltar, and, potentially, Tyrol/Cally, Cylon/human love, sex, and interbreeding rank highly on the Cylon's agenda, preoccupations with romance and reproduction further coding their culture feminine. Indicative of various models' repeated attempts to place Starbuck in traditional feminine positions, "The Farm" reveals the Cylons' interest in Starbuck's birthing potential. It is through this capacity that the female body—according to a range of discourses—achieves greatest affinity with nature. Such narratives, while emphasizing Starbuck's natural human body, paradoxically, in feminizing the fighter pilot, evoke suggestions she may actually be a Cylon.

A fascinating scene in this respect occurs in "Final Cut" (2.8), where Starbuck is briefly interviewed by D'Anna Biers, before her revelation as Cylon model Number Three. Prior to the episode's denouement, Biers has already been marked as suspect, an outsider to Adama's masculine military order. The character's bright civilian clothes, sculptured hair, and unintimidated familiarity signal her as threatening Adama's authority. The TV journalist's association with the electronic media reflects the Cylon's relationship with technology, echoing public relations manager Aaron Doral's unmasking as Number Five ("Miniseries"), and spin doctor Tory Foster's membership of the final five in Season Three's finale ("Crossroads, Part 2," 3.20). The modern media of Hollywood spectaculars, glossy magazines, and stylish advertising is often constructed as female, and the Cylons are frequently associated with digital media technologies—downloading into bodies, manipulating close circuit camera, infecting computer networks with viruses—technologies forbidden by Adama, whose Ludditism is exonerated by his crew's continued survival.

This encounter between D'Anna and Starbuck foregrounds the pilot's healthy human physique. Starbuck is seen sparring against a punchbag in a display of taut fitness, bodily control, and lean muscularity. While recognizably feminine, little of the traditional Hollywood techniques for emphasizing the femininity of active women are evident: no slow motion, no lingering shots of fetishized body parts, no objectification of breasts, bottom, or crotch.

The camera momentarily looks up Starbuck's body, a movement authored by the camera's presence within the scene, and by D'Anna's scrutinizing gaze, which structures the episode. With retrospective knowledge of D'Anna's true nature, this glance typifies the investigation into human ways which motivates the

Cylons' documentary—maybe their entire post-war project—and links the filmmaker's actions with Number Six's curious scrutinization of the human ambassador in the miniseries' opening sequence. D'Anna's gaze investigates Starbuck's body as human, and as woman.

Leoben's obsession with Starbuck appears part of this ambivalent project. Hardly libidinous, his actions appear founded on a sexless spiritual mania, centered on her capacity for fulfilling more traditional female roles. In kidnapping Starbuck following the invasion of New Caprica ("Occupation," 3.1), the Cylon clearly seeks to manufacture the same amorous circumstances as successfully created between Sharon and Helo on the new colony's namesake. While probably desiring sexual congress of a kind, more significant to Leoben is the induction of love within a construction of the human nuclear family.

Therein lies the series' more explicit engagement with gender politics. Off *Galactica*, Starbuck is able to mobilize more recognizably feminine and feminist discourses. The prison home, a particularly sterile domestic space characterized by cold blues, frosty lighting, and expressionistic shadows, can easily be understood as a critique of the heterosexual family unit. Within such arrangements—according to feminist critics—women are subjected to domestic slavery, emotional blackmail, and physical and sexual abuse. Given its position in the series, Starbuck's domestic prison reflects a growing dissatisfaction with civilian life and marriage to Anders in particular. It is no coincidence Leoben's trump bid for Kara's cooperation involves the production of a (fake) daughter, Kasey—Starbuck's newt—and her injury while in Starbuck's care coerces the nearest thing to physical and emotional closeness between this Cylon and human ("Precipice," 3.2). Equally, the nearest Starbuck gets to a *Thelma & Louise* moment, an expression of feminist rage, is when she stabs Leoben in the neck with a sharp object. The Cylon's repeated return symbolizes the circle of violence enacted in situations of domestic abuse.

More problematic is Starbuck's own growing obsession with her Cylon captor. In fantasizing about the very act of sexual passion Leoben sought to elicit ("Maelstrom," 3.17), Starbuck's character appears to confirm mythologies that such victims are actually complicit in their victimization. The independent action heroine's acceptance of the Cylons' image of her is indicated in visual terms by the revealing shirt and underwear Starbuck sports in her own dream. A male (Cylon) gaze infiltrates Kara's subconscious, structuring her soft-core writing in white paint, suggestive of male bodily fluids. The Cylon's words, and her mother's domestic violence, are exonerated by the female oracle who insists Starbuck embrace her "special destiny." Leoben's switch from abusive husband to benevolent spiritualist—part therapist, part ghost of Starbuck's past—absolves the Cylon of past sins, while Starbuck is forced to redefine herself in Leoben's terms.

True to form, early in the episode the action heroine asserts, "I write my own destiny." Starbuck's ending in Season Three would suggest otherwise.

Starbuck's Humanity

Starbuck represents a compelling addition to the action heroine hall of fame. She combines the toughness of Ripley with Sarah Connor's knowledge of weaponry, the superheroism of Xena with Charlie's Angels' broad and adaptable portfolio of skills and abilities, the defiance of Thelma and Louise with—in her lighter moments—the playfulness of Buffy.

While amalgamating these recognizable characters and characteristics, Starbuck never verges on cliché, testimony to the long-running TV format's facilitation of more nuanced characterizations than traditional film and TV heroines. For nearly three seasons Starbuck manages to navigate the binary gender constructions that threaten to masculinize her heroism on the one hand, or constrict her agency and activity through traditional conventions of femininity on the other. In "Flesh and Bone"

(1.8), Starbuck shows traditionally male ruthlessness in torturing a Cylon prisoner physically and emotionally, but in "Scar" (2.15) is seen distraught to the verge of suicide at having to abandon her Caprican lover. "Act of Contrition" (1.4), where Starbuck is shown to have compromised her professionalism for love, is immediately followed by "You Can't Go Home Again" (1.5), where the hotshot pilot escaped a hostile moon unaided by Adama and his fleet. In "Resurrection Ship, Part 1" (2.11), Starbuck pledges unquestioning allegiance to the patriarchal Adama against a woman commander—perversely representing the worst excesses of militarized masculinity—offering her the world; but in "Kobol's Last Gleaming, Part 1" (1.12), Starbuck deliberately goes against the old man in accepting President Roslin's mission to find the Arrow of Apollo. Starbuck may return for Kasey in "Exodus, Part 2" (3.4), but the range of emotions she experiences upon realizing the girl is not her own—a remarkable performance from Katee Sackhoff—bears testimony to the action heroine's conflicting attitude toward maternity.

Humanity, as embodied by Starbuck, is tough, resilient, heroic, athletic, fertile, potentially life-bearing, and female. If Starbuck represents the most human character—and at the time of writing, she may still turn out to be a Cylon—this represents a curious inversion, given the show's investment in normalizing *man*kind. If *BSG* establishes masculinity as the signifier of being human, the incorporation of a female fighter pilot as its pinnacle might constitute a sly inoculation against charges of phallocentrism. Maybe the body of the action heroine represents a more stable site than that of the action hero, who is now too far associated with "unnatural" body-building activities, steroid consumption, and homoeroticism. That figure's abnormal hypermusculinity hinted at certain masculine insecurities even at its apotheosis in the *Rocky*, *Rambo*, and *Die Hard* movies, subject to Schwarzenegger parody and revision even before it achieved archetypal status.

The future, *BSG* suggests—despite itself—is female. An alternative brand of humanity constructed by the show, a flawed feminized masculine one, is represented by Gaius Baltar, whose claim to being a man relies upon duplicity, murder, and self-interest ("Fragged," 2.3). His is the humanity Adama questions in his retirement speech; Starbuck's is the humanity deserving to be saved.

IN SPACE, NO ONE CAN HEAR YOU LAUGH: *BATTLESTAR* DOES THE FUNNY

"Relax, Will. I was making with the funny."

—BUFFY, *BUFFY THE VAMPIRE SLAYER*
("BECOMING, PART 1," 2.21)

"Lighten up! It's only the end of the world."

—SAM ANDERS, *BATTLESTAR GALACTICA*
("THE FARM," 2.5)

In a time that will not go down as a golden age for the sitcom, some of contemporary American TV's finest recent dramatic series have also been among the funniest. Mixing pathos, action, and "the funny" (as Whedonites call it) ("Becoming, Part 1" [2.21]), all of Joss Whedon's series—*Buffy the Vampire Slayer*, *Angel*, *Firefly*—were often hilarious without ever being jokey. On HBO, "not-TV" like David Chase's *The Sopranos* (1999–2007), David Milch's *Deadwood* (2004–2006), even David Simon's *The Wire* (2002–2008) are, despite their often dark subject matter, full of character-derived humor. Even shows like *Lost* or, more rarely, *24*, can be occasionally funny, thanks to characters like Hurley and Sawyer or Chloe O'Brian.

It must be admitted that, despite Sam's injunction to Kara Thrace in "The Farm" (see the epigraph above), *BSG* is not often light and seldom does the funny. In their DVD commentaries, podcasts, videologs, and especially R & D TV Logos, Moore and David Eick show themselves to be truly, ironically, mordantly funny (on the podcast for "Lay Down Your Burdens, Part 2" [2.20] Eick identifies himself as "court jester"), but the humor of the creators of *BSG* does not, for the most part, translate to a show which is, after all, about "the end of the world."

Which is not to say that *Battlestar* is devoid of comedy. The established-in-the-miniseries rebel-against-authoritarian antagonism between Starbuck and Colonel Tigh is potentially humorous: think of that brief moment when Starbuck, allowed out of the brig after war breaks out with the Cylons, gestures toward the XO as if to ask, "How's that nose I smacked" before saluting and reporting herself "ready for duty, sir." The blowsy, over-the-top Ellen Tigh is, despite her tragic end, an inherently comic character. When Laura Roslin gets the giggles just before her presidential debate with Gaius Baltar ("Lay Down Your Burdens," 2.19), we almost get them too—and have we ever loved her more? (Moore discloses on the podcast for the episode that Eick didn't approve of Laura's uncontrollable mirth and had to be convinced.)

And thanks to James Callis' wonderfully protean portrayal, Gaius Baltar is as often a stitch as he is a son of a bitch. Particularly in the miniseries and in Season One, when the conceit was still new, his continuing colloquy/affair with Six was often very funny. That moment in "Tigh Me Up, Tigh Me Down" (1.9), for example, when Starbuck discovers the crazy scientist apparently masturbating to a Six fantasy when he is supposed to be developing a Cylon detection test is deliciously comical. "What's up, doc?" she asks, incredulously. "Keeping up with the old exercises," he responds in a lame attempt to cover up. To his question, "What can I do for you?" Kara Thrace replies, "You can zip up your fly."

Even the addition of one of *Buffy the Vampire Slayer*'s prime funny bringers, Jane Espenson, did not exactly amp up *Battlestar*'s humor quotient, though as David Kociemba shows in Chapter 4, her two episodes do offer some comic moments.

If, in Season Four, the human race makes it to the end of their epic journey, then, and only then, will humor—down-to-earth-humor, if you will—become a real possibility. But at that point, should it come, *Battlestar Galactica* will be over.

Chapter Eight

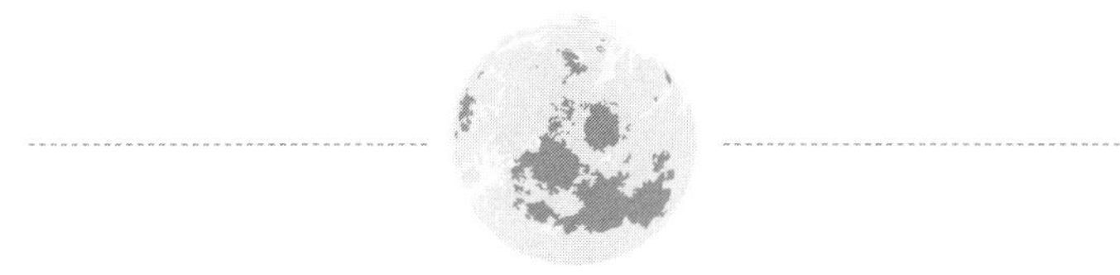

WOMEN ON TOP

"What a wonderful world this would be."[87] So sang Sam Cooke in describing how great life would be if the one he loves would love him back; it's up to the woman to make his world go round. But what if women really could make the whole world revolve around them? When global chaos becomes too oppressive, it's often said (and not always by women) that the world would be different (i.e., better) if women ruled it. The longed-for gentle, loving, nurturing utopia created by women, however, may be just as much a fantasy as, well, a TV series like *Battlestar Galactica*. More than most series ever have, *Battlestar Galactica* presents a world in which women are on top, and not just during sex, although that seems to be a favored position. They also take control in politics, the military, and the home just as much as in their sexual encounters, romantic relationships, and rivalries. But so far, their world is far from wonderful.

Women decide to love or not, and the men who are their love/sex objects often seem helpless to determine their own romantic fate. Even Dualla, a quieter, gentler woman than most on this series, leaves husband Lee when she becomes tired of ignoring a stronger woman's (Starbuck's) claim to him and, apparently, doesn't want to fight for him openly; Lee is left wavering between two women who may or may not want to keep him around. Although Caprica Sharon grows to love Karl "Helo" Agathon, she first calculates how to win his affection as part of her Cylon job; only later, and especially when she becomes pregnant, does she begin to love him passionately. Even so, she controls their relationship and makes it clear that her child is her first priority. Cooke's simple "wonderful world" is far from reality even among lovers and spouses. Like everything else in a post-apocalyptic society, love isn't easy and may not be completely satisfying or all-encompassing, no matter who is on top.

WOMEN'S LIB IN THE *BSG*VERSE

The new *Battlestar Galactica* shows women's advancement toward equality in ways still unrealized in real-world politics or employment, and it is light-years ahead of the women's roles portrayed in the 1978–79 series. In the 1970s *Battlestar Galactica*, women, like children, were more often seen and not really heard. They speak dialogue, but it often is of the adoring Serina or, later, Sheba "Oh, Apollo" variety or Athena's catty comments when Starbuck double-times her. Women are primarily in the story for sex appeal, even if that appeal—in the form of socialator (sanctioned hooker) Cassiopeia—soon had to be covered up to be suitable for an early Sunday evening family viewing hour.

What do women do in the original series? Athena works on *Galactica*'s bridge as a communication officer (more reminiscent of *Star Trek*'s Uhura than the reimagined series' Dualla, who makes the job seem much more tension filled and time consuming), but her best scenes are with Starbuck as they flirt and try to maintain their pre-war romance. Her other roles as Adama's daughter and Zac's and Apollo's sister seem forced, but, after all, this was former model Maren Jensen's first acting job; Athena's role became further reduced in later episodes as her romance with Starbuck fizzles.

Other women have more to do. Cassiopeia takes over as Starbuck's main love interest, but as soon as she does, she is covered from neck to toe and converted from sexy socialator to nurse-aide (two stereotypical roles for women). Even Viper pilot Sheba, a late arrival in the series, seems more of a replacement for Apollo's soon-dead wife Serina than a hotshot rival pilot; she giggles as much as Cassiopeia and pines away for Apollo, at last winning a slightly more than platonic kiss in the last episode. In the late 1970s, men rule—whether in the gentle paternal style of Lorne Greene, best known as Ben Cartwright on the long-running *Bonanza* (1959–1973), or through the gentle banter of action heroes/good buddies Starbuck and Apollo. Although Dirk Benedict and Richard Hatch's reported off-screen chemistry was nil, their on-screen camaraderie was a high point of the original series. In fact, *Battlestar Galactica* was as much a buddy show as traditional sci-fi fare. The emphasis was on the friendship and adventures shared by the male leads; women played supporting roles and were greatly outnumbered.

The twenty-first century's series includes more female characters, and the flashy, meaty, pivotal roles go to women. They are the interesting characters to watch, not just because they're female. They face even more conflicts and receive more development than the male characters. With the exception of Baltar, whose debates, love scenes, and mood swings manipulated by Number Six are wildly entertaining, the male characters seem little different from other beleaguered soldiers from dozens of other TV series or movies.

The series also provides plenty of good supporting roles for women:

- Cally Tyrol, the competent technician who becomes a devoted mother and, surprisingly, union instigator
- D'Anna/Three, a Cylon masquerading as an investigative reporter and a soul-searching leader striving to learn what's between life and death
- Ellen Tigh, seducer, manipulator, castrator, victim, whose love-hate relationship with her husband influences all his command decisions

- Dualla (Dee), a gentle soul who advises two generations of Adamas and often finds herself in a "love him *and* (not necessarily *or*) leave him" relationship with her husband.

These and other women, by their sheer number if nothing else, show audiences a society in which women take equal responsibility and receive equal benefits or, conversely, share the same dire consequences as men at every level in society. It may not be an ideal world, nor an adamantly feminist one, but *Battlestar Galactica* is one of the few TV series today that feature such a wide array of strong female characters.

Each woman is different in strengths and vulnerabilities; each is flawed and far from perfect; each is so much more than physical appearance, although beauty and sex appeal obviously are factors in TV casting. Without so many and such interesting female characters, *Battlestar Galactica* would be just another sci-fi show, or weekly drama, or remake. It might just be (gasp) boring, a retread of what audiences have seen before. Although Moore and Eick may not have set out to liberate *BSG*'s women, they have been credited with giving female characters a wide range of important roles and interesting characteristics. The characters are definitely female, not male wannabes, and they often go beyond "typical" portrayals of women on television.

Reflecting a Stereotype or Breaking One?

On television or in movies, women have often been portrayed as a "type": spinster schoolteacher, female president (played as novelty or comedy), tomboy, whore, smart seductress sleeping her way to the top, good wife, working mother, immigrant/socially inferior wife who doesn't fit into her husband's family. Although *Battlestar Galactica* casts women in these stereotypical roles, the resulting characters don't quite fit the traditional archetypes audiences might expect. In fact, the male characters could be perceived as just as stereotypical: handsome athlete Sam Anders, gruff military leader Bill Adama, older man with trophy wife Saul Tigh, blue collar worker/union leader Galen Tyrol, flyboy Lee "Apollo" Adama. What makes these characters different is that, although they may display some title- or role-based characteristics of the stereotype, they go far beyond what's anticipated. They stretch the boundaries of their proscribed "type"; female characters transform the labels of "spinster schoolteacher" or "tomboy" so that audiences develop broader expectations for these roles. And isn't that what breaking stereotypes is all about?

The following sections highlight common stereotypical roles for women on television but illustrate how the women thrust into these roles on *BSG* often defy audience expectations.

Spinster Schoolteachers

Auburn-haired Laura Roslin might fit someone like Billy Keikeya's or even Lee Adama's boyhood vision of the perfect schoolteacher: pretty enough to warrant a crush, stern enough to keep unruly boys in line, but with a twinkle in her eye or a sly smile indicating a warm personality beneath the "teacher" facade. She loves books, a joy she shares with Adama, and she, like he, occasionally wears glasses. (Unlike Six/Shelly Godfrey, whose glasses seem like a prop to make her look highly intelligent, Roslin's seem more a signifier of the aging eyes of a scholar.) When Baltar becomes president and Roslin lives on New Caprica, she returns to teaching children, a job that creates a haven of peace and security for youngsters during the Cylon occupation. Roslin does seem to be a natural teacher and easily falls back into that role.

The "spinster" part of the stereotype also technically fits; she isn't married and has no children. She tells Adama that Billy is the closest she has to a son, and she grieves over his body after he dies in a hostage standoff on the *Cloud Nine* ("Sacrifice," 2.16).

Although Adama and Roslin develop a close friendship bordering romance as the series progresses, she is one of the few women so far who hasn't had a steamy sex scene.

At first Roslin seems defined as a shy, quiet former teacher who falls into the cutthroat world of politics. On Colonial Day, a few reporters debate whether she's fit to be president because she's only a schoolteacher; her classroom experience defines (and limits) her, and her experience in government as secretary of education doesn't seem to count for much in public opinion. Even her colleague and friend Wallace Gray finds her presidential demeanor surprising; she encourages him to run for vice president one day, only to request that he withdraw from the race the next. Her reason? She now wants Gaius Baltar to stand for election because he can win more votes and, post-election, be easier to control. The disgruntled Gray tells her, "I never thought you'd fit in with the bare-knuckled, backstabbing politicians. I guess I was wrong" ("Colonial Day," 1.11). The shy teacher obviously learned how to play hardball in the schoolyard. She defies the typical schoolteacher persona by becoming a decisive, sometimes ruthless leader, which surprises those who only knew her as a compassionate, low-key, but minor cabinet member.

Whereas Laura Roslin initially is portrayed as a soft-spoken, nurturing teacher, a role to which she returns on New Caprica, other "teachers" have a decidedly more aggressive approach to education. If Starbuck's role as flight instructor classifies her as a "schoolteacher," she certainly breaks the stereotype. She is a tough-love teacher who cares deeply about the "nuggets" under her command. Even more difficult is the "spinster" label. Although Kara Thrace may never really settle down, even though she technically is a married woman, her frequent sexual encounters nevertheless seem unfulfilling beyond a momentary pleasure. For the sheer number of times she's had intercourse, she remains surprisingly loveless. Her mostly unrequited love for Lee could tip her into the lonely older woman category at some point in her life, just like the proverbial spinster. Although Starbuck might technically be placed in this category, she obviously stretches the stereotype to its limits.

FEMALE PRESIDENT

Mary ("Roslin") McDonnell found her role as humanity's first appointed, then elected president post-apocalypse apt for women of her generation:

> [W]e were right on the cusp of being truly prepared for power. We weren't quite prepared for it. And as we were growing up, things began to change. I fortunately was raised in a family of strong women, but a great deal of my peers were not ready to be in the work world or ready to be Presidents or heads of companies. ... So the story was very relevant to me as this middle-aged woman steps into a position of leadership.[88]

Initially the idea of a female president is a hook to get viewers, as well as McDonnell, interested in the story. Compared with the curiosity bestowed on real-world presidential candidate Hillary Clinton or the critical acclaim (but commercial failure) surrounding Geena Davis' portrayal of President McKenzie Allen in the short-lived *Commander in Chief* (2005–2006), *Battlestar*'s Laura Roslin has received little notice. The way the series is written, she becomes president because of a fluke—the long line of elected officials in front of her die in the Cylon attacks. Thus the former secretary of education becomes humanity's civilian leader. She clearly understands politics and, once she gains power, becomes reluctant to relinquish it without a fight. Her male opponents, including terrorist/revolutionary Tom Zarek and Gaius Baltar, run against her in elections and, although they gain temporary public support, eventually lose; President Baltar gladly returns the job to

Roslin after his nightmarish term during the Cylon occupation of New Caprica ends in his trial as a war criminal.

Laura Roslin provides a balance with military-minded Bill Adama. Their relationship truly is the meeting of two minds; their yin and yang creates the perfect symbolic balance. Their discussions show two often-oppositional viewpoints about any situation, but the views represent more than gender issues. Roslin stands up for civilian authority and has little initial understanding of military protocol or strategy. She becomes the people's priestess with visions coinciding with scripture. She sees the need to change society into what it should be. Adama, on the other hand, lives, breathes, promotes, and maintains the military lifestyle. He thinks of religion as a useful political tool but indicates his doubt in its daily value. He strives to maintain the status quo and keep humanity running with military precision, which often means giving and following orders.

Laura becomes more than a political leader who matures on the job; she is a middle-aged love interest, a woman facing death, a savvy plotter—she is as capable and as flawed as any male president. She learns from her experiences. A flashback shows her having an affair with President Adar, who then asks for her resignation after she negotiates a peaceful end to a teachers' strike on Caprica. Adar claims she overstepped her role as a presidential advisor and secretary of education; she bound him to a course of action he didn't want to follow. When President Roslin faces a miners' strike, led by Galen Tyrol, she, too, takes a hard line, just as Adar once did; her actions seem to oppose her long-ago stance about the need for negotiating with workers who strike only to improve their lot. Once the strike is broken, however, Roslin meets with Tyrol to change the system, so that everyone in the fleet takes a turn at harder labor and the children of miners are no longer left "in the dark" but can climb the socioeconomic ladder ("Dirty Hands," 3.16).

As this progression moves Roslin from a teacher and lover of a powerful leader (stereotypical female roles) to powerful leader, her persona doesn't become more masculine; instead, Laura Roslin becomes "more" of herself. She still is interested in her appearance, asking Billy how she looks before her first protocol visit to *Galactica* ("Water," 1.2). She can giggle and flirt after a few drinks on New Caprica ("Occupation," 3.1). She cries over her cancer diagnosis but becomes determined to fight the disease her way—with alternative medicine chamalla instead of more traditional medical treatments. Although her experiences give her new perspectives on politics and the best way to guide her people, she gains depth as a character without becoming someone she wasn't at the beginning of the series.

A female president sometimes is played for laughs on television, or else the novelty of having a real-life president who is also female often results in more emphasis on the candidate's gender than her qualifications for office. Even another "groundbreaking" series, *24*, received a lot of attention during summer 2007 with its announcement of a female president to be introduced in the 2009 season; critics and reporters breaking the news usually started their story featuring the character's gender. "The rumors are true: *24* has gone with a woman to be the President of the United States for its upcoming season" was the first line of TV Squad's announcement.[89] Weeks before the official announcement, well-known *TV Guide* reporter Michael Ausiello blogged that "Word on the street is that the Commander in Chief on next season's revamped *24* will likely be a (drumroll, please) *woman* [his emphasis]."[90]

Being a "first" sets off all kinds of emotional responses in real- and televisionary world constituencies, but on *Battlestar Galactica*, only Roslin's political experience becomes debatable; her ability or inability to lead because she's a woman never becomes a hot topic. In this way, as well as the way Roslin handles the presidency (notably better than male president Baltar), *Battlestar* makes Roslin seem a good choice for leader of the last of humanity; the fact that she's a woman is just an incidental detail.

Tomboy

Initially the gender change between the original character of Starbuck and the reimagined version was the hook, but because Kara "Starbuck" Thrace is uniquely intriguing, she has emerged as possibly the most important character in the *Battlestar Galactica* saga. She displays typical "tomboy" tendencies—she drinks, swears, has casual sex, advocates adultery to suit her libido, is a crack pilot, plays cards, hates the idea of being valued as a potential childbearer, is a terrible wife and a not-so-hot surrogate mother—but she is more than this collection of tendencies and preferences. In some ways she very much resembles Colonel Tigh; both enjoy baiting each other about their obvious flaws, lose themselves in alcohol when troubled, are loyal to a fault to Adama, and often enjoy acting superior to others.

Starbuck is tomboyish in that her actions often seem masculine, yet she never strives to "become" a man. She has some female-only concerns, such as whether she should, or even can, have a child, and perhaps whether men are attracted to her because she's more like them than she is a "typical" woman. Even best-friend/sometimes-lover Lee questions her hygiene and responds with a sarcastic "Let me know when" after Kara says she sometimes can "clean up good." So she does, leaving Lee open-mouthed in wonder and disbelief when she shows up at the Colonial Day celebration wearing a form-fitting green dress and carefully applied makeup. Unlike the stereotypical tomboy who one day learns that acting feminine gains her a different, more desirable kind of attention from men, Kara admits as Lee takes her onto the dance floor that he should take advantage of her once-in-a-lifetime appearance in a dress ("Colonial Day," 1.11). Kara, unlike the stereotypical tomboy, isn't going through a phase or planning to dress and act more like a girl in the future; she knows how to morph into a gorgeous babe but prefers her more usual attire and lifestyle.

Kara also isn't "butch"—yet another pigeonhole for women who wear their hair short, prefer masculine or gender-neutral clothes, and forego makeup. If her choice of lovers to date accurately reflects her sexual orientation, she is all heterosexual. She even values the institution of marriage so much that she refuses to divorce her husband Sam to devote all her romantic attention to lover Lee ("Home," 2.6). In these ways Kara is a traditional woman/wife, at least in her ideals if not her actions.

Unique on both *Galactica* and television, Kara/Starbuck is so much more than a stereotype, in appearance, attitude, or role. If, as Katee Sackhoff hinted at Comic-Con 2007, the returned-from-a-visit-to-Earth Starbuck becomes a savior of humanity, her role transcends that of any archetypal label. Sackhoff teased that the returned Starbuck isn't dead but not really alive, not a god but could be like a god.[91] Whatever is revealed during Season Four about Kara's true nature should make her even more difficult to categorize.

Smart, Sexy Businesswoman

In the first season, Tricia Helfer played three versions of Number Six. Most often Six interacts with Baltar on the *Galactica* through a series of visions/hallucinations that make viewers question whether Baltar is imagining his lover and her often disturbing advice or sharing mental encounters via an implanted computer chip. Another Number Six monitors Helo's activities on Caprica, where he is marooned shortly after the Cylon attack. The third Six masquerades as a human member of the fleet, Shelly Godfrey ("Six Degrees of Separation," 1.7). Each Six is a product of environment and job, but Helfer easily differentiated among them: Caprica Six is "the base model—she's stronger and more militaristic"; Baltar's Six is "more seductive, and she wants to be loved by Gaius" (prompting her to wear revealing or no clothing); Shelly is "more intellectual" (illustrated by her conservative attire and glasses).[92] The bigoted cliché that "they all look alike" may be true at first glance, but the subtleties of each "clone" reveal important differences. During a Comic-Con 2007 interview, Helfer said yet another Six will be revealed in Season Four. Natalie will be an important Six early in the season, and not all Sixes may be in love with Baltar.[93] Logically, unless Baltar receives a personality transplant, he seems unlikely to "commit" to any of the Sixes; if any Six is going to experience true love, she'll need to find another partner. Season Four may very well take one or more of Helfer's characters in that direction.

Number Six is neither a Stepford Wife—the perfect spouse/goddess/sex machine, an object of desire and her husband's slave—nor a vapid but beautiful blonde, nor the smart woman as bitch. Baltar's first Six, who (temporarily) gives her life to protect him during a nuclear blast, acts like a bright woman who sleeps her way to the top, using her relationship with Baltar to open doors at the Ministry of Defense for her own research. Shortly before the Cylon attack, she instead reveals that she's been using Baltar for much more—to learn how best to infiltrate humanity, procure its secrets, and destroy it. Still, to her lovelorn chagrin, she becomes ensnared by love for Gaius, a glitch in her programming that, like a computer virus, spreads to the rest of the Sixes: even if one dies only to be downloaded into a new body, the entire model seems to have become flawed with Baltaritis.

Smart women who make bad choices, especially with their love lives, are another cliché on television. The Sixes, however besotted they might be with Baltar, are independent thinkers who have a larger worldview than their relationships. Whether religion or pragmatism motivates a Six, she stays faithful to a global game-plan that involves Cylon evolution and long-term political and military strategy. The Sixes play for keeps, and those who underestimate these smart, sexy "businesswomen" are likely to lose not only the battle but their lives.

Whore

In many ways Ellen Tigh's reputation places her in this category, and for many episodes, she neatly fits the modern label of "whore" (in quotation marks)—a promiscuous woman having multiple partners without any transfer of money. When Adama fetches her from the *Rising Star*, where the amnesiac Ellen slowly regained her memory, he admits that she has the reputation of sleeping around the fleet. Her actions at a get-reacquainted dinner hosted by Adama portray her as a wild partier: she drinks too much, says the wrong things, loses a shoe playing footsie with Lee, and later gropes him when he returns her footwear ("Tigh Me Up, Tigh Me Down," 1.13). She flirts with any male in range of her batting eyes and, as she tells Tom Zarek while he mixes her a drink, her agenda is like his: to promote herself first. She tries (and fails miserably) to play politics so that she, and secondarily her husband, will be able to get ahead ("Colonial Day," 1.11). On New Caprica, after Saul has been incarcerated and tortured by the Cylons, Ellen becomes the degraded sex slave of Brother Cavil, all in the hopes of freeing her husband. She later divulges secrets from the human underground, leaving her husband with no option other than to "mercy kill" her ("Exodus," 3.4).

Although the character of Ellen Tigh is defined by her sexuality, she becomes more multidimensional during the "Exodus" two-parter. As a woman who truly does love her husband, despite all her past problems and infidelities, she offers her body to the Cylons in barter for Saul's freedom. This really is the first time she truly fits the whore (no quotation marks) designation. Her previous assignations are designed to get attention from her jealous husband, who much of the time seems married to the military; she gets no real gratification from her flirtatious and promiscuous behavior unless it makes her husband crazy and reaffirms his desire to keep her. When Ellen sells herself to a Cylon, she seems cheap and dispirited for the first time. She performs a variety of "tricks" to keep the Cylon interested (see

"Jump: The Swirl") and to make her value seem higher; she clearly hates what she's doing, but it's a "job" that must be done. Ironically, her life as a whore leads to her death; her life as a promiscuous wife on *Galactica* and even before the Cylon attack kept her vibrant and alive. Although Ellen seems to be a harpie/"whore" in popular vernacular from the moment she steps onto *Galactica*, the disintegration of her character on New Caprica reveals just what the term really means.

Good Wife and Mother

Female characters often are mothers and caregivers, but that's not all they are. Proud of their children and status as mothers, they also have many other roles.

No matter how much *Galactica*'s mothers may want to spend more time with their children, they have other jobs that take them away from quality time with the kids. Daycare is a necessity for both Sharon Agathon and daughter Hera and Cally Tyrol and son Nicky. Yet no matter how busy they are with their "regular" jobs, their children are a top priority. These women often take care of their offspring because the men will not or somehow forget about their children when they get busy. Even a doting father like Galen Tyrol still puts his job first, and he wants his wife with him, not only because she's the best at her technical specialization but because he likes her by his side. Cally is the one who, under duress, decides where her son should be placed if she and her husband die ("A Day in the Life," 3.14); she is the one who remembers what Nicky needs for daycare. Cally fights for family time—not just because she's the mommy, but because she sees the importance of the family unit. She doesn't spend all her time with her child, however; her on-screen time is split between work and home, reflecting a typical modern split for working mothers.

Caprica Sharon spends even less on-screen time with Hera, but the time they do share seems high quality. She becomes angry when husband Helo becomes too busy with work-related crises of his own to check on their daughter—she reminds him to do so just before she flies her morning mission. When she returns, her first instinct is to check on the baby, and when she finds Hera ill, she's the one to take the child to the doctor ("The Woman King," 3.13). But even more than Cally, Sharon spends more on-screen time working, involved with rescue missions, routine patrols, or crises-of-the-moment.

Even when these women are shown "at home," domestic bliss is still elusive. The couples fight, threaten to split up, do so, and then reunite. They are passionate, but not always in good ways. The happy family moments are hard won, largely the result of wives and mothers making home life as much a priority as possible within war machine *Galactica*.

Sharon is an especially interesting example of the good wife and mother. Initially Boomer's gender change was a potential way to hook new viewers, but the more important revelation quickly became that she's Cylon. Ironically, she seems "more human" when audiences try to discern what is, and always has been, alien about her. As the episodes progress, audiences, and characters like Helo, discover that she's far more like humans than like any "villain" previously encountered, which makes her a very powerful, scary character. Would we want her to be our mother, or the mother of our child?

As Caprica Sharon further morphs into Athena, a more acceptable Boomer look-alike, she joins the ranks of immigrant women who find themselves facing prejudice from their husband's family and friends. No matter how much the *Galactica* crew seem to accept her, they still recognize her as Cylon and, perhaps deep down, harbor doubts about her loyalty. Grace Park (Sharon) acknowledged fans' feelings toward her character; they mirror what the *Galactica* crew must also sense: "[A] lot of viewers will be conflicted about how they should feel about her and whether they should view her as a villain." After all, first-season

Boomer also has to come to grips with being a Cylon, leaving her "quite vulnerable, emotional, and in heavy denial."[94] By Season Four, Sharon "Athena" Agathon has returned to her "rightful" place among *Galactica*'s pilots, with the additional blessing/burden of being Helo's wife and Hera's mother. Despite her ever-deepening roots within humanity, she will always be perceived as strange or outcast in some ways.

SEXY OR SEXIST?

Despite this wide range of roles for females, human or Cylon, some fans and critics complain that the series exploits women by emphasizing beautiful bodies, sometimes scantily or revealingly clad. Is *Battlestar* sexy or sexist? Does it give women just enough to do on screen so that audiences take notice without the series really being all that groundbreaking? Does it denigrate women by showing them in various stages of undress too often compared to the number of their "serious" (i.e., fully clothed) scenes? Is not the decision whether *Battlestar Galactica* is meant to be a feminist show better left to the audience, not the writing staff or series creators?

Viewers aren't used to seeing so many women, even in an ensemble cast, in so many different roles. *24*'s Chloe is smart if not always sociable and plays a major role, and women often take charge of CTU. *Lost*'s ensemble cast boasts many women in a variety of roles that also bend stereotypes, and female superheroes are just as common as male on *Heroes*. *Desperate Housewives* is mostly about women, but the title alone sends signals that this might not be the ideal show for feminists. The difference with *Battlestar Galactica* is that it presents a whole society, and women actively work in each sector. (Even within *Lost*'s little society, strong female characters like Kate or Juliet often bow to the will of Jack or Other mastermind Ben; the recognized or self-appointed leaders of the castaway and Others societies are men.) In contrast, women are at least half the workforce at every level with the fleet, especially evident on *Galactica* and *Colonial One*. They work not just at the top levels of business and politics or at home, as in so many other TV series.

If *Battlestar Galactica* is sexist, it is in its portrait of men as more stereotypically strong and stoic—only Baltar really breaks this mold, and his character even gets to be macho and heft a weapon now and then. When Lee Adama seems wimpy, his indecision and vulnerabilities often stem from being unsure how to live up to a famous, Alpha Male father or from choosing to stand on the side of "law" against anyone, male or female, who wants to bend it far out of shape. Lee might be a stronger character more often if he were allowed to follow his idealized career path; he seems miscast as a pilot when, as several characters note after Season One, he acts more like a lawyer than a hotshot fighter. Even Starbuck initially belittles his leadership abilities as CAG. She laughs at his choice of words to close the ready room briefing; "Be careful" isn't nearly as forceful (as manly) as "Good hunting." Starbuck then bullies Apollo into ordering her to do what he needs her to do ("33," 1.1). She expects to follow his orders, but she has to show him how to earn her respect as her commanding officer.

Ronald D. Moore, who was responsible for writing Starbuck as a woman, and co-creator David Eick believe that audiences find women in roles more traditionally played by men to be more interesting to watch. After all, audiences have already seen male Han Solo characters, but a female (Hannah Solo?) doing the same things is more fun to watch. Nevertheless, Eick insisted early in the show that gender "isn't the main issue. It isn't what drives us." Moore agreed that theirs is "a more balanced show,"[95] whereas most sci-fi stories are all about the men.

Whether gender equality or just simply interesting storytelling is the impetus for more women playing more dynamic characters, perhaps women's most important role in this series is as catalyst; female characters prompt the major and minor plot shifts. The entire episode "You Can't Go Home Again" (1.5) revolves around Kara, who is missing in action after presumably crash landing. Adama *tells* son Lee that if he were lost in space, the fleet would never stop looking, but what is *shown* in that episode? Adama loses sight of reason and risks not only his career but all humanity's security to keep looking for the missing Kara well beyond the time when her oxygen should've run out. Throughout the saga, many people anger him, but who makes him cry? Kara again, when she disappears a second time and is declared dead ("Maelstrom," 3.17). Even such a pillar of authority as Commander Adama is made vulnerable by one woman who has become both daughter and friend.

The mythical power of a woman behind a powerful man comes true especially in the Tigh household. As long as Ellen Tigh is an active force in her husband's life, she determines his actions; he is weak and ineffective when he gives over all decision-making power to her. Saul, a problematic leader who never should be in charge of a nation, takes the "man's" way out of his problems—hiding in a bottle. During the time that Adama is sidelined, next-in-command Tigh is so henpecked that he sadly leads the fleet far astray and into all kinds of political traps as he tries to show his wife that he can be a man. He becomes jealous and grasping while trying to hold on to his sleep-around wife. Only when Ellen goes too far in giving away secrets to the Cylons in a misguided attempt to keep her husband from further harm does Saul "act like a man" and take charge of the couple's destiny. He has to kill Ellen to become his own person. Women may not always be good influences, but they are powerful catalysts. They drive the action and often become the most compelling characters on screen, as well as on TV, today.

Battlestar Galactica's women are decidedly sexual beings and unafraid to show it. Even Laura Roslin occasionally flirts with Adama—if their potential relationship were left to him, it would never get off the ground. As previously mentioned, women are usually shown on top during sex (and not just to show their glowing red spines), a role reversal for most movie or TV depictions of sexual activity. Is it sexist or pragmatic for Six, in particular, to use her body as well as her mind to control Baltar?

Without reimagining *Battlestar Galactica* so that women have more integral roles—and making those roles much more interesting than those of their male counterparts—the 2000s version might not have lasted any longer than the 1970s original. Much has been written about the story reflecting current global issues—genocide, terrorism, conflicting religious beliefs, political turmoil, abortion, prisoners' rights in wartime, survival with dwindling resources, lack of confidence in political or military leaders, etc. But who is at the crux of these storylines? Laura Roslin, former teacher and political cabinet member, beleaguered president, religious prophet, cancer patient, budding love interest; Kara "Starbuck" Thrace, ace fighter pilot, take-charge soldier, torturer, wife, lover; (in two Cylon incarnations) Sharon Valerii/Boomer and Sharon Agathon/Caprica Sharon/Athena, newbie pilot, not-so-secret lover, traitor, assassin, mother; Number Six (also in many versions), seductress, mother wannabe, political rebel, religious zealot, spy.

Battlestar Galactica shows us what a gender-equal society (as much as it is possible) might be like. (Gender differences in who begets babies and who bears them will always create some differences, or inequalities, between men and women.) The series has been called groundbreaking for mirroring our world as it is, but it also may be groundbreaking because, like the best of science fiction, it shows us what our world may become, not just in the sphere of science and technology but in the relationships between men and women. The women who take charge of the fleet (Admiral Cain), lead their people (President Roslin, but also Eights, Sixes, and—before being deactivated—the Threes), step forward as religious leaders (Roslin again, but also Elosha, the Gemonese priest), become legendary for their battle prowess (Kara "Starbuck" Thrace), or give birth to a new race (Sharon

"Athena" Agathon and Cally Tyrol) may not find their lives completely fulfilling, even though their schedules certainly are full and filled with drama. Perhaps that's the lesson girls and women who watch this series are learning; even if the glass ceiling or pink-collar professions don't limit them, they still might find themselves less than satisfied with their careers or lives. But in the *Battlestar Galactica* world, and perhaps someday in our own gender-unbiased society, women and men have the same opportunities to be happy or miserable as they scramble to survive.

THE FINAL FIVE

What roles do women have yet to play in *Battlestar*'s mythology? As the series winds down with Season Four, speculation about that fifth Cylon includes an all-important question about Leoben's prophesy. Who is the Adama that Leoben tells Laura Roslin is a Cylon? Although a previously unseen Cylon model could look just like the Commander, the more likely interpretation is that *an* Adama will join Saul Tigh, Sam Anders, Galen Tyrol, and Tory Foster ("Crossroads," 3.19) to make the Final Five. Of the four "surprise" Cylons, only Tory is female, and her role in Season Three as Roslin's press secretary/aide is small. Roslin likely will rely on Tory more in Season Four; Mary McDonnell indicated during a Comic-Con interview that Roslin's health declines during this season and Tory becomes more important to her because she's very detail-oriented. A scatterbrain pre-"awakening," Tory apparently becomes a much more efficient assistant after she realizes she's Cylon.[96] Having a Cylon double-agent next to the president could be a very interesting development.

With so much emphasis on female characters and their equal role in the series so far, the "Adama" prophesied by Leoben to be a Cylon might not only be one of the Final Five but could be female. Leoben's prophesies are laced with accurate plot twists; his words are never as straightforward as they seem. Dualla, married to Lee, is an Adama by marriage. Lee, always halfway in love with Kara despite his desire to make his marriage work, could divorce Dualla and marry Kara, which would make her an Adama; she long has been a leading fan candidate to be revealed as a Cylon. Even Roslin, Bill Adama's close friend and colleague, could potentially become an Adama by marriage, far-fetched as that seems. There might even be another as yet unknown female Adama to step forward and surprise audiences.

For *Battlestar Galactica* to maintain its equal footing with fans who now expect to see women in high places, another important female or two must be revealed in Season Four. To leave the fate of humanity up to the Final Five, and make four out of five male, seems to be a betrayal of all the series has done to date for gender equality. But then, determining who should ultimately come out on top just because of gender is sexist thinking, isn't it?

THE SWIRL, OR, THE INTERTEXTUAL *BATTLESTAR*

"All this has happened before, and all of it will happen again."

—**Leoben, *Battlestar Galactica*, "Flesh and Bone" (1.8)**

"All this has happened before, and all of it will happen again."

—**Peter, *Peter Pan* (Walt Disney, 1953)**

Early in "Precipice," the back end of Season Three's two-part premiere, we find Brother Cavil telling Ellen Tigh, post-coitus, "That was really something." "I thought you might like that," she replies. This time, the notoriously nymphomaniacal Mrs. Tigh is not going to the mattresses for her own gratification. Her bedding by the sleazy monotheist is intended to get her husband out of prison, where Saul has already lost an eye to his Cylon torturers. Her sacrifice will soon prove fatal when the XO poisons her in an agonizingly touching scene for betraying the Resistance.

Cavil has a question for his coerced partner, though:

> You didn't do the twist this time. What do you call … What's that deal you did right at the end? What do you call that?
> Ellen: You mean *the swirl.*

If the well-established Cylon knowledge concerning everything human extended to "terrestrial" television, Cavil might have recognized Ellen's allusion to a certain sexual technique perfected by the eponymous star of NBC's megahit *Seinfeld* (1990–1998). In the Season Six episode "The Fusilli Jerry," Jerry's old girlfriend Elaine, who has been sleeping with his mechanic David Putty, reports on their sexual activity:

> Elaine: He did the move.
> Jerry: What move?
> Elaine: You know … *the* move.
> Jerry: Wait a second. *My* move? David Putty used *my* move?
> Elaine: Yes, yes.

Angry that his move has been stolen, he vows to put an end to the rip-off, but Elaine, hedonistically anxious for her new lover to retain the satisfying technique, seeks to convince Jerry that it is not outright plagiarism:

> Elaine: Well, he doesn't even do it exactly the same. He—he—he uses a pinch at the end instead of *the swirl*!

Already famous for its regendering of Starbuck, *Battlestar Galactica* has clearly switched sexes in other ways as well, here giving—in an episode written by none other than Ronald D. Moore himself—a woman a move pioneered by a sitcom-man on the far-away, in space and time, home planet both Cylons and humans long to find. (Inexplicably, the swirl conversation is missing from the UK DVD version of *Battlestar*. Whether as a result of censorship or a concession to the Sky audience—*Seinfeld* never caught on with British audiences and thus the joke might have been lost—we do not know.)

Today's "postmodern" popular culture is nearly as promiscuous as Ellen Tigh herself, sleeping around a lot and regularly passing on/aka "stealing the moves" of its partners: jokes, references, scenes, narrative developments, etc. Now *Battlestar* is by no means the most licentious of television series. *Buffy the Vampire Slayer*, for example, was more wantonly intertextual, as was the just-completed *Sopranos*, the ever-brilliant, long-running *The Simpsons*, or *BSG*'s true contemporary *Lost*. Careful watching, reading, and listening to *BSG* episodes, official companion books, and podcasts reveal it to be a "swirl," if you will, of its own genius and allusions, quotations, homages to other filmic and televisual texts, literature, and music.

Battlestar's intertextuality is not typically as overt as that of these other TV texts: explicit *Seinfeld* references (in addition to the Swirl, Brendan "Hot Dog" Costanza borrows his last name from the sitcom's infamous schlemiel George); deliberate sharing of a name, Six, between *BSG*'s Cylon femme fatale and a memorable character on the cult classic *The Prisoner* (BBC, 1967); unambiguous referencing of a famous novel by Thomas Wolfe—in the title of the episode "You Can't Go Home Again" (1.5); or the clear-cut appearance of *Serenity*, the spacecraft from Joss Whedon's *Firefly* (FOX, 2002) in the sky over Caprica in the miniseries—these are hardly the norm.

More typically, we learn from a podcast, a website, a DVD commentary, or one of the official companion books that a scene, a theme, a plot element, even an entire episode has drawn inspiration from another "ship" in the intertextual fleet. *Black Hawk Down* (Ridley Scott, 2001), *2001: A Space Odyssey* (Stanley

Kubrick, 1968), *Band of Brothers* (HBO, 2001), and *Alien* (Ridley Scott, 1979) (Bassom 1: 28) are acknowledged influences on *BSG*'s naturalistic science fiction. Without Moore's generous podcasting, we might never have realized that Adama cutting himself shaving in "33" (1.1) was an echo of Donald Sutherland's razor-induced bleeding in *Don't Look Now* (Nicholas Roeg, 1973) or that Colonel Tigh's battles with the bottle were shared by Paul Eddington, Kirk Douglas' character in *In Harm's Way* (Otto Preminger, 1965). The design of *BSG*'s distinctive handguns was suggested by similar weapons in *Blade Runner* (Ridley Scott, 1982) (commentary on miniseries DVD). That fight between Leoben and Adama in the miniseries was inspired by Scorsese's films from the 1970s (Bassom 1: 32). The flashbacks in "Act of Contrition" (1.4) were indebted to *The Getaway* (Sam Peckinpah, 1972) (Bassom 1: 58); writer Toni Graphia had *Dead Man Walking* (Tim Robbins, 1995) and *Silence of the Lambs* (Jonathan Demme, 1991) in mind as she fleshed out "Flesh and Bone" (1.8) (Bassom 1: 74).

The germ for "Tigh Me Up, Tigh Me Down" (1.9) was the submarine drama *Crimson Tide* (Tony Scott, 1995) (Bassom 1: 76), although the title also plays off a Pedro Almodovar (1990) film title (*Tie Me Up, Tie Me Down*). The battle scenes of "The Hand of God" (1.10) owed a considerable, quite conscious debt to war movies like *Tora! Tora! Tora!* (Richard Fleischer and Kinzi Fukasaku, 1970), *Sink the Bismarck* (Lewis Gilbert, 1960), and *Midway* (Jack Smight, 1976) (Bassom 1: 82). "Colonial Day" (1.11) originated in the desire to do *West Wing* (NBC, 1999–2006) on a spaceship (Bassom 1: 84).

"Valley of Darkness" (2.2) owed a conscious debt to *Aliens* (James Cameron, 1986) (Bassom 2: 28), and Sergio Mimca-Gezzan, who had been an assistant director on Spielberg's *Saving Private Ryan* (1998), was willing in "Fragged" (2.3) to reprise the scene from that film in which Captain Miller (Tom Hanks) thinks he has blown up a Nazi tank with a handgun in Tyrol's rescue by Raptors in a battle with Centurions (Bassom 2: 34).

"The Farm" (2.5), in which Starbuck finds herself in a nightmarish Cylon hospital and discovers she is part of a breeding program, is full of echoes of many an episode of *The X-Files* and a film like *Coma* (Michael Chriction, 1978). Kara Thrace's pyramid ball bouncing in "Home, Part 1" (2.6) was a nod to *The Great Escape* (John Sturges, 1963). That Mexican standoff—Starbuck/Helo v. Anders and the Caprican resistance ("Resistance," 2.4)—is unmistakably John Wooish. Six's naked straddle of a chair in "Home, Part 2" (2.7) is "right out of *Scandal*" (Michael Caton-Jones, 1989), as Moore tells us in the DVD commentary, and in the same episode Laura Roslin's reinstallation as president was "a fairly faithful" borrowing from *Brubaker* (Stuart Rosenberg, 1980) (Bassom 2: 51). "Flight of the Phoenix" (2.9) took its title from a 1965 Jimmy Stewart film (directed by Robert Aldrich) and was inspired by the "War of Nerves" episode (6.4) of one of Moore's favorite television shows: *M*A*S*H* (Bassom 2: 59). Admiral Cain's assassination orders in "Resurrection Ship, Part 1" (2.11) evokes *Apocalypse Now* (Frances Ford Coppola, 1979). The interrupted beatings of Tyrol and Helo in "Ship's" second part (2.12) was modeled after similar scenes in *Full Metal Jacket* (Stanley Kubrick, 1987) and *The Grifters* (Stephen Frears, 1990) (Bassom 2: 71). "Black Market" (2.14), Moore acknowledges, was partly suggested by Conrad's *Heart of Darkness* (Bassom 2: 77). The strategic use of European cars—that Citroën in "Downloaded," for example (2.18)—to impersonate SFish vehicles was, as Moore suggests, borrowed from *Gattaca* (Andrew Niccol, 1997). Does sleeper-Cylon Sharon Valerii's agonizing visit in the same episode to her Caprican apartment—filled with mementos of her illusory human past—evoke the situation of the replicant Rachel in (the already cited) *Blade Runner*? Eick reveals that *McCabe and Mrs. Miller* (Robert Altman, 1971) provided the visual template for the scenes on New Caprica at the end of "Lay Down Your Burdens, Part 2" (2.20).

Season Three continued to evoke other texts. "Exodus, Part 1" (3.3), for example

- borrows its oracle (Amanda Plummer) from *The Matrix* (The Wachowski Brothers, 1999);
- pays a visit to Sam Peckinpah's *The Wild Bunch* (1969) in the scene in which Number Three, channeling Ernest Borgnine, counters Sharon's "I gave my word" with "It depends on who you made it to" (David Weddle, the co-author of the episode, has penned a definitive biography of the director);
- acts like Arnold in *Terminator 2* (James Cameron, 1991)—"He'll live"—when Sharon then shoots Three in the knee rather than kill her;
- suggests *The Longest Day* (Ken Annakin, Andrew Marton, Bernhard Wicki, 1962) in the scene in which the humans in Cylon internment recognize that their battle, like D-Day, is "on";
- and is thinking of the famous Saint Crispin's Day speech of the eponymous hero of Shakespeare's *Henry V* when Adama rallies the forces for the rescue mission at the episode's end (Moore discusses all these on the episode podcast).

In "Hero" (3.8), the "End of the Line" hatch ID Number 3 finds during her fatal dream visit to *Galactica* will seem familiar to those who remember *Tron* (Steven Lisberger, 1982), and Bulldog's workouts in his cell on the Cylon basestar recall Max Cady's crazed calisthenics in *Cape Fear* (Martin Scorsese, 1991). In the two-part finale of Season Three, "Crossroads" (2.19–2.20), other films are cast as supporting *Battlestar* texts. In Part 1, President Roslin's recurring dream sequence in the opera house was meant to be, as Moore informs, very *Don't Look Now*ish (Nicholas Roeg's 1973 film was about a man who has ESP but doesn't know it), and in Part 2 Baltar's "Now what do we do?"

after being found innocent would reiterate the query of Bill McKay (Robert Redford) after an election day success in *The Candidate* (Michael Ritchie, 1973). (For those who lost count, that was four *BSG*-influencing films from the Scott brothers: Sir Ridley—3; Tony—1.)

Battlestar's intertextuality does not end before the credits roll. A viewer who fails to stay tuned until the final frame may be oblivious to one of *BSG*'s cleverest uses of intertextuality.

R & D TV Logos

The "R & D TV Logos" (sometimes repeated) that end each episode of *Battlestar* in all three seasons are wonderfully, playfully intertextual. Viewers who have never experienced the gruesome violence of the logos' ur-text, MTV's grand guignolish *Celebrity Death Match* (1998–2002; 2006–), in which real (e.g., Lucy Lawless vs. Calista Flockhart), fictional (e.g., Scully and Mulder vs. the Men in Black), and historical (e.g., Attila the Hun vs. Gandhi) opponents fatally slice, dice, and crush each other, may not recognize the essential parody.

Those unfamiliar with *Jaws* (Steven Spielberg, 1975), ["Litmus"], or *American Idol* (FOX, 2002–) ["Flesh and Bone"], or homemaking advocate and felon Martha Stewart ["Kobol's Last Gleaming, Part 1"], or the SF film *Westworld* ["Scattered"], or Verizon Wireless ads ["Final Cut"], or John Carpenter's horrific remake of *The Thing* ["Black Market"], or *Jurassic Park* (Steven Spielberg, 1993) ["Lay Down Your Burdens, Part 1"], or the shrivelling Wicked Witch of the West in *The Wizard of Oz*) ["Occupation/Precipice"], or *The Exorcist* ["Exodus, Part 2"], or Jack Nicholson as Randall Patrick McMurphy in *One Flew Over the Cuckoo's Nest* (Milos Foreman, 1976) ["Collaborators"], or the famous cover of The Beatles' *Sgt. Pepper's Lonely Hearts Club Band* album (1967) ["Hero"], or Ray Harryhausen's fencing skeleton *The 7th Voyage of Sinbad* (Nathan Juran, 1958) ["Crossroads, Part 2"] may well experience visceral enjoyment watching the two key figures in *BSG*'s reimagining do violence to one another, but they are not likely to fully understand their clever intertextuality.

All Along the Watchtower

We cannot jump away from this discussion of the intertextual *Battlestar* without noting one other significant way in which the series depends on other texts. As we have discussed elsewhere,[97] the literary critic Harold Bloom has argued that all great writers must do battle with their literary ancestors—must, in effect, slay the ancestral father—in order to overcome the "anxiety of influence" and establish their own creative space. (Think, for example, of the way twentieth-century American poets wrestled with the powerful authority of their nineteenth-century ancestor Walt Whitman.) Even if, as we discuss in Chapter 5, *Battlestar* co-reimaginer Moore had not actually been prominently involved in the *Star Trek* franchise for both television and the movies, the series would have had to do battle with its powerful SF footprint. *Star Trek*, of course, was not the only father figure with which *BSG* has had to do battle. First, it had to eliminate the original *Battlestar*.

Throughout both parts of "Crossroads," Tigh, the Chief, Anders, and Tory are haunted by phantom music seemingly reverberating throughout the *Galactica*. A kind of Pied Piper, the music, which is incrementally revealed to be Bob Dylan's "All along the Watchtower" (as covered not by Jimi Hendrix, who made the song famous, but by *BSG* composer Bear McCreary), leads the quartet to a clandestine meeting in which they come to the startling realization—they are, in fact, sleeper Cylons.

Not all *Battlestar* fans were amused by the OMG audacity of the narrative strategem. Television Without Pity's *BSG* chronicler would write "Oh my God! My stoner boyfriend from high school wrote the season finale of *Battlestar Galactica*!

> How did that happen? Why did Ronald D. Moore take a break and hand over responsibility for the finale

> to a guy who spent most of his time doing shots of Bacardi 151 Rum and noodling Hendrix on his guitar? Was that wise, really? Didn't Moore realize that my ex would make Bob Dylan the Cylon God?
>
> Can you believe it? This is science fiction, it's pure made-up, imaginary, insane fantasy, the sky's the limit, you can do whatever you want, and you *do* whatever you want, and it's *working*, for the most part, and you want to take a little break from that to indulge your jones for Dylan? It's worth it to you, to alienate the vast majority of your audience at the end of your finale, just to reference a pretty cool song that, frankly, no longer seems all that cool since most of us have heard it, oh, fifty million times in the last twenty years?

A more charitable viewer might see it as a magical, transcendent TV moment in which the series' customarily latent/tacit intertextuality sprang to the fore, asserting itself as a real player, no longer a sleeper, in the *Battlestar*verse.

Chapter Nine

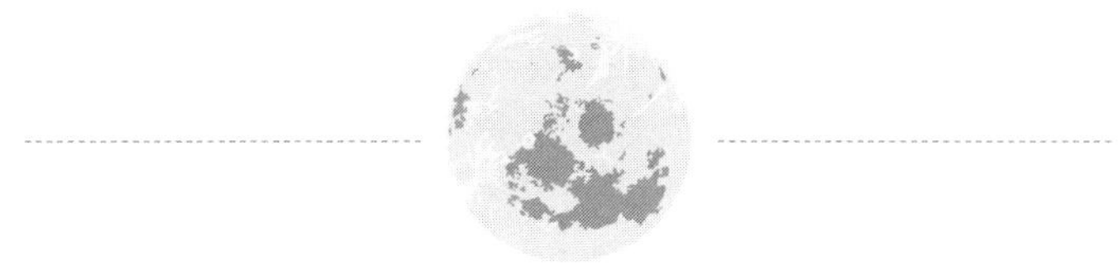

BLOOD WILL TELL

"Blood is life. ... It's what keeps you going, makes you warm, makes you hard, makes you other than dead."

—Spike, *Buffy the Vampire Slayer* ("The Gift," 5.22)

"Blood will tell" is a popular saying handed down since the Middle Ages. Always-important bloodlines revealed genealogy and established family lines for the transference of power and inheritance; their importance drove societies. To a certain extent, that interest in bloodlines continues today, even in popular entertainment through the titles of video games[98] and novels.[99] *Battlestar Galactica* hasn't yet used this phrase as an episode title, but the significance of bloodlines and the sheer volume of blood dripping through episodes are unmistakable. Like a thematic drum beat, blood pulses through each episode.

Like Parent, Like Child: The Importance of the Family Line

Early in Season Three, Anastasia Dualla (Dee) lovingly motivates husband Lee Adama and tries to assuage his self-doubts as a leader; she asserts that he'll complete his mission to lead the remnants of humanity to Earth, simply because he's an Adama. She reminds him of his father's legacy and assures Lee that, more than he may choose to accept, he's very much his father's son. "You're an Adama," she explains, "and that's one reason why I married you" ("Precipice," 3.2). The qualities in the Adama bloodline, passed from father to at least one son, receive a great deal of attention, not only among *Galactica*'s crew but within the remnants of humanity. Being an Adama ensures certain privileges but also requires levels of competence, sacrifice, and dedication. Lee spends much of his adult life trying either to live up to or live down what his father has done and, therefore, who he is supposed to become.

Other episodes reveal Bill Adama's differences with his own father, a famous lawyer on Caprica. Father and son never got along, a pattern often repeated in Bill and his son. Bloodlines have a way of passing on traits, even if they sometimes skip a generation. Bill had no use for his father's profession, but Lee once wanted to become a lawyer, and on *Galactica*, as Baltar's trial nears, the admiral gives him a set of law books belonging to his father, Lee's grandfather ("A Day in the Life," 3.15). In subsequent episodes, Lee both warms to and fears the role of a successful attorney. It becomes clear that he could be either a fine lawyer or a fine military leader, even if—or perhaps especially because—his approach differs from his grandfather's or father's. In fact, Lee is a new "hybrid" of the various leadership qualities displayed by his forbears. Lee's bloodlines would seem to ensure the continuation of a "ruling class" of Adamas—if he ever settles down to father a child with either Dee or Kara.

There's no reason to believe that Lee isn't Bill Adama's biological son, no challenge to his parentage or question about his human status (at least yet). Bloodlines in the Adama family signify leadership, although perhaps not exclusively in the military. Lee becomes so incensed that his late younger brother Zac[100] was pressured into the military—where he quickly lost his life—because the younger man wasn't cut out for the life that Bill, and later Lee, have come to embrace. Family qualities, whether real or imagined, are important to humans, and those serving on the *Galactica* are no different.

Having a human bloodline is important not only to humans. Caprica Six yearns for her and Gaius Baltar's child, believing it a divine gift ("Fragged," 2.3), even when, as she later admits, the little girl might not be their biological child but that of another human-Cylon couple. Sharon Valerii, also known by flight call sign Boomer, has no reason to believe she's not human until she experiences inexplicable time gaps and finds disconcerting things like explosives in her flight bag; only when she does something "inhuman"—shooting Commander Adama in a almost successful assassination attempt—and sees her "sisters" (a batch of Eights chanting "We love you, Sharon") during a flight mission ("Kobol's Last Gleaming, Part 1," 1.13) does Sharon Valerii really suspect she's not who she thought she was. Her proof that she's human? She remembers her "biological" family and, when reincarnated after being downloaded into a new body, has difficulty feeling "Cylon" on Caprica. She returns to her old apartment, filled with mementos of her "human" life, and, like Caprica Six, sets herself apart from the rest of the Cylons. Her "human" experiences have tainted her, leading to other Cylons' suspicion of her and her newfound mission to bring Cylons and humans together in peace ("Occupation," 3.1).

The Eights may not have real human blood, but Sharon Valerii/Boomer likes to trace her lineage to a human family and, indeed, seems to share traits with the humans who have loved her. Caprica Sharon/Sharon Agathon gives birth to a half-human daughter and, despite often overwhelming obstacles, remains married to a human Raptor ECO pilot. The couple eventually earns the right to raise their daughter together, just as any other couple on *Galactica* would.

On and off *Galactica*, blood will tell many other things, too. Sharon and Karl "Helo" Agathon's baby initially is feared not only because it will be half Cylon, but because it's unique,[101] as

Dr. Cottle's early blood tests reveal. This baby literally has a "clean slate" because she has no blood type—the Cylon characteristics blending with human DNA give the baby's blood healing properties for humans: indeed, Laura Roslin's late-stage cancer is immediately cured after she receives a transfusion of the fetus' blood ("Epiphanies," 2.13). (Hera gives the concept of a "universal" blood donor or type a new spin.) The blood test reveals previously unconsidered benefits from a human-Cylon hybrid; it offers a new world for scientists and geneticists to study and becomes a hopeful metaphor for the future of human-Cylon interactions.

With the revelation in the Season Three finale ("Crossroads, Part 2," 3.20) that Galen Tyrol, *Galactica*'s chief engineer, is a Cylon—and one of the elite Final Five at that—another half-human, half-Cylon baby is onboard *Galactica*. Tyrol's marriage to Cally produces a chubby baby boy, Nicholas, named for Cally's grandfather (a choice that indicates Cally's belief in the power of bloodlines; "Occupation," 3.1). With the audience's (and Tyrol's) newfound knowledge that he has been a sleeper agent, Nicky's bloodline takes on even greater significance. How ironic it is, too, that Tyrol long agonized over his relationship and post-"outing" treatment of former lover Sharon Valerii, another sleeper agent "awakened" on *Galactica*.

Recent revelations make viewers wonder which other children, or adults, may be part (or all) Cylon—and what that ultimately means for the future of humanity. The news also calls into question Dr. Cottle's ability to determine who is half-Cylon on the basis of blood tests. Surely little Nicky's blood has been drawn and typed at some point; does he also have "clean-slate" blood with no discernible human blood type, and if so, why hasn't Dr. Cottle mentioned it? Furthermore, will Cally feel as much love for her son and husband once she knows that they're Cylon? After all, she became the emblem of vigilante justice by murdering newly revealed Cylon and Adama assassin Sharon in cold blood.

Baltar's Cylon detector requires a blood sample: if the analysis turns the screen green, the test subject is human; if the result turns red, the subject is Cylon. Before being "awakened" as a Cylon but heavily suspecting something may be different about her, Sharon Valerii/Boomer volunteers to beta test Baltar's system. With Six goading Baltar as he analyzes the results and warning him of just what Sharon might do if he announces that her test turned red, he lies to Sharon ("Flesh and Bone," 1.8). The bright red results on his screen, carefully hidden from Sharon's view, clue in Baltar and the audience that something bad is likely to happen soon.

Soon everyone is being tested. Roslin is especially concerned about Adama's blood test, fearing that, as Leoben told her, he might be a Cylon in disguise. Adama likewise harbors suspicions about Ellen Tigh. In what passes for comedy on *Battlestar Galactica*, Baltar is inundated with blood samples and forced to start and stop various tests as he's pulled different directions by Roslin's and Adama's commands. Surrounded by 905 vials of blood that he figures will take sixty-one years to analyze, he is dwarfed by the task before him and has a mini-breakdown, relieved only by Six's promise of sex. Of course, only Baltar can see Six bent across the lab table, her dress tantalizingly lifted over her derriere, and when Kara abruptly enters the lab, Baltar is literally caught with his pants down ("Tigh Me Up, Tigh Me Down," 1.9). Making Baltar the arbiter of who is or isn't Cylon may not be the wisest decision.

Bloodlines may be "tainted" in the humans' future world, leading them to question just who or what they are if blood *won't* tell—or if it reveals something they'd rather not know.

A Persistent Trail of Blood

Blood tells many other tales, too—of military defeats and losses, self-defense and survival, murderous intent, unfortunate accidents, personal fortitude. *Battlestar Galactica*'s camera shots frequently focus on blood, providing close-ups of a smear, a droplet splattering in slow motion, a pool congealing on a table or floor; the obvious emphasis not only transfuses a burst of color in often-drab, dark scenes but graphically illustrates life-or-death, emotional issues and outcomes. As much as a *CSI* episode, *Battlestar Galactica* is colored by and covered with blood in nearly every episode, which provides multiple metaphors for life in a post-apocalyptic society. The lifeblood of humanity not only is prized but becomes a sacrificial sacrament—the ultimate icon of life.

The following table highlights bloodletting in the first three seasons. Clearly both human and Cylon characters have been "blooded" during their many personal and war-based clashes; more than sixty lingering close-ups of blood thematically unite these episodes.

TABLE 4. BLOOD, BLOOD EVERYWHERE

Episode	What's Bloody	What Happened
"33," 1.1	Adama's neck	Adama nicks his neck while shaving.
"33," 1.1	Caprica Six's lips	After Caprica Six kisses Helo, she is shot by Caprica Sharon, a close-up of Six's bloody lips indicate her death as she falls back from the kiss.
"33," 1.1	Caprica Six's back	The gunshot leaves a gaping bloody wound on Six's back.
"Bastille Day," 1.3	Lee's face	Blood trickles down Lee's face after he's injured in a prison riot; later, his other cheek sports bloody scores.
"Bastille Day," 1.3	Mason's ear	Cally bites off a prison leader's (Mason's) ear when he tries to assault her.
"Bastille Day," 1.3	Cally's hand	After Mason shoots Cally, her bloody hand presses against the wound.

Episode	What's Bloody	What Happened
"You Can't Go Home Again," 1.5	Cylon "body" in a damaged cockpit	The gory remains of the Cylon Raider "pilot" are more animal than human-like. Kara cuts through the goo when she tries to hotwire the downed Raider.
"You Can't Go Home Again," 1.5	Kara's leg	After successfully flying the Raider back to *Galactica* after her Viper is destroyed during a crash, Kara is pulled from the Raider. The camera first lingers on her bloody leg when she lies on a stretcher.
"Litmus," 1.6	Caprica Sharon's face	To make Helo believe that she was captured by and escaped from Cylons, Six beats Sharon until her face is bruised and bleeding.
"Flesh and Bone," 1.8	Leoben's head	At the beginning of the interrogation, an officer hits Leoben, leaving a bloody gash on top of his head.
"Flesh and Bone," 1.8	Leoben's face	As the interrogation continues, Leoben's face is repeatedly hit until it becomes a mass of bloody cuts.
"Flesh and Bone," 1.8	Bucket of water	When beatings fail to elicit information, Leoben is nearly drowned in a bucket. The water becomes progressively redder with each dunking.
"Tigh Me Up, Tigh Me Down," 1.9	905 vials	Baltar, surrounded by 905 vials of blood to be tested, figures it will take 61 years to finish analyzing the samples.
"Colonial Day," 1.11	Bound prisoner's hands	An apparent would-be assassin is found dead, his wrists slashed, after Lee and Kara leave him alone following an interrogation.

Episode	What's Bloody	What Happened
"Colonial Day," 1.11	Caprica Sharon's nose	Blood runs from Sharon's nose down her face after Helo shoots her.
"Kobol's Last Gleaming, Part 1," 1.12	Bandage on Boomer's cheek	After a botched suicide attempt, Boomer is shown with a blood-soaked bandage taped to her cheek.
"Kobol's Last Gleaming, Part 1," 1.12	Pilot's head	The dead pilot's bloody head drops forward as the Raptor begins a collision path for Kobol
"Kobol's Last Gleaming, Part 1," 1.12	Bullet hole in the Raptor's broken windscreen	A close-up of the bloody glass shows where Cylon gunfire entered the Raptor.
"Kobol's Last Gleaming, Part 1," 1.12	Baltar's head	An angry Six (seen only by Baltar) slams his head against a mirror, leaving a bloody mark on his forehead.
"Kobol's Last Gleaming, Part 1," 1.12	Steps outside a building	Sharon's blood pools on the steps where her faltering body falls after Helo shoots her.
"Kobol's Last Gleaming, Part 2," 1.13	Adama's torso	Sharon/Boomer shoots Adama point blank, his blood soon covering the CIC's tables and floor.
"Kobol's Last Gleaming, Part 2," 1.13	Starbuck's face	In a fight to the death, Starbuck is beaten by Caprica Six.
"Scattered," 2.1	Tarn, in particular, but lots of battle wounds	Tyrol's downed Raptor, carrying Cally, Crashdown, and Baltar, is attacked by Cylons. In the bloody combat, Tarn is shot several times, his body riddled with bullets.
"Fragged," 2.3	Lieutenant's body	Baltar shoots the lieutenant who points a gun at Cally, saving her life during a tense situation. "Now you're a man," Baltar's vision of Six tells him.

Episode	What's Bloody	What Happened
"Resistance," 2.4	Tyrol's face, one drop splashing on the floor	Tigh slugs Chief Tyrol when he denies knowing Sharon/Boomer is a Cylon. The camera focuses on one drop of Tyrol's blood as it hits the floor.
"Resistance," 2.4	Sharon's torso, one drop splashing on the floor	A similar shot of a single drop of Sharon's blood slowly splashing on the floor signals her imminent death after she has been fatally shot. The sound effect of a slowing heartbeat accompanying the slow-mo blood loss emphasizes this sudden, shocking death.
"The Farm," 2.5	Kara's abdomen	On Caprica, Kara is shot during a surprise Cylon attack. As the human resistance fighters retreat, the wounded Kara is left behind; she falls in slow motion.
"The Farm," 2.5	Cylon doctor's neck	To escape from a Cylon hospital, Kara stabs her doctor in the neck with a broken mirror; she slashes his aorta.
"The Farm," 2.5	Kara's hands and face	Covered in her victim's blood, Kara next unplugs a roomful of women who have become Cylon baby machines. Although the women beg to be killed rather than forced to bear Cylon children, Kara still has the blood of innocents on her hands.
"Home, Part 2," 2.7	Zarek's colleague's head	In a standoff, Sharon shoots Zarek's colleague point blank when he threatens to kill Adama.
"Final Cut," 2.8	Sharon's abdomen	Sharon fears a miscarriage when she begins bleeding. Her bloodied gown is glimpsed by D'Anna Biers as she films a documentary.

Episode	What's Bloody	What Happened
"Flight of the Phoenix," 2.9	Sharon's arm	Sharon "mainlines" a cable into her arm to avert a computer virus problem plaguing *Galactica*. A close-up shows the increasingly bloody arm as Sharon inserts the cable.
"Pegasus," 2.10	Sharon's face	A *Pegasus* interrogator beats Sharon. He then is beaten and killed by Tyrol and Helo.
"Epiphanies," 2.13	A blood-filled syringe	Laura Roslin receives a life-saving blood transfusion from Sharon's fetus. A close-up shows a blood-filled syringe about to be injected into the president.
"Black Market," 2.14	*Pegasus* Commander Fisk's slashed neck	Commander Fisk, Cain's replacement on the *Pegasus*, is garroted by a black marketer. When Lee investigates, the murder site is readily apparent: Fisk's blood covers a tabletop.
"Black Market," 2.14	Black marketer's chest	When Lee confronts the leader behind the black market, a bloody ending is expected. Lee shoots the man, and blood spurts from his chest.
"Sacrifice," 2.16	Billy's mouth	The death of President Roslin's aide, Billy, is quiet, the only obvious sign of his passing a thin line of blood trickling from his mouth.
"Sacrifice," 2.16	Lee's chest	A hostage crisis leaves Lee, blood spurting from his chest, critically injured.
"Sacrifice," 2.16	Dee's hands	Trying in vain to stop Lee's blood loss, Dee's hands become covered in his blood.

Episode	What's Bloody	What Happened
"Sacrifice," 2.16	Kara's hands	When Kara tells Adama that Lee has been injured, and that she may have accidentally shot him, the camera focuses on her bloody hands.
"Sacrifice," 2.16	Lee's body	Adama hovers over Lee's bloody body in a scene similar to that when Adama was shot and Lee hovered over his wounded father.
"The Captain's Hand," 2.17	Dead pilots' faces seen through the cockpit	Pilots on a rescue mission find the missing Raptor, its pilots obviously dead inside. Bloody faces are all the would-be rescuers see in the cockpit.
"Downloaded," 2.18	Caprica Six's scratched face	Caprica Six scratches herself, leaving a bloody welt across her beautiful face, as part of a ploy to win Caprica Sharon's sympathy and possibly her friendship.
"Lay Down Your Burdens, Part 1," 2.19	Tyrol's hands, Cally's beaten face and body	Chief Tyrol beats Cally when she awakens him during his nightmare. He carries her bloodied body to find help, his hands covered in her blood.
"Occupation," 3.1	Kara's hand	After stabbing Leoben, Kara wipes her bloody hand on the floor and eats dinner, blood still on her hands.
"Precipice," 3.2	Kacey's head	When toddler Kacey is left alone, she falls and hits her head. Kara finds the child, blood from the head wound pooling on the stairs.
"Precipice," 3.2	Six's head	Six is shot in the head when she defends Baltar, who doesn't want to sign the death warrants of human detainees on New Caprica.

Episode	What's Bloody	What Happened
"Exodus, Part 1," 3.3	Dr. Cottle's lab coat	On New Caprica D'Anna/Three asks Dr. Cottle about his blood-soaked lab coat, wondering if the blood is from humans or Cylons. After all, "this stuff all looks the same."
"Exodus, Part 1," 3.3	Cavil's hands	After being shot during an ambush and rescue of human prisoners, Cavil presses his hands against the wound.
"Collaborators," 3.5	Cavil's abdominal gunshot wound	Cavil presses a hand against his bleeding abdomen, then lays his bloody hand against his thigh. The humans he plotted to kill turn against him and leave him to die, "in the hot sun," he later incredulously tells other Cylons after his next download.
"Torn," 3.6	Virus-infected Cylons' samples	Baltar takes blood samples from dying Cylons in an exploration vessel sent near the Lion's head nebula he believes will provide them clues to Earth's location. Analyzing the blood might indicate what caused a whole ship's crew to become infected.
"A Measure of Salvation," 3.7	Virus-infected Cylons' samples	Once the humans have learned about the lethal Cylon virus, Dr. Cottle studies the blood work of infected Cylons, the human crew who found them, and "rescue" crewperson Sharon Agathon in order to learn who carries the virus.
"Hero," 3.8	D'Anna's nose, mouth, and forehead	When D'Anna/Three torments a caged Danny Novacek, he strikes back, punching her in the face. The camera shows a close-up of blood tricking from her nose, mouth, and forehead until her face becomes a gruesome mask.

Episode	What's Bloody	What Happened
"Hero," 3.8	Adama's face	Danny "Bulldog" Novacek beats Commander Adama when he learns that Adama left him behind to be captured by Cylons during a pre-invasion Black Ops mission.
"Unfinished Business," 3.9	Lee's ear	During an early boxing match with Helo, Lee is punched, and the blood on Lee's ear is captured in close-up.
"Unfinished Business," 3.9	Lee's eye	A gash next to Lee's eye makes blood stream down his face as the match progresses.
"Unfinished Business," 3.9	Kara's & Lee's battered and bleeding faces	They fight each other, but end up smiling, as they resolve personal conflicts in a boxing match.
"Rapture," 3.12	Splattered wall	Sharon asks Helo to shoot her so that she'll be downloaded inside the Cylon ship, where she can find Hera. Helo reluctantly does, splattering Sharon's blood all across a wall.
"Rapture," 3.12	D'Anna's nose	Before dying in the temple of Athena, D'Anna sees the Final Five. Her nose begins to bleed while the temple is destroyed.
"Taking a Break from All Your Worries," 3.13	Baltar's neck, and thus the water in the resurrection tank	Six scratches Baltar during a dream in which he wakes up in the Cylon resurrection tank. Saying he's not a Cylon, Six pushes Baltar beneath the water, which turns progressively redder with his blood.
"Taking a Break from All Your Worries," 3.13	Murdered bodies, surrounded in a large pool of blood	Roslin shows Baltar a photograph of a family murdered on New Caprica; their blood is a prominent image in the photo.

Episode	What's Bloody	What Happened
"Taking a Break from All Your Worries," 3.13	Baltar's neck	Gaeta stabs the incarcerated Baltar during a "visit" observed by Roslin and Adama.
"Dirty Hands," 3.16	Cabot's hands	Incarcerated strike leader Cabot scratches the walls of his cell until his hands are bloody.
"Dirty Hands," 3.16	Boy's bloody arm	A close-up of a boy's mangled arm shows how dangerous old mining equipment has become; the accident prompts Tyrol to call a strike.
"Maelstrom," 3.17	Young Kara's nose	Kara envisions herself as a child sitting in her cockpit. The close-up emphasizes blood streaming from her nose, prompting a vision of Kara's abusive childhood.
"Crossroads, Part 2," 3.20	Adama's neck	Once again Adama nicks himself shaving.

Humanity's leaders are bloody conversationalists, whether during top-level political maneuvering or friendly bantering. Blood is a powerful metaphor, providing a powerful subtext for conversations about other subjects:

- "You want a bloodbath," Lee accuses Tom Zarek at the start of a prison riot. Zarek plans to use his death to bring down the government; dying a martyr seems better than living as a forgotten prison inmate ("Bastille Day," 1.3).
- One of the most significant scenes uses red paint as a stand-in for Zac's blood. Lee and Kara knock over a paint bucket as they laughingly decorate helmets to wear in an impromptu

parade celebrating a pilot's one-thousandth landing. The red paint spills across the floor, pooling and congealing into a sticky mess. When Adama asks who is at fault for the spilled paint, Lee and Kara giggle and point fingers at each other. "Somebody has to clean that up," the parental Adama tells them. Although this scene begins playfully, the spilled paint highlights the mess Kara and Lee have made of Zac's death (as well as foreshadows the untimely death of the pilot being celebrated). They point fingers of blame at each other for causing his untimely end, the paint like so much spilled blood between them. Adama is right: somebody has to clean up the mess, and by the end of the episode, Kara confesses to Adama that she passed Zac in flight school when he should've been washed out. His inability to fly well likely led to his accidental death ("Act of Contrition," 1.4). Even such a lighthearted scene takes on dark undertones and can weaken (or ultimately strengthen) ties of blood and friendship among characters.

- "Machines shouldn't bleed," Starbuck dispassionately tells Leoben during her torturous interrogation of him ("Flesh and Bone," 1.8). If the Cylons wish so much to be human, to the point of "appropriating" human physiological responses, Starbuck wants Leoben to feel as much pain as possible.
- President Roslin understands just how brutally Admiral Cain could treat civilians (even before Cain's side of the story is told in *Razor*). Roslin also correctly predicts that Cain will move to kill Commander Adama and end his threat to her "regime," prompting the president to suggest Cain's murder. Adama incredulously asks the former schoolteacher, "What's gotten into you? You've become so bloody minded" ("Resurrection Ship, Part 1," 2.1).
- Roslin and Adama's growing personal relationship involves the ritual of exchanging books. Roslin's latest gift to Adama is entitled *Blood Runs at Midnight*, a story she assures him is very good ("A Day in the Life," 3.15).

- Roslin calls Adama early one morning during Baltar's trial, asking him to use his "military" voice to get her out of bed. The couple share an oddly intimate conversation, discussing nothing important but offering moral support to each other. Adama comments on a nick received during shaving, and the camera focuses on the bloody mark on his neck, but the commander spends more time than necessary detailing his progress in stemming the blood ("Crossroads, Parts 1 and 2," 3.19–3.20). Again, irony is prevalent: Adama's vote as a member of Baltar's jury indeed allows him to "stop the blood"; by the end of the two-parter, Adama reveals to Roslin that he couldn't convict Baltar after realizing how decisions he and so many others made on New Caprica and during the exodus have bloodied and nearly exterminated humanity.

The list goes on and on. Each episode offers anything from a glimpse to a camera-forced stare at the bloody mess of the humans' and Cylons' lives. The "modern" (i.e., "like ours") world of constant warfare, fight-to-the-death confrontations with internal and external enemies, and even day-to-day minutiae (e.g., shaving) provides mostly painful experiences. How much blood should be shed just to get through the day? How much lifeblood is risked on everything from routine military patrols to solving problems with friends and co-workers? Although many action sequences involve warfare, and battles are commonplace throughout the series, bloodletting is just as, if not more, likely in the everyday world as on the battlefield. Space or land battles might be expected to be gory (as illustrated by scenes of injured and dying soldiers in episodes like "Fragged," 2.3)—war is *supposed* to be painful and bloody; audiences might hope that an average day, however, even on a battlestar, shouldn't have quite so much bloodshed. *Battlestar Galactica* indicates that such naiveté is very old school. Every act has a cost, and often, according to this series, payment in blood is required.

The Blood of Innocents

As series co-creator David Eick has mentioned many times in interviews, the revisioning of *Battlestar Galactica* is appropriate to a post-9/11 world. The initial 9/11 attacks took the lives of many people and spilled innocents' blood—actions to which Eick and viewers liken the Cylon attack on the Colonies, which precipitated all future plotlines in *Battlestar Galactica*. The humans' initial and continuing anger at the Cylons for this unprecedented level of violence directed at them—and the Cylons' victorious successive attacks on all twelve human home worlds—makes people feel like the victims in their long relationship with the Cylons. As the series progresses, however, with some Cylons portrayed sympathetically, determining just who is innocent in the complex history of Cylon-human relationships becomes a matter of perspective.

At various times throughout three seasons, different characters seem, alternately, innocent victims and culpable instigators. Commander Adama trusts and likes Boomer, a member of his crew for more than two years before she attempts to assassinate him. In this scenario, Adama seems the almost-martyred victim, yet another human attacked, without provocation, by a Cylon. In the aftermath of this act, Sharon/Boomer is reviled by her friends and co-workers, attacked by her former lover, incarcerated and brutally interrogated, and finally shot to death. Is Boomer unjustly killed, or does she just get what she deserved?

That this Cylon has been perceived as human for all her life, and even believes that she is human, causes Sharon's human friends great distress. What are they if they believed her to be human? What if they still like her, even if they abhor what she did to Adama? Is her story—that she didn't know until she was "activated" that she was Cylon—to be believed, or is it just another ploy by those sneaky Cylons?

The story continues to evolve, with Sharon/Boomer becoming the "innocent" victim of human prejudice, a problem another Eight, Caprica Sharon, also endures because of her relationship with Helo and subsequent pregnancy. In later episodes, after Caprica Sharon helps her human friends on *Galactica* by, for example, providing information, reversing a Cylon-created computer virus, and eventually returning to duty as a pilot (taking the call sign Athena to differentiate herself from the "other" pilot, Boomer), the humans who mistrust her seem like unjust, racist perpetrators of violence. Identifying innocent victims is as problematic as pinpointing sleeper Cylons among *Galactica*'s command or crew.

Perhaps the only true "innocents" in *Battlestar Galactica* are children, and the spilling of innocent blood means that children are also among the injured and dead. Kara, caught in Leoben's web of deception, doubts that Kacey is really her daughter, a child Leoben says he created by inseminating an egg from Kara's amputated ovary ("The Farm," 2.5). Still, the child's blonde hair and approximate age could indicate that Kara is indeed Kacey's mother. Leoben shrewdly leaves toddler Kacey alone with Kara, forcing her to deal with the child she has carefully avoided in their apartment. Perhaps the childhood traumas the Cylon doctor hypothesizes during "The Farm" are correct (a theory proved true in flashbacks during the later episode "Maelstrom" [3.17]): Kara was physically abused as a child, a good and likely reason for her reluctance ever to bear children. While Kara locks herself away from Kacey, she hears the child fall—and to her horror discovers an unconscious, bleeding toddler on the stairs.

Feeling guilty that her actions, or lack of, led to Kacey's injury, Kara becomes a good mother to the little girl, a resolution that Leoben happily takes advantage of while he can. During the human exodus from New Caprica ("Exodus, Part 2," 3.4), Kara's husband, Sam Anders, finds her and tries to carry her to safety. Kara, however, refuses to leave without Kacey. She becomes more warrior Starbuck than Kacey's mom when she takes the little girl away from Leoben and, for the last time, kills him.

Kacey is an innocent victim of Kara's disquieting past and fears of motherhood and, it turns out, abduction by Cylons. After Kara and Kacey come aboard *Galactica*, Kacey's biological mother sees them and gratefully retrieves her child. Kacey again becomes a victim when the bitter, angry Kara refuses to have anything to do with the child, despite Kacey's mother's entreaties that Kara visit. Innocent Kacey doesn't realize that "mom" Kara no longer wants her and is understandably hurt when she fails to visit. Only when Kara begins to overcome her revulsion at Leoben's deception does she put aside her own emotions and visit the little girl, who is happy to see her ("Torn," 3.6).

Although Kacey retains her innocence, at least as much as possible after her abduction by a Cylon, Kara also is an innocent victim of Leoben's deception. Just when it seems that worlds-wise, often worlds-weary Starbuck couldn't possibly have any more innocence to lose, audiences see yet another side to her character. The "blood of innocents," in this case Kacey's head injury, reveals Kara's innocent desire to believe—in the bond between mother and child, in her ability to be a good mother despite her upbringing, in the power of love. To have those hopes shattered is a cruel emotional wound that undoubtedly leads to some internal bleeding. Although Kara often has blood on her hands, for one reason or another, and usually seems impervious to pain, it takes the blood of innocents like Kacey to show just how caring she can be.

Blood on Their Hands

On New Caprica, Leoben enjoys playing mind games for god, one way that he likely believes he can mesh his desires to convert the heathen humans and win Kara Thrace's affections. Day after day he woos her in a weirdly logical, Cylon-ingenious way in the apartment/cell where she is incarcerated. He sees to her comfort; he fixes her dinner and displays admirable patience in the face of yet another refusal. After all, he prophesies that she will come to love him. Day after day, Kara finds another way to kill him; once during dinner she stabs him in the neck after he cuts her meat for her ("Occupation," 3.1). Although her hands are bloody, Kara delicately begins to dine, genteelly dabbing her mouth with a napkin. She knows her would-be lover will simply download his consciousness into another body and soon reappear at the door with an ironic "Honey, I'm home!" Still, she enjoys her only way of fighting back—finding new and innovative ways to kill Leoben, a gleefully gory way to pass the time.

Although many, perhaps most, characters' choices lead to someone's death at least once in this series, Kara Thrace/Starbuck best represents the often illogical complexity of humanity, with its abhorrence of unprovoked violence on the one hand but, on the other, belief in the need for retaliatory attacks or pre-emptive strikes. Although she at times is vulnerable, she often revels in having blood on her hands. As a warrior she glories in her ability to fly dangerous missions and take out Cylon raiders. She becomes so focused on one, Scar, that only a last-second decision to abort a suicide run at her enemy gives rival Kat the coveted kill. Before the mission, Kara learns from incarcerated Cylon Sharon that Scar likely has been killed by Starbuck many times before (only to be regenerated to fight yet again). Kara is both horrified that she can keep killing Cylons, only to have them return in a never-ending cycle until she dies trying, and appalled that her victim may remember several deaths by her hand; nevertheless, she enjoys the hunt and the kill ("Scar," 2.15). Having blood on her hands, if the blood is her enemy's, doesn't bother Kara at all. She views killing as a regular part of her job.

When the blood is a friend's, however, Kara may try to maintain her tough facade, but she harbors fears and guilt that eventually wear her down. An early episode ("Act of Contrition," 1.4) reveals that Kara's early promotion of her lover Zac Adama may have led to his death during his first mission as a pilot. Even more damning is Kara's friendly fire shooting of Lee. During an attack on *Cloud Nine's* bar, Lee and several civilians and soldiers from *Galactica* are held hostage. Already on *Cloud Nine* on leave, Kara volunteers to disguise herself as a repair person in order to gather information on the situation and, perhaps, bring in the marines. In an ensuing melee, Lee lunges into crossfire, and Kara accidentally shoots him. The wounded Lee, bleeding profusely, is left behind when the marines are forced to abandon the attack. Sitting in the hallway with blood on her hands from a fellow soldier's wound, Kara fills in Adama about the latest developments in the hostage crisis. She first tells him that Lee's been wounded but soon admits it was friendly fire and, she fears, she was the shooter ("Sacrifice," 2.16). Kara's resulting guilt further strains her relationship with Lee, which only is resolved more than a year later, after numerous complications and estrangements, in yet another bloody battle ("Unfinished Business," 3.9).

This time Lee and Kara face off in a boxing match. By the time the two work through their sexual frustrations, latent guilt, and deeply buried friendship and love, they are emotionally and physically battered. The final scene summarizes the heart of the Kara/Lee and Starbuck/Apollo dynamic: the camera freezes on a close-up of Kara and Lee leaning into each other, their bloodied faces close together as they smile. In many symbolic and experiential ways, Kara/Starbuck and Lee/Apollo are bonded through blood; they can hurt each other more deeply than anyone else could wound them, but their lives are so completely entwined that when one is cut, the other bleeds.

The Color of Life

Red as a highlight color not only makes scenes more interesting—after all, the favored color scheme in this dark drama is usually shades of gray—but it also focuses viewers' attention on details. Whether red emphasizes innocuous clothing worn by extras in the background or a bar radio hinting that the music Tigh and Sam desperately try to tune in might be an important clue that they're "different," this color becomes a prominent stylistic and storytelling device used throughout the series.

During the Cylons' first reintroduction into this reimagined *Battlestar Galactica*, Number Six saunters into the room where a human ambassador awaits, but doesn't really expect, a meeting with a representative of the Cylon race. The sexy Six is a surprising testament to Cylon evolution; not only is she blonde, incredibly well built, and eerily humanistic, but she wears a form-fitting red dress. She kisses the human ambassador, assuring him that everything will be all right, just as the assault on the Colonies begins ("Miniseries").

In color symbolism, red can represent everything from deep, sometimes violent but always passionate emotions to lifeblood. The Sixes, especially Baltar's "angel," typically wear red. When they don white, black, or, much less frequently, blue clothing, the shift in wardrobe signals an important change in the emotional tenor of Six's and Baltar's relationship, as well as a shift in the plotlines involving Baltar. Most often, however, Six wears a variety of stylishly revealing blood red dresses, symbolizing her sexuality.

Red light bathes the faces of those making emotional speeches or facing some kind of emotional trauma: Baltar's face is bathed in the glow of red lights in his quarters on the Cylon ship; his face "lights up" when he pleads his case before D'Anna and an increasingly wary Six ("Torn," 3.6). Adama's face "turns red" when he overhears Apollo's distress in tracking Starbuck; the bridge's alert alarm is reflected on his face as he learns of Starbuck's apparent death when her Raptor disintegrates ("Maelstrom," 3.17). Carolanne Adama, the Commander's ex, pours yet another drink during Adama's "flashback" to his broken marriage; her face glows in the red bar lights, and her anger soon erupts as she begins to yell at her husband ("A Day in the Life," 3.15). Fear, grief, and anger are clearly three intense emotions colorfully highlighted in these scenes, and the use of red facial highlights is prevalent throughout the series.

Red spotlights the following details, only a few of the many examples throughout each episode:

- Red lights in the black market's bar indicate its status as a "red light" district ("Black Market," 2.14).
- A dead pilot's girlfriend is wearing a red sweater in the snapshot his friends pass around after his death ("Scar," 2.15).
- Scar's roving red eye is shown in a close-up as the raider stalks Starbuck ("Scar," 2.15).
- Red lights flicker across Starbuck's face while she plays chicken with Scar during a space battle ("Scar," 2.15).
- Red lights on the Cylon ship pulse behind Baltar, who tries to figure out the safest way to deal with his captors ("Collaborators," 3.5).
- The Cylons and Baltar sleep on red beds ("Collaborators," 3.5; "Torn," 3.6).
- Lee's boxing gloves are red ("Unfinished Business," 3.9).
- Baby Hera sports a red blanket as her mother carries her around the ship ("The Woman King," 3.14).
- On New Caprica, during ground-breaking festivities, Laura Roslin wears a red sweater, a color that Adama notes looks good on her ("Unfinished Business," 3.9). Adama also mentions his fond memory of that dress in "A Day in the Life" (3.15).

These examples subtly layer details about the characters or emotions in these scenes: Laura Roslin's choice of red clothing, which heightens Adama's interest in her as a woman, indicates the potential for romance. Her auburn hair is yet another shade of red, and although Roslin's responses as president are controlled and calculated, her private emotional responses to situations are much richer and deeper than those of her military counterpart Adama. Red provides a visual focal point for viewers and, almost subliminally, subtext for a scene or relationship.

Intense emotion is the lifeblood of *Battlestar Galactica*. What the characters feel passionate about propels the audience into episodes filled with death-defying plot twists and conflicting character development. Even the "quiet" moments between parents and children, best friends, or lovers thrum with turbulent emotional undercurrents. Pride, devotion, envy, jealousy, lust, regret, determination, hatred, joy, hope, but, most of all, love brightly color this series and elevate the characters and their life stories above the expected or mundane.

Battlestar Galactica redlines every human and Cylon emotion. Such depth of feeling, for good or bad, helps them survive even as it threatens to undo them. It binds every character—women and men, parents and children, officers and subordinates, governors and governed, humans and Cylons—in an uneasy truce. The series traces our social bloodlines as we—and the series' writers—struggle to make sense of the riveting but terrifying emotional world that envelops us all.

GODS & STARS: MYTHOLOGY AND ASTROLOGY IN *BATTLESTAR GALACTICA*

"As flies to wanton boys, are we to the gods.
They kill us for their sport."

—Gloucester, *King Lear* (Act 4, Scene 1)

"Men at some time are masters of their fates:
The fault, dear Brutus, is not in our stars,
But in ourselves, that we are underlings."

—Cassius, *Julius Caesar* (Act 1, Scene 2)

The overarching concepts of religion, astrology, and the history of the Lords of Kobol, so strongly prominent in the contemporary *Battlestar*, are relatively underdeveloped in the original series. The few astrological references (to Caprica and Geminon, specifically) were perhaps more a sign of the times—the 1970s—than representation of a true mythos. Similarly, religion is another undeveloped concept in the original *Battlestar*: while the Lords of Kobol play a central role, their religion seems oddly monothesistic (the only plural reference to "god" is in an episode title: "The Planet of The Gods I and II"), and the colonists' religion embraces a holy book, a unifying scripture entitled *The Book of the Word*.

In the contemporary *Battlestar*, the human race is more obviously polytheistic: actively worshipping the Lords of Kobol (presumably Greek and Roman gods of classic mythology: Apollo, Hera, Zeus, Aries, Artemis, Athena, and Aurora have been specifically named) and venerating the *Sacred Scroll* that details how the colonists fled from Kobol after war erupted as a result of one of the gods demanding superiority above all others. (While not specifically stated, it seems the Cylons may worship this fallen God, a Christ-like figure that celebrates the tenants of peace, love, and understanding.)

Humans and Cylons alike appear to heed a recurring theme of renewal: humans believe in the fates and the significance of recurrence. The psalm-like phrase from Pithia—"All this has happened before. All this will happen again"—is an utterance repeated by both humans and Cylons. The Cylons, however, take the saying quite literally upon death, experiencing a near-instant "reincarnation" and rebirth of their psyches, via download, into other, identical bodies.

To understand both the parallels and dichotomies of Cylon and human religions requires a brief historical overview. While the term "polytheistic" comes from the Greek *poly theoi*, "many Gods," the concept predates Greek culture. Earthly human religion began as polytheistic, a construct represented in countless creation stories. The Egyptians, Sumarians, and Mayans were all polytheistic, along with the indigenous tribes of Central and South America, Africa, and Asia. Many of these religious beliefs had a societal impact, with hierarchical structures of power distribution, beginning with a "main" or primary god (for the Egyptians, the god of the Sun—Ra, for the Greeks, Zeus) that either sired or created the other deities from their own flesh or from will alone.

In *Battlestar*, the Lords of Kobol, named after their Greek counterparts, lived in a rich, verdant, Earth-like world where gods and men lived in unity for an undisclosed period of time before the war resulted in a massive exodus from the planet to the twelve disparate colonies. For the humans, the Lords of Kobol serve as sacred recipients of specific, action-oriented prayers—Artemis is beseeched before a hunt, for example; Athena is asked to bestow wisdom—in a way similar to that of the ancient Greeks and Romans.

Understandably, the contemporary *Battlestar*'s mythos seems to have the threads of mythology heavily weaved into its central narrative, giving the viewer a greater understanding of who the central characters are based on the gods and goddesses that they call upon in times of trouble or use as their call sign while in flight. In the first section of this jump, we'll examine those explicitly referenced in the series in detail.

The Greek Pantheon

The Greek pantheon of gods was organized by a sort of social hierarchy beginning with the father of all gods and creator of the world, Chronos, down to lesser and lower gods that were half-human. To the Greeks, this deity system was not only religious: day-to-day life was severely impacted by the gods themselves, requiring a great amount of prayer and praise. The Greeks (and later Romans) would often adopt a favorite god or goddess for worship, and would place a small statue of this god on display in their homes. They also carried small trinkets that represented the gods or goddesses on their persons to represent their constant devotion to the gods. Of all the Greek and Roman gods, the one held in often highest esteem was Zeus.

Zeus/Jupiter (Son of Chronos, Ruler of Mt. Olympus)

In the earliest Greek mythology, Zeus was a celestial god, symbolized by the changing weather. Over time, he was viewed as the "king" of the gods of Mt. Olympus, and sired many of the most prominent offspring in Greek-Roman mythology. Named as the "father of Gods and Man," Zeus ruled over both heaven and earth, preserving justice for all. Recognized as the first Lord of Kobol in *Battlestar*, Zeus has offered several omen-like portents of things to come: in the Scrolls of Pithia, for example, Zeus warns that a return to Kobol will result in bloodshed ("Home, Part 2," 2.7); and in "Exodus, Part 1" (3.3), the drugged oracle Dodona Selloi tells Number Three that Zeus has revealed that all the gods weep for her. Commander Adama is referred to as "Zeus" by Tom Zarek upon his first meeting with Lee Adama ("Bastille Day," 1.3)—a dual reference to the son's call sign, Apollo, and the Old Man's rule over the ship both physically and spiritually.

Apollo (Son of Zeus and Leto) and Artemis, Twins

Apollo, Greek god of music, disease and medicine, light and intellect, colonization, and archery, was known for his ability to shoot disease-carrying arrows but was most famous for his skill at prophecy. He had many loves, all which ended badly. In *Battlestar*, Apollo is one of the Lords of Kobol, and celebrated for his healing powers and as god of the hunt. Lee Adama's call sign is perhaps an allusion to his skills as CAG and leader of the hunt, as well as his familial association to Zeus/Bill Adama.

Artemis, twin sister to Apollo, goddess of the hunt, is also associated with fertility in Greek mythology. She was known for her jealousy and possessive nature and her vengeful attacks against those who betrayed her. She had an equally soft side, serving as protector of small children. Artemis is a favorite god of Kara Thrace, often the recipient of her prayers prior to a hunt, and the similarities between Kara and Artemis are striking: like Artemis, she has a willful and somewhat vengeful streak when betrayed, but she softens to the idea of having her own child when she is led to believe that she is a mother by Leoben.

Ares/Mars (Son of Zeus and Hera)

Ares, god of war and destruction, was disliked by all the gods for his warlike nature. In Greece, he was most revered in the region of Thrace, where cult-worship of the god flourished. A Lord of Kobol and namesake to Galen and Cally's son, Ares has scarcely been mentioned otherwise in the course of the series. The connection of the region of Thrace to the often bellicose nature of Kara Thrace may be mere coincidence, but worth noting.

Aphrodite

The goddess of love and lust was said to emerge from sea foam into existence, though Homer considers her the offspring of Zeus and Dione. Aphrodite possessed an irresistible beauty, wit, and charm and was worshipped for her ability to bring forth powerful emotions. She, too, serves as one of the Lords of Kobol, and has been the recipient of prayers uttered by Kara Thrace.

Athena

Athena, worshipped for her ability at logic, war, reason, and justice, is another child of Zeus who sprung forth, full grown, from his head. Zeus' favorite offspring, she carried the symbol of the owl. In the *Battlestar* mythos, Athena commits suicide following the massive exodus from Kobol, and her tomb contains a constellation "map" to Earth. Athena is the call sign of the Cylon Sharon, Number Eight, who has willingly disenfranchised herself from her kind and is mother to Hera.

Hera (Zeus' sister and wife)

When Chronus, Zeus' father, feared that Zeus would one day rebel and overpower him, he swallowed all his children, including Hera, and a stone wrapped in a blanket he thought to be

Zeus. The son lived to confront and defeat his father, however, demanding that he vomit up his swallowed children, including Zeus' sister Hera, who thereafter became his wife.

Hera was known for her jealousy and rage over her husband's affairs and often punished all potential rivals or anyone who had betrayed her in any way. A mountain ridge on Kobol is named for Hera, as well as Caprica Sharon and Helo's hybrid child.

Mixing of Culture and Faith: Astrology

It's not surprising that astrology and mythology are intertwined into *Battlestar*: historically, the practice of astrology and polytheism go almost hand in hand. While no one race or culture specifically created astrology, some of the earliest records trace back to the Egyptian and Greek cultures. The blend of astrology practiced in *Battlestar Galactica* is based upon the central themes of so-called "horoscopic" astrology, a blend of Indian and Western astrology involving the twelve constellations of Aries, Taurus, Gemini, Cancer, Leo, Virgo, Libra, Scorpio, Sagittarius, Capricorn, Aquarius, and Pisces. In turn, modern astrology is based upon the Greek version of the now-discredited science, as combined from Babylonian and Egyptian practices. The Greeks first learned of astrology as a result of conquests in Babylon, where astrology looked to the significance of omens in the sky to correlate to specific natural events, and were exposed as well to the more organized form of Egyptian astrology. Throughout Western history, astrology had remained influential, and belief in omens represented in the skies as portents of things to come has persisted for centuries. The popularity of sun-sign astrology as indicative of individual personality traits continues in modern society, with most daily newspapers in the United States carrying weekly, even daily horoscopes.

In *Battlestar*, the twelve colonies are based upon the twelve constellations, each "ruled" in turn by a specific planet:

Astrological Sign	Planet	Colony
Aries, "The Ram"	Mars	Aerilon
Taurus, "The Bull"	Venus	Tauron
Gemini, "The Twins"	Mercury	Geminon
Cancer, "The Crab"	The Moon	Canceron
Leo, "The Lion"	The Sun	Leonis
Virgo, "The Virgin"	Mercury	Virgon
Libra, "The Scales"	Virgo	Libris
Scorpio, "The Scorpion"	Pluto	Scorpion
Sagittarius, "The Archer"	Jupiter	Sagittaron
Capricorn, "The Sea Goat"	Saturn	Caprica
Aquarius, "The Water Bearer"	Neptune	Aquaria
Pisces, "The Fish"	Jupiter	Picon

Many of the colonies in the series have yet to be developed, and some only receive brief mention (appearing during the quorum of twelve meeting, for example, in "Colonial Day" [1.11]). We will discuss the colonies directly mentioned in the series and identify their similarities to modern understandings of astrology.

ARIES/ARIELON

Aries, the Ram, is considered the "child" of the Zodiac: ruled by the first sign of the zodiac, Aries are the most immature, quick to catch fire and become angry, but they also struggle at finishing projects. They have a tireless energy and are hard workers. According to Gaius Baltar, Arielon was a colony populated by poor, uneducated, underprivileged workhorses that primarily provided food to other colonies ("Dirty Hands," 3.15).

It is the Aries personality that is most clearly exhibited in the series: Aries can be quite tenacious, determined, and strong-willed when put to a challenge and can often overcome long odds based on sheer determination. Gaius Baltar reinvented himself from country bumpkin to esteemed scholar; reporter Sekou Hamilton also beat the odds to become a renowned reporter. Aries can be quite egotistical (again, Gaius Baltar is a prime example) but also extremely giving when it comes to their friends or loved ones—deckhand Socinus nearly gives up his freedom to vouch for Chief Tyrol when "caught" colluding with the Cylons ("Litmus," 1.6), and later gives his life when the Raptor crashes on the deserted Kobol ("Valley of Darkness," 2.2).

TAURUS/TAURON

Taurus, the bull, is well known as the most obstinate, stubborn sign of the zodiac. Strong willed and not easily bullied (pun intended), a Taurus can be a formidable enemy when provoked out of a seemingly docile shell. The colony on Battlestar *Tauron* is represented as one that constantly strained against authority.

Tauron tenacity, struggle for power against all odds, and legendary obstinacy are best reflected in *Pegasus* commander Helena Cain. Her abrasive aggressiveness and fixated belief that she's constantly right cause more than a little conflict on both battlestars, and her brutality against the tortured Number Six/Gina trapped in her brig results in her death ("Resurrection Ship, Part 2," 2.12).

GEMINI/GEMINON

Gemini, the twins, is ruled by the planet Mercury, named for the messenger of the gods, who was representative of swift thought and communication. Geminis are quite a lively bunch, very enthusiastic and kind when those around them agree with them, but quite quarrelsome when they are met with any sort of opposition. The Gemini trait for interpretation and analysis is represented in the somewhat controversial and extremist readings of the Sacred Scrolls. When Laura Roslin seems to disagree with their strong anti-abortion beliefs, she is met with the strong, antagonistic reproach by Sarah Porter ("The Captain's Hand," 2.17).

Sagittarius/Sagittaron

Those under the sign of Sagittarius, the archer, are said to possess a great love for philosophy and religion with a strong independent streak. Sagittarians are best known for being brutally honest and are sometimes considered harsh and abrasive because of boldly honest answers. They are natural-born speakers and communicators, with a natural talent for persuasion. Tom Zarek is a prime example of the sometimes rebellious, always morally minded Sagittarius frame of mind.

On *Battlestar*, Sagittaron natives possess a traditionalist approach to their religion and their personal health. As we learn in "The Woman King" (3.14), they refuse to take modern medicine, preferring homeopathic and natural remedies, and they bear a fierce independent streak that others, even a native of their own colony like Anastasia Dualla, view as stubborn.

Capricorn/Caprica

Capricorn, the Sea Goat, is associated with the planet Saturn, astrologically the planet associated with the benefits and success of hard work and dedication. Caprica is the center of the colonies, the seat of art, literature, and leisure, the home planet of the most affluent members of society. Hard work and tenacity is the mark of the Capricorn personality, a trait mirrored in its native inhabitants William Adama and Kara Thrace.

PISCES/PICON

Represented by two fish swimming in opposite directions, one upstream, one down, Pisces embodies constant internal struggle: doing the right thing with an upbeat attitude or indulging in drink and excess and succumbing to a strong tendency for melancholy.

Asha Janik is a strong advocate for Cylon rights, and the "Demand Peace" movement is representative of the strong Pisces need to do "good" while inadvertently doing bad. Asha tampers with rounds on the Vipers and is later arrested by Adama. Playa Palacios, reporter and Picon native, is quite serious about her position as a highly respected reporter—but that doesn't stop her from having a quick bathroom rendezvous with Gaius Baltar to get the "exclusive" that he plans to run for president. This dichotomy in the strong Pisces will—usually pulling the subject in opposite directions—is often portrayed in the series.

Mythology and astrology may prove a mere narrative device that serves to provide unity and continuity to certain understandings about the storyline and characters, but both are worthy of discussion and speculation. While we'll not know the final outcome of the search for Earth until the final season, we will know that the twelve constellations, the eye of Jupiter, and Athena's Arrow played a role—deepening the mystery of the unique and multilayered *Battlestar* mythos.

Part IV

EPISODES

This section—four chapters and three "jumps"—takes as its subject a variety of *BSG* episodes. "Carrying 'Water': An Interview with Marita Grabiak" goes behind the scenes with the director of the second episode of Season One. Chris Smiley's "'Kobol's Last Gleaming, I and II' as Quality Television" considers the Season One finale. "Frakking Up: When *Battlestar* Goes Awry" contemplates the causes of the series' weakest episodes. "Cylon-Vérité: Monotheism and Polytheistic Stories in 'Final Cut'" revisits the place of monotheism and polytheism in the series in an examination of one of its best episodes: Season Two's "Final Cut." Justin Door's "Weaving a Story through Webisodes" reflects on the role of *Battlestar's* use of supplementary Internet-only miniature narratives. The series pre–Season Four stand-alone "made-for-television movie" is the subject of "This *Razor's* Edgy." "Taking the Last Shot: The Endings of *Battlestar* Episodes" contemplates and catalogs the distinctive, signature final shots of each *BSG* installment.

Chapter Ten

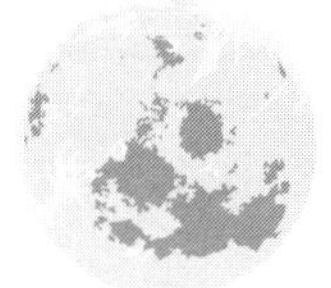

CARRYING "WATER": AN INTERVIEW WITH MARITA GRABIAK

"I grew up in a small town in Pennsylvania, with a mother who was an avid reader of books, both classic and modern, from whom I inherited a love and respect of stories and movies. My father was a dentist whose passion was reading about geography, history, science, and lives of explorers. I wanted to be an anthropologist, or archeologist, and photography, art, and movies were my passions, so I combined all interests and went to film school at UCLA."

—Marita Grabiak

After working as a production assistant on *The Men's Club* (1986) and as script supervisor on *Nights in White Satin* (1987), *Bat*21*

(1988), *Young Guns* (1988), *The Night Before* (1988), *D.O.A.* (1988), *The Hot Spot* (1990), *Men at Work* (1990), *Soapdish* (1991), *Super Mario Bros.* (1993), *Chasers* (1994), and *Mother's Boys* (1994), Marita Grabiak has become an in-demand TV director, having helmed to date episodes of the following series:

- *ER*: "Survival of the Fittest" (2001); "Viable Options" (2000)
- *Angel*: "Fredless" (2001); "The House Always Wins" (2002); "The Price" (2002); "Unleashed" (2003); "Shiny Happy People" (2003)
- *The Division*: "Hide and Seek" (2001)
- *Firefly*: "Jaynestown" (2002)
- *Smallville*: "SkinWalker" (2001); "Relic" (2003)
- *Buffy the Vampire Slayer*: "End of Days"; "Storyteller" (2003)
- *Cold Case*: "Hitchhiker" (2003)
- *Strong Medicine*: "Heartbeats and Deadbeats" (2003)
- *Gilmore Girls*: "The Reigning Lorelai" (2004)
- *Battlestar Galactica*: "Water" (2004)
- *Lost*: "Raised by Another" (2004)
- *Everwood*: "Your Future Awaits" (2004)
- *Wonderfalls*: "Karma Chameleon" (2004)
- *Alias*: "A Man of His Word" (2005)
- *The Inside*: "Point of Origin" (2005)
- *One Tree Hill*: "Locked Hearts and Hand Grenades" (2005)
- *Point Pleasant*: "Waking the Dead"; "Who's Your Daddy?" (2005)
- *Law & Order: Special Victims Unit*: "Intoxicated" (2005)
- *Eureka*: "Alienated" (2006)
- *In Justice*: "The Public Burning" (2006)
- *Surface*: "Episode #1.12" (2006)
- *Drive*: "Let the Games Begin" (2007)
- *Bones*: "Mummy in the Maze" (2007)

When Grabiak directed "Water" (1.2), she became the first *BSG* director other than Michael Rymer, who had helmed the entire miniseries and the premiere episode of Season One as well.

She generously answered the authors' questions in September of 2007.

What creative pressures did you encounter when directing this episode? How much did the script penned by Ronald Moore inspire you, and what kind of tone did you initially hope to convey when you arrived to direct "Water"?

The pressures I encountered at *BSG*? First of all, I am a die-hard *Star Trek* fan, and I never watched [the original] *BSG*, never saw the show. I was in college, and working a full forty hours a week job, and didn't even own a TV when the show was on. So, there was pressure when I interviewed for the show (which was set up with the producers over the phone).

Producers look to hire directors who are good storytellers, who have a nice well-rounded résumé, and know how to move the camera in a way which would suit their ideas for the show. I had that and had done *Firefly*, a futuristic kind of cowboys-in-space, done by the genius Joss Whedon, whom I had worked for on a number of occasions. I was known as a female director who had broken into and done well in genres, like *Buffy* and *Angel*, which were male dominated. Producers want intelligent directors who use the camera to tell the story, and understand editing as a tool, no matter what the genre.

I immediately got on the phone with my brother, a *BSG* expert, and from my deep conversation with my brother, was prepared for my interview with the producers of *BSG*. The main thing I sensed, and my brother confirmed, was that I needed to know in detail the past story and honor the concerns and needs of the die-hard original *BSG* fans. I went into the interview stating that as my goal.

After I was hired, my research on original *BSG* began in depth. I watched the miniseries, I studied the synopses, and I read the fifty-page research bible compiled by the new producing staff. Only then was I ready to begin prep on "Water," when I know every twist and turn of the past story plots and all about the original actors, and the characters they played. When that was done, I went to location in Vancouver, with a sense of confidence and purpose.

I was happy with the script [by Ronald D. Moore], which was a relief. I thought it was done well in plot advancement, with good dialogue, conflict, and danger. If you don't get good elements in the script, then your job is ten times harder, because you don't have much to work with. The more challenging a script is, the better—that is what I always hope for, to showcase what I can do as a director. I think having a good script brings up everybody's game, and that is what I always hope for.

The tone I hoped to convey was of respect to the original show, with modern advancements that would meet the needs of a sophisticated modern audience. Not unlike when, instead of tearing down a beautiful, classic old building that is obsolete, you save its facade, and build around and behind it a wonderful, state-of-the-art, comfortable new superstructure that honors the classic beauty of the original architecture. We don't have the ability to recreate what artisans did in the old days, and they couldn't do what we do today with computers, so it is wisest to combine the best of both what was old and what is new.

Did you know when filming that the episode was going to air back to back with "33"? How does that add to the pressure of directing an episode when they are aired back to back?

I didn't know [about] the airing of the shows until I was done shooting. Change of order of shows has no impact on a director at all. And when I did find out about it, my response was "Cool."

A show's airing order and change of order would only affect the producers who have to juggle budgets. Not all shows cost the same to make[;] more effects and action, or days out of the stage will add to the budget. If one show's costs are way over, then the following show's budget would need to be more restrained[;] it would be more of a "bottle show," that is filming more on stage, with less action or effects. Bottom line, these decisions are the producer's territory, and do not involve the television director, unless the director is "in house" and carries the title of producer/director, which I did not.

The original concept of the episode was (we have read) to deal with a paper—and not water—shortage. Is that true? How did the concept evolve?

The concept of an episode storyline happens months before the visiting director comes onboard. I am supposed to be guaranteed to have the script by my first day of prep. That is the first I hear of my story. I have seven days' prep, and eight days' shooting. If it was paper, and not water, I am very glad of the change, but I never heard that rumor. I am glad, because water is life.

How a story evolves happens in a secret inner sanctum called the writers conference room, and is top secret. Even the actors don't know until the script comes out (with rare exception).

Does the director of an episode have any hand in the "previously on"?

No, a director does not have a hand in "previously on." Never, ever. It is merely the show's creator, and head writer, who tell the editor what to hit on. Then they tweak it together. And that only happens after you have a final cut of this week's show. Based on usually being over by three to seven minutes, many things hit the cutting room floor, from line cuts, to entire scenes. So, first the final cut, then the "previously on" can be compiled to make sense of things.

How many days did you have to complete filming? Did you bring it in on time?

Seven days' prep, eight days' shooting. Yes, I always bring my shows in on time. I believe directing to be 90 percent preparation, and I am really very thoroughly adamant in my prep.

How sequential was the filming—how close to the order of events in the narrative?

Filming is never, ever sequential to events in the narrative. The schedule is dictated by location and actor availability. A massive juggling strategy. Locations you can only get on certain days, or even hours, like you can't start until 4:00 p.m., or you have to be out, taillights by 10:00 p.m., etc. We will have so many days "out" (off the lot and stages), a certain amount of sets make sense to be "a build" (swing sets) on the lot.

Early in "Water," Laura Roslin comments to Billy, "You don't know anything about women, do you?" The viewpoints of female characters are extremely important in *BSG*, much more so than in most TV series. Do you think female writers and directors have a larger say in this series about the way women are portrayed?

I don't think female writer/producers have a larger say at *BSG;* I just think that they have the equal say that any female has on any show. The change that I do see occurring is that male writers are writing more, and better, for female parts. The male awareness is growing both for female characters, and for ethnic characters. And as far as female directors having more of a say, I just tend to think, male or female, they like you or they don't. You can do a good job as a storyteller, and still not be invited back. And I don't blame the male/female thing. Really to me, that is a myth. We women owe so much to the women's activist movement in the seventies. I have benefited so much from their political strife and pain. I NEVER felt I had more or less of a say because I am a woman. And that is true equality. You either are liked, or not, and you could be a good filmmaker, a tremendous filmmaker, either way.

What's the best part about directing a *Battlestar Galactica* episode?

The best part about *BSG* for me was working with Baltar (James Callis). He is gifted and very talented with many facets and levels. He never makes the obvious choice, and that is what I dig. I had many time pressures on a TV schedule, but he requested going again for more takes quite often. I assured him I had what I wanted, yet every time I let him go again, even greater things would be discovered. I did feel sorry for him, because I sensed he was never quite happy, always thinking he could do better. The sign of great artists—they are never satisfied. I loved watching him.

The card game: how do you shoot a scene like this to keep it interesting? The episode is full of "two shots." Are these difficult to make interesting?

We rehearsed the moves in the card game to have it make sense. I went handheld to give some tension. I did many moves with the camera, without making it look false or contrived. I always try to move camera, if actors can't logically, or organically, be moving.

Did you know that Starbuck and Baltar would sleep together by season's end?

I didn't know Starbuck and Baltar would sleep together, later in the show, but I liked that there was sexual tension, and I thought she should be smoking, and blow smoke in his face as a power move, and I thought it would be cool if he were not repulsed by the smoke, but was inhaling it, as if he were inhaling her.

The attention to detail, especially about liquids (such as the water droplets falling off Sharon, the level of booze in Tigh's bottle, the little bottle from which Starbuck drinks during the card game), is important in this episode. How did you

decide which details you'd emphasize and how you'd emphasize them visually?

Thanks for noticing!

The use of water to me was very important, and although the first scene with Sharon, sitting there, dripping wet, had a small, partial page count, I needed to spend extra time to enhance the water dripping from her. The script said she was wet, and I thought "OK, time to go slo-mo, and wide, tighter, tighter, tighter, and ECU [extreme close-up], with big old drop of water falling off her hair, rolling down her face, and bang, spilling in giant slo-mo to the floor before. In my original cut, I made a meal of it; I wanted to really create some cool images while she was in this suspended, mysterious state. And keeping the water dripping and showing was difficult and took too much of my scheduled day. But I was kind of relentless. Every time props would pour the water, it would instantly disappear. I had to roll camera, and try to hide the prop person to pour more on her as we were rolling, but just couldn't even do that in the WS. It was one of those little scenes that just are harder to do than you imagine in prep.

Remember the scene in Adama's quarters, where he carefully measures some water as an offering to his lady President? That was all about reminding us of how precious water was, and was a sign of respect.

***Battlestar Galactica* has a specific "look"—very dark, lots of interesting camera angles, handheld camera shots, extreme close-ups of facial features, and so on. As a director, were you given specific guidelines to ensure the consistency of the "look" among episodes, or were you allowed to put your unique stamp on the episode?**

As on every show, you are given guidelines on use of photography. I try to leave my mark in choice of shots and angles, and design of coverage and use of cranes, and the pace created in the editing.

How do you direct the model sequences? How does the director's role differ from directing people in live-action sequences to directing blue or green screen sequences or models and special effects?

I had a great deal of fun directing the model sequences, which you don't get to do on every show. For instance, I didn't on *Firefly* (but I had no complaints as they were brilliant). *BSG* began with a concept meeting, in which I explained how I wanted variety of angles, with no repetition, and I had an idea for the water spilling out of the spaceship, like the intro to the show *Hawaii Five-O*—like you were riding into the curl of a wave while surfing. I loved the visual FX team, and I called them my loveable Super Geeks. I am sure that some of them carried *Battlestar Galactica* lunchboxes to school as kids. We held a little toy spaceship to talk shots and angles, and we had storyboards (artist sketches) made to refer to and tweak and make adjustments. Then they had to work on their budget, and we had further meetings for final decisions.

I have to mention one thing that blew me away, which first occurred to me in my concept meeting for *BSG*. In dealing with CGI, I was always very limited regarding visual FX b.g., set extensions, or if you will, in our script, seeing outer space, from a hole in the inside of the water storage tank, our heroes walk into to inspect and investigate. We were talking about the set we were building for the tank, and I assume we would have green screen behind it, where the hole was, and I would have to design the shots with the hole behind it with a stationary camera, as was always done in TV to that point. I saw the floorplans for the set, and I said, "Where are the rest of the walls?" "There aren't any" was the answer—"just the entry door; the rest is CGI." "But how can I deal with not moving the camera with a one-wall set?" I asked. "Oh, you can move the camera, either handheld or stedicam." "WHAT!? We can do that here?" Yes, they had pick points, like little green tennis balls to lock on to, and I had so much freedom to move actors and camera. It was exciting. That is much more in common use now, but *BSG* was so ahead of its time in the first season.

To answer the rest of the question ... once you have in mind what the CGI b.g. looks like, directing is exactly the same. You plan your angles, and coverage, you direct the actors, walking them through what they are looking at, showing them the storyboards, and you light it, taking careful planning to consider what and where the light sources are, and then you call action and shoot it. Not much different, just planning.

Compare directing *Battlestar Galactica* to directing other television series.

It is so hard to compare shows, because they are comprised of their own cast of characters (meaning writers, producers, crew, and editors), and each has its own style and ways of doing the same job. Each show has its own blueprint you must study as an outsider, and then try to fit in.

By the time I directed my two *Buffys*, it was a secure show, a well-oiled machine in its last season. It was a pleasure working for Joss Whedon, who helps you prep, gives you the tone, and then steps back completely and lets you be a real director without interference. A supreme pleasure.

I directed *Lost* early in its first season—in fact my first day of shooting was their first day on the air. The show at that time was just finding itself, with a lot of experimentation. I had a lot of supervision. I would be told to do a scene a certain way, then when setting up the scene, a producer would give me specific details on how something should be done, which was great, but then, and the next moment, another nearby would say the exact opposite to me. Not uncommon for a new show. It is in fact easier to come on to a show after it has been up and running for a while—the kinks are worked out. The actors were outstanding to work with there.

Smallville—I adored the subject matter; I relished the challenge of the action and stunts, and special FX. I gave my heart and soul to work on it. The cast was a dream—they were all supercool. I was especially proud of the show I did about the flashback to 1960, when Tom played his own father, Jor-El, as a young man visiting Earth, and Kristin played Lana's aunt as a young woman. The actors were worried that the writers were jumping into a convenient sex scene too early in the season, and I made it work, by giving them an embellished back story to justify what I perceived as a great and powerful real love (like in the movie *Ryan's Daughter*) that could not and would not be denied, despite social barriers and politics. Lana was in kind of an arranged, loveless marriage to someone who wasn't very kind, or loving, and she wanted a bigger world, and lost herself in Hollywood fan magazines. *Smallville* was a great show to work on, but also hard to survive very long at, because of a rumor mill with shaky merit, and politics that could hurt or damage a director.

Alias: a very nice job to have. They really had their act together, in terms of action, and finding locations to work at around the world.

Do you continue to follow *Battlestar Galactica*?

The best part about directing *BSG* was embracing and completely losing myself in a show and topic that is so historical and meaningful to so many people. I loved this particular challenge of making the original audience like the new version and making it accessible to [a] new, younger audience who had grown up in the computer age, with all the sophistication they possess. I loved the crew, and the cast was wonderful, and I respected and benefited from the dedication of the producers to making this a worthy show.

I have received more glowing feedback and e-mails about this show than all the other shows I ever directed combined. So many people have said it was their favorite episode. I have visited Vancouver several times, directing other shows, and stopped by to visit my crew friends, and was pleasantly gratified to hear how they enjoyed their time with me, and wished I was on regular rotation there. I would have been overjoyed to go back and direct any time.

And yes, I continue to watch and really enjoy the series.

Chapter Eleven

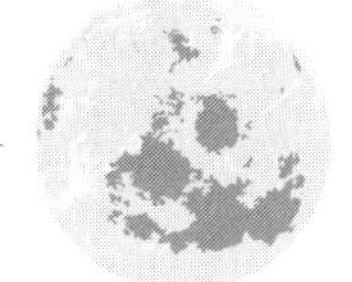

"Kobol's Last Gleaming, I and II": *Battlestar Galactica* as Quality Television

—Christopher Smiley

"Though very few critics went so far as to see the 1980s as the start of a new 'golden age,' many did recognize that a new type of programming was emerging that they thought was better, more sophisticated, and more artistic than the usual network fare. They called it 'quality television.' This descriptive if unimaginative term started regularly appearing in the 1970s. ... Journalists now use the term 'quality TV' almost as regularly as they use programming neologisms like 'sitcom,' 'infomercial,' and 'docudrama.'

Yet even today, no one can say exactly what 'quality television' means. ... Though it may have originally been used just to describe unusually good shows, the

'quality' in 'quality TV' has come to refer more to a generic style than to an aesthetic judgment."

—ROBERT J. THOMPSON,
TELEVISION'S SECOND GOLDEN AGE: FROM HILL STREET BLUES *TO* ER (1996)

Once upon a time, the governing paradigm for American television was the idea of "Least Objectionable Programming" or LOP. As late as the 1970s, the networks remained convinced, in a time before remote control devices eliminated the major impetus for couch potatoes to get up from the sofa, that the best TV shows they could put on the air were those that gave viewers no good reason to change the channel. The invention of "quality television" and the advent, in the wake of TV's new paradigm, of "television's second golden age"—as TV scholar Robert J. Thompson deemed it in a definitive book on the subject—now seem so last century, a sea change in the medium contemporary with the original *Battlestar Galactica*.

Perhaps the most remarkable achievement of Ronald D. Moore and David Eick's *Battlestar Galactica* is just how quickly it manages to establish itself as something different, not only from its seventies predecessor, but from most current television. In fact, arguing the case for *BSG* as quality television, one is tempted to look no further than the opening few minutes of an episode: its impact is that sudden. Certainly those who tuned into "*Battlestar* reimagined" wanting no more than a weekly appointment with easily accessible sci-fi frivolity probably left disappointed. For anyone else, however, the new *Battlestar Galactica* is practically a revelation. Joss Whedon, creator of TV's *Buffy the Vampire Slayer*, *Angel*, and *Firefly*—each huge critical successes in its own right—describes the show as "humbling"; magazines like *Time* and *Rolling Stone* have labeled it the best show on television. So what makes it stand out?

An excellent illustration of *BSG*'s status as a quality TV show in accordance with Thompson's defining characteristics is the two-part finale of Season One: "Kobol's Last Gleaming." What Moore describes in the podcast[102] as a "two-hour movie split into two parts" makes an interesting case study because it not only matches many of Thompson's criteria, but in some ways exists beyond them, thus highlighting some ways in which television, and, in parallel, quality television, have evolved since Thompson defined it in the mid-nineties.

* * *

As one might expect from a season finale on a serialized drama, the episode inevitably deals with the culmination of several key narrative threads. This expectation in itself could be seen as an example of how television has changed over the years. Thompson's observation that "Quality TV has a memory. ... Characters develop and change as the series goes on. Events and details from previous episodes are often used or referred to in subsequent episodes" (14) is now almost conventional.

The idea of TV drama without a memory nowadays seems almost strange, so while it is hard to imagine a quality TV show existing without it, one could certainly argue that a memory is no longer a characteristic unique to quality television. After all, series like *Smallville* and *The O.C.* are regularly capable of working with events and details from deep in their pasts without ever feeling like quality shows. True quality TV shows at this point in their evolution, however, have an unshakeable, unrelenting memory, a memory used not only for plot purposes, but permeating every action of the show, ensuring that nothing that happens is without a perceivable consequence. It is also important to recognize that the audience assumes this to be the case. In the teaser to "Kobol's Last Gleaming, Part I" we see such an example of how memory can be utilized in different ways.

With very few words the teaser intercuts quickly among four different scenes. We see Commander Adama and his son Lee sparring, Starbuck and Baltar engaging in an altogether different sort of physical engagement (after which we see Number Six looking devastated), Boomer seriously contemplating suicide, and Helo running from and eventually shooting the other Boomer on Caprica. The fast-paced sequence not only demands the audience to recall previous events, but it perceptibly progresses at least six relationships on the show. Starbuck and Baltar's relationship is turned on its head, Baltar and Six's relationship is affected, Starbuck's feelings for Lee are made clearer, Boomer's state of mind and intent are made clearer, Helo's relationship with the other Boomer is hugely complicated, and Commander Adama's conversation with his son sets up a very important plot point in the second part of the episode—all in twenty-five words or less, so to speak. Without memory, or more specifically without the kind of unrelenting memory modern quality television demands, such depth could not be plumbed in such an artful manner.

Moore speaks proudly about the teaser in his podcast commentary for the episode, comparing it to his other favorite teaser, for the episode "33":

> It was challenging, it was provocative, it sort of grabbed the audience and said, "Okay, catch up, 'cause we're in the middle of a crisis. We're not going to explain anything to you, we're not going to spoon-feed you all the plot. You're just going to have to figure it out and we respect that you're intelligent and that you can figure it out."

Moore's further assertion in the following episode's podcast commentary that he should not have to "write loathsome lines of exposition that will do nothing more than reiterate points [the audience] should already know intuitively" represents the new standard of quality television—that if we can prove capable of always remembering, it will prove worthy of remembering always.

The teaser also exhibits other hallmarks of quality television. Structurally and aesthetically, the way in which it cuts among four narrative threads, underscored throughout by a classical theme, is certainly not what one could call "regular" TV. This is in keeping with Thompson's first characteristic of quality television: "In a medium long considered artless, the only artful TV is that which isn't like all the rest of it" (13). This statement remains apt because it allows for the shifting standard of television. Although television is no longer as artless a medium as it may have been, it is easy for an audience to recognize the different levels of craft different shows exhibit. This teaser certainly stands out in a crowd.

It also emphasizes the use of *BSG*'s "large ensemble cast"—another Thompson criterion. Because ensemble casts are not as unusual on television today, again it is important to clarify what makes *BSG*'s ensembling unique. Two great examples within the teaser are the scenes in which Boomer is contemplating suicide and Number Six cries because Baltar has slept with Starbuck. Evoking the series' memory makes it possible to advance characters' stories efficiently but meaningfully. When we see Number Six in tears we gain a new understanding of both her own and Baltar's feelings without so much as a word being spoken. When we see Boomer putting a gun in her mouth, we immediately understand why and sympathize—perhaps even support—her intent; it is a complex yet immediately clear scene that manages to evoke a complex emotional reaction without so much as a hint of exposition.

In contrast, if an episode of *One Tree Hill* opens with a kid holding a gun to his mouth, the only thing a savvy audience might know to expect is an hour-long lecture on the tragedy of teen suicide and the value of good friends. In a modern quality TV series, not only the number of characters matters, but the depth of character with which each is imbued. *BSG*'s many characters are as full and complex as any on television.

Immediately following the teaser are the opening titles, which are worth mention in their own right. From the haunting operatic music that's juxtaposed with images of explosive space battles, to the startling highlighting future events from the impending episode, *BSG*'s credits are a very different experience. They also serve to quickly highlight *BSG*'s fulfillment of another of Thompson's principles: that it boasts a "quality pedigree." While Moore's background led him from working on *Star Trek* spin-offs to producing HBO's well-received *Carnivale*, *BSG*'s two lead actors, Edward James Olmos and Mary McDonnell, are both Academy Award nominees, undoubtedly an impressive hand for any TV show to hold.

After the titles the next great scene of note features Baltar simultaneously conversing with President Roslin and Six. Most interesting is the complete ambiguity of the latter character. At this point in the series we still do not understand exactly whether she is real or simply a figment of Baltar's imagination. Such ambiguity, routine on *BSG*, is certainly an unusual feature in a lead character on television, and another example of *Battlestar* not being "regular" TV.

In a subsequent scene, as President Roslin looks at an inhabited city in a photo of Kobol's ruins, we see an interesting example of the way in which *Battlestar* matches the specs of yet another Thompson quality trait:

> The subject matter of quality TV tends toward the controversial. *St. Elsewhere* presented the first prime-time series story about AIDS, and other quality series frequently included some of television's earliest treatments of subjects like abortion, homosexuals, racism, and religion, to name a few. (15)

As we explore elsewhere, *BSG*'s treatment of religion is nothing short of fascinating. Initially we are presented with a world (and a race) destroyed by what seem to represent right-wing Christian fundamentalists. The Cylons are devoutly monotheistic and deeply unforgiving of alternative beliefs, while those positioned to fight in humanity's corner are a mixture of pagan and secular, mystical and logical. This in itself offers a relatively controversial reading in the context of the time it was made, especially when keeping in mind science fiction's long-standing tradition of producing social commentary.

However, it is also interesting to consider *BSG*'s audience and question whether such beliefs would be marked as controversial among them. Is the average fan of a genre that speaks almost entirely in the language of social concern and liberalism going to be offended or delighted by the portrayal of religious fanaticism as dangerous? I suggest the latter. The story becomes even more controversial when President Roslin's motivations also become based in religion. It is easy to imagine an audience who reveled in the show's early stance against religion being troubled by the idea that they must support their heroine as she treads similar ground. Such a narrative move displays a willingness on *BSG*'s part to be controversial not only in the larger social landscape, but within the niche audience it is targeting—a move that relies on their audience's desire to be challenged more than its desire to be placated. In today's deeply competitive TV industry, the potential willingness to subvert audience expectations is perhaps as controversial as a TV show can be.

The scene that immediately follows, in which Baltar essentially advises Boomer to kill herself, also leans towards the controversial. Again the situation is complex enough to negate any petty moral outrages, but condoning suicide in any context, let alone advocating it, is not something that has much of a place in "regular" television.

The way the first part of the episode ends demonstrates an interesting merger of two more of Thompson's characteristics: that quality TV shows must (1) engage in a "noble struggle" against both networks and non-appreciative audiences and (2) "tend ... to be literary and writer-based." In his podcast commentary on the episode, Ronald D. Moore explains the need to overwrite his scripts so readers looking over his shoulder at the Sci Fi network can understand his vision more clearly (when "the suits"—my word, not his—read scripts, Moore notes, they tend to skip descriptive passages). Considering how supportive Sci Fi, and Sky in the UK, which provided essential funding, have been with regard to finance and ratings success, it's a somewhat amazing irony that the network happens to be, at least at the creative stage, the non-appreciative audience Thompson is talking about. Moore, of course, manages to find a way around the opposition: as he puts it, after securing network approval, he can transform the story back to its "true fighting weight," replacing heavy-handed exposition with defter, more artful touches. In this episode's case, it allowed him to lead into the next episode with emotion instead of action, prioritizing Starbuck's feeling of betrayal by Commander Adama over the Raptor's impending crash on Kobol.

Finally, the second part of "Kobol's Last Gleaming" perfectly exemplifies Thompson's insistence that quality television "creates a new genre by mixing old ones" (15). While retaining all the other qualities *Battlestar Galactica* possesses, the second part of the Season One finale offers an immense range of attractions: intense political drama between Roslin and Adama, family drama between the two Adamas, relationship drama between Helo and Boomer, and even metaphysical drama between Six and Baltar—and that's before even mentioning the epic fight scene between Starbuck and Six, the *Independence Day*–style nuking of a Cylon Basestar, or the assassination attempt on Adama by Boomer.

The reason *BSG* is able to fuse such elements so seamlessly is because its focus has never been on genre. Moore's sole concern has always been on developing human drama, and in this sense it is easy to suggest without reservation that a TV show that deals in a world of truly fantastic science fiction manages to achieve "realism"—another Thompson criteria—far more convincingly than in most TV shows set in the "real" world.

That *Battlestar Galactica* is a quality TV show by Thompson's standards is a no-brainer. If it can continue its high standard in its final season, it may well become an important touchstone for critics testing future understanding of the nature of quality television.

FRAKKING UP: WHEN *BATTLESTAR* GOES AWRY

No doubt about it, *Battlestar Galactica*, like any long-running TV series, has generated its share of weaker, if not downright bad, episodes. Given the tremendous pressures—time! budget! network interference! multiple seasons! censorship!—the creators of even the best series must battle, it should not surprise us the original *Star Trek* descended to the level of "Spock's Brain" (3.1); that *Buffy the Vampire Slayer* was forced to offer us the occasional "Go Fish" (2.20) or "Beer Bad" (4.5); that *Lost* lost its way with "Stranger in a Strange Land" (3.9); that *Heroes* failed to save its Season One finale, "How to Stop an Exploding Man" (1.23) [see *Saving the World*, pp. 165–179]; or *Grey's Anatomy* resorts to airing "Grandma Got Run Over by a Reindeer" (2.12). (No doubt some of you reading these pages will disagree with our examples.) The existence of such forgettable episodes of ordinarily fascinating series does not necessarily constitute shark-jumping: they need not be taken as proof-positive that a good show has gone bad.

Jacob, recapping *BSG* on Television Without Pity, was ready to declare, with "Torn" (3.6) in mind, "this season freakin' rocks." By "A Measure of Salvation" (3.7), he can hardly contain his enthusiasm:

> Lest you forget Gaius Baltar is the creepiest motherfrakker ever written, though, he spends the entire episode getting off in a sex-type way with Chip Six in the middle of—and spurred on by—the torture itself. And then I think he fools Three into thinking he, or she, or both of them, are God. It's a whole God-sex-torture-threesome-projection-crazy thing, as we've come to expect from the basestar storyline. Which is either awesome or horrible, depending where you stand, but I say: "Bring on the God and sex and torture! Bring on the threesomes, with robots both incarnate and imaginary! *This is the best season ever!*"

Eight episodes later ("A Day in the Life," 3.15), his fervor has dimmed dramatically: "The long, boring, pointless back half of another disconnected, once-promising season limps painfully forward, exhausting and embarrassing by turns, holding out the trial of Baltar like it's the fucking second coming when really it seems likely to be just as boring as this episode right here, and yet *never arriving there*." Still, Jacob cautions his readers not to give up hope, not to assume the worst, not to fear television's vicious marine predator:

> Don't freak out that the show has jumped the shark—the same thing happened last year, and it doesn't mean we turn our backs on the show. Unless it does, in which case, I bid you a fond *au revoir*, and wish they'd tried a little harder again this week. It's been 49 days since the Cylons were last seen, and you know what that means: shitty episodes of this show. …

Like a tall ship with the wind in its sails progressing toward its destination at a rapid clip, a TV season must fear finding itself caught in the doldrums, succumbing to inactivity or stagnation. Bad episodes are often the waste product of such narrative languishing.

Jacob identifies another one of the prime movers of *BSG* frak-ups when he singles out the Cylon-absentia of Season Three's nadir. That sans-toaster-and-skin-job *Battlestar* tends to bore should not surprise anyone who found Dante's *Purgatorio* and *Paradiso* a snooze compared to *Inferno*'s hell of a tale, or was more enthralled by *Paradise Lost* when Satan himself took center stage. Evil has always been more dramatically captivating than good.

As we observe earlier, thanks to Ronald D. Moore's prolific podcasting and three informative companion books, we may know more about the making of *Battlestar* than just about any TV show ever made, and one of the many things we learn is that there are episodes of which Moore himself is not fond. Moore reveals to David Bassom (2: 78–79), for example, that "'Black Market' [2.14] is not an episode I particularly like." Taking all the blame himself, careful not to insult its writer (Mark Verheiden) and director (James Head), he goes on to characterize the episode—correctly in our opinion—as too conventional and predictable and hence not up to *Battlestar* standards. David Eick agreed. Both liked the concept but felt "Black Market" never really "gelled." Moore also acknowledges disappointment with "Sacrifice" (2.16).

We would like to suggest two other possible reasons *Battlestar* sometimes goes awry. "I think this line's mostly filler," Willow sings, self-referentially, in the *Buffy the Vampire Slayer* musical "Once More with Feeling" (6.7). Like any long-term TV narrative, *Battlestar* has produced some subpar, filler episodes simply because of the necessity to generate the extraordinary number of episodes network television requires. Now the first three seasons of *BSG*—thirteen, twenty, and twenty episodes in length, respectively—hardly constitute a long run by American standards: most American dramatics series, after all, come in well-seasoned (if you will) allotments of at least twenty-two episodes. By contrast, consider the transient duration of the extraordinary UK series *Life on Mars* (BBC, 2006–2007), which ran for only two seasons of a mere eight episodes each: the need for filler obviously decreases dramatically with a run that short.

The narrative burdens of the required American season brought Damon Lindelof and Carlton Cuse to negotiate a determined-in-advance end date for the wildly complicated story of *Lost* (ABC, 2004–2010). If some episodes of *Battlestar* seem like Moore, Eick, and company are treading water, well, it's because they are. The *Battlestar*verse is not capable of generating an inexhaustible number of episodes, which is why its makers were more than ready to make Season Four its last. "The secret of life," the philosopher Nietzsche once observed, "is to die at the right time." The rule applies to television as well. (We're talking to you, *X-Files*!)

Joss Whedon once pledged that there would never be a "very special episode of *Buffy*" (Wilcox, "Very Special *Buffy*"): *Buffy* would not, in other words, address socially relevant themes in essentially didactic, after-school-specialish episodes. (We knew the consistently brilliant *Veronica Mars* was floundering in Season Three when it took on the issue of child soldiers in Africa and even included the cast in a public service announcement at the end of the episode ["I Know What You'll Do Next Summer," 3.18].) *Battlestar* sometimes fraks up when it abandons its otherwise brilliant commitment to "naturalistic science fiction" to steer in the direction of the very special episode. "Bastille Day" (1.3), with its focus on prisoner's rights, "The Woman King" (3.14), an episode about discrimination against immigrants, "Dirty Hands" (3.16), a look at labor strife within the fleet—all drift into "very special" territory, and none are likely to be fondly remembered episodes.

Chapter Twelve

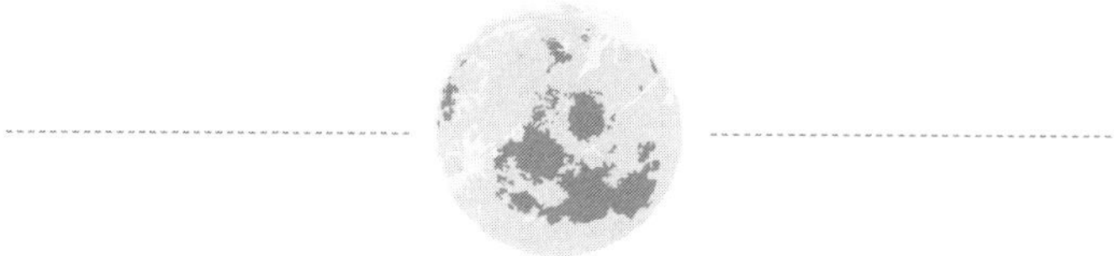

CYLON-VÉRITÉ: MONOTHEISTIC AND POLYTHEISTIC STORIES IN "FINAL CUT"

"I'm not sure I've found a story in all this yet."

—D'Anna Biers (Number 3) in "Final Cut"

"[T]here's a religion in narrative."

—Joss Whedon

In the podcast for "Occupation"/"Precipice" (3.1–3.2), the Season Three premiere double episode of *Battlestar Galactica*, Ronald D. Moore speaks of an abandoned plan to begin with a D'Anna Biers propaganda film about how the Cylons had brought peace and happiness to the troubled lives of the human colonists of New Caprica. Moore tells us little about his intentions for the film-within-a-film, though he does makes reference to Centurions handing out candy—a sharp contrast to that disconcerting scene of toasters goose-stepping into the human settlement at the end of Season Two (much like the Nazis marching into Paris in World War II).

The film would not, of course, have been Biers' first. In "Final Cut" (2.8), which had introduced us to the sleeper Cylon, Biers, a Number Three model, is given full access to *Galactica* and "final cut" privileges,[103] as she and her camera man Bell shoot a behind-the-scenes documentary about life onboard the *Battlestar*. In the wake of the *Gideon* Incident (in which marines had shot indiscriminately into a civilian crowd struggling over supplies), her intent then had been to "blow this thing wide open." The motives behind President Roslin's surprising willingness to cooperate provoke suspicion in the uncompromising Fleet TV journalist: "[A]ccess won't buy you a propaganda piece," Biers insists.

That insistence on journalistic independence came before we learn, in the episode's final scene, that Biers is in fact a Cylon with a hidden agenda ("They have a plan"). Since the imagined "Occupation" documentary would have revealed Biers/Three more than willing to propagandize, the question must be asked: how did Biers, the modeled-on-CNN's-Christiana-Amanpour journalist, become the speciescidal, virulently monotheistic cyber beings' Leni Riefenstahl?[104]

THE SELF-REFERENTIAL

"Get out of my face!"

—Colonel Tigh in "Final Cut"

Part of the DNA of modernism and postmodernism in all the arts is the tendency to become self-referential. More and more novels (those of John Barth or Paul Auster, for example) take as their subject the writing of novels and become metafictions. Movies about making movies—*8½* (Federico Fellini, 1963) is the urtext—become all the rage. In the hands of a Luigi Pirandello or a Tom Stoppard, theatre becomes about the theatre. Television takes on television as its focus: think *30 Rock* or *The Simpsons*. On television, an episode like *Buffy*'s "Storyteller" (UPN, 2003—written by Jane Espenson, the subject of Chapter 4) and directed by Marita Grabiak (interviewed in Chapter 10) turns the camera around, as daft but adorable Andrew tries to make a behind-the-scenes documentary about "Buffy, Slayer of the Vampyres." A show like Gary Shandling's *It's Gary Shandling's Show* (Showtime, 1986) took this tendency to its TV limit.

The tendency, clearly alive in the *Battlestar* DNA as well, manifests itself in "Final Cut." Written by Mark Verheiden (whose script for the Season Three finale "Crossroads, Part 2" would prove to be among *BSG*'s most critically debated) and directed by veteran documentary (and feature film and television) director Robert M. Young (eighty-one years of age at the time of filming!), "Final Cut" follows a documentary film crew given carte blanche in order to, in Laura Roslin's words, "show people what life aboard the *Galactica* is really like" and, in so doing, "put a human face on the officers and the crew who protect us against Cylons and guard our freedoms every day."

The episode becomes a vehicle for some fine Verheiden-authored speechifying, all captured as face-to-face soliloquies by major and minor characters. For example, in response to Biers' taunt that Apollo "seem[s] to think that your pilots deserve special consideration," Adama's son replies eloquently:

> Actually, I do. Like everyone else, my pilots have lost their families, and their friends, everyone they ever cared about. But on top of that, they're asked to put their lives on the line every single day for a fleet that seems more interested in what they do wrong than in what they do right. They're not asking for your pity, but they damn well deserve your respect.

To Biers' reasonable question, "Are you afraid when you go into combat?" Racetrack gives a "whistling past the cemetery" bold response:

> First thing they tell you is to assume you're already dead. That sounds ghoulish. Yeah, maybe. But dead men don't get scared or freeze up under fire. Me, I'm just worried that hell's gonna be a lonely place. And I'm gonna fill it up with every toaster son of a bitch I find.

In a similar vein is Kat's blustery insistence that "When you come back after a successful run, let me tell you. It is better than a great meal. Better than hitting a jackpot. It's better than sex." Helo's answer to the question "What's been the hardest for you?" goes to the core of the series' major themes: "They try to turn off the human part of you because that's what'll get you killed. But ... when you're out in the field, it's not that easy. Nothing's that easy." Along the way we also learn things about some of the characters that we didn't know before—for example, that Gaeta is a chain smoker and sports a tattoo.[105] A subplot in which a marine who seeks revenge against Tigh for the *Gideon* Incident provides some mostly routine tension.

"Final Cut" remains memorable, however, not for these moments but for the metafictional questions it raises about Cylons, humans, and storytelling.

The Finale of "Final Cut"

"Visual. The first thing that will leap out at viewers is the dynamic use of the documentary or cinema verite style. Through the extensive use of handheld cameras, practical lighting, and functional set design, the Battlestar Galactica will feel on every level like a real place."

—Ronald D. Moore, "*Battlestar Galactica*: Naturalistic Science Fiction or Taking the Opera Out of Space Opera"

In the penultimate scene of "Final Cut," Roslin, Adama, and Tigh screen Biers' documentary with the filmmaker. The response of the XO, whose "mean drunk" side is prominently featured, is not favorable: the first words of the scene are his emphatic "I've seen enough." "It's a hatchet job," the Colonel continues: "The fleet already thinks we're a bunch of trigger-happy assassins. This just confirms it. You show us with our pants down and our asses hanging out."

The old man's review, solicited by Tigh, is very different. "I think it's great. I think she did exactly what we asked her to do. That she put a human face on the guardians of the fleet. Warts and all. I'm proud of it. You can show it to the entire fleet." Their thumbs clearly raised, the Admiral and the President ask to see the remainder of the film. We see it too.

Over various black-and-white scenes of life on *Galactica* and shots of the crew watching, Biers, the film's narrator, confesses her growing realization that the story she had planned to tell—of "an arrogant military [which] let their egos get in the way of doing their job safeguarding the lives of the civilian population"—was simply untrue: "*These people aren't Cylons*. They're not robots blindly following orders and polishing their boots. They're people. Deeply flawed, yes, but deeply human too ..." (my emphasis). And they do not have the luxury of surrender:

> They wake up in the morning, put on their uniforms, and do their jobs. Every day. No pay. No rest. No hope of ever laying down the burden and letting someone else do the job. ... Not a single member of *Galactica*'s crew has asked to resign. Not one. ... The story of *Galactica* isn't that people make bad decisions under pressure. It's that those mistakes are the exception. Most of the time, the men and women serving under Commander Adama get it right. The proof is that our fleet survives. And with *Galactica* at our side, we will endure.

During these scenes, cutaways reveal even Tigh warming to Biers' themes, seemingly won over by the film he had initially despised.

"Final's" final scene, however, takes us to yet another screening. In a seamless transition, the frame of the film Adama, Roslin, and Tigh are watching becomes the screen of a movie theatre in "Cylon-Occupied Caprica." Five (Aaron Doral), Eight (Sharon Agathon), and Six sit talking of Biers' film: Six observes that "Their resilience is remarkable"; Eight, however, wants to see the footage that (for security reasons) was cut from the film, and they watch outtakes of Sharon's pregnancy emergency. As an astonished Eight affirms, "I'm still alive. She's still alive," and Six rejoices that "It was saved," a familiar voice responds from the left of the frame: "We lost two Raiders relaying the images back to the fleet ... but I think the sacrifice was worth it." The voice of the now visible Number Three/Biers gets the last line: "It truly is a miracle from God." The cinéma-vérité documentary[106] of "Final Cut" has been Cylon-vérité.

Monotheism, Polytheism, and TV Storytelling

"And a person who had never listened to nor read a tale or myth or parable or story would remain ignorant of his emotional and spiritual heights and depths, would not know quite fully what it is to be human. For the story from Rumpelstiltskin *to* War and Peace *is one of the basic tools invented by the mind of man, for the purpose of gaining understanding. There have been great societies that did not use the wheel, but there have been no societies that did not tell stories."*

—Ursula K. LeGuin, *The Language of the Night*

"Warts and all"—Adama's words of praise for Biers' documentary reveal his aesthetic (and Laura Roslin's as well) to be surprisingly similar to that espoused in Ronald D. Moore's series bible—with its "reinvention" of the sci-fi TV series in the direction of "naturalism." "Our characters," Moore writes, "are living, breathing people with all the emotional complexity and contradictions present in quality dramas like *The West Wing* or *The Sopranos* ... everyday people caught up in an enormous cataclysm and trying to survive" (Ash 41). The bible, the podcasts, and the DVD commentaries are likewise full of talk of creating a documentary look and feel for *Battlestar*, which would make "Final Cut," described by Moore and Eick as a "stand-alone" episode, of central, self-referential importance.

Such an understanding of story might likewise be deemed, in keeping with our discussion of religion in an earlier Jump, polytheistic, for it comes down on the side of the "warts and all" multiple truths of full-of-contradiction characters, not on the "take captive every thought for Christ" single-truth obsession of monotheists. In contrast, Tigh's initial resistance to such an approach puts him on the side of monotheists or at least the monotheistic story, not all that surprising given his realization at the end of Season Three that he may in fact be a Cylon.[107]

The motives behind D'Anna's Cylon tendencies, however, her willingness to make a film that praises humanity for not being Cylons, for not being "robots blindly following orders and polishing their boots," remains unfathomable. Clearly, her hidden agenda was to learn if Caprica Sharon and her in-utero miracle child (by Helo) were still alive (they are). Caprica Six would seem to be aware of her real identity. Does she not tell Baltar, "You'll do whatever is necessary to protect our child. ... Trust me. This one [Biers] can help us"?

From the start, one of *BSG*'s recurring themes—brilliantly explored ten episodes later in the long-promised Cylon-point-of-view episode "Downloaded" (2.18)—has been Cylon envy, despite their self-righteous claim of being the chosen "people" of their One True God, of the distinctly human: our ability to reproduce, our capacity for love. Caprica Six's seduction of Gaius

Baltar leaves her changed, infatuated with the possibility of a real relationship. Both the sleeper-Cylon *Galactica* Sharon, who knows both agape (in her strong feelings for Adama) and eros (in her affair with Chief Tyrol), and Caprica Sharon, who falls hard for the father of her child Helo, a man she was under assignment to seduce, are clearly under the influence.

At the end of "Final Cut," the pro-human film which D'Anna Biers has made—"These people aren't Cylons. They're not robots blindly following orders and polishing their boots"—strongly suggest she too has been seduced by the enemy, not by the promises of love, but by the distinctly human appeal of narrative possibility.

WEAVING A STORY THROUGH WEBISODES

—Justin Door

Long hiatuses between seasons pose problems for any serialized TV program, but the ways a series creators and a network handle these breaks are vastly different. After some amazing TV storytelling, Ronald D. Moore and David Eick had set a high standard for themselves. Their solution to the hiatus problem went above and beyond the typical "forget about the series until we finish our new episodes." They instead created ten webisodes, brief clips of *Battlestar Galactica* action freely available online. In order not to alienate their more casual viewers, they made sure these webisodes were not integral to the overall plot of *Battlestar Galactica*, while still moving the plot along and showing more of the complex world in which the characters live.

The reimagined *Battlestar Galactica* not only breaks new ground on television but over the Internet. Although many sci-fi or fantasy shows such as *Heroes* have released already-broadcast episodes on the Internet, and *Lost* has long promised "mobisodes" for download via cell phone, new *Battlestar Galactica* episodes were created solely for release at the Sci Fi Channel's website.

The webisodes initially "aired" between Seasons Two and Three, with a new batch appearing in weekly installments between Seasons Three and Four. The first webisodes, although not vital to *Battlestar*'s overall plot, explain what happens after the events at the end of Season Two and before the abandonment of the New Caprica settlement at the beginning of Season Three. They show how the Cylons impose their will through political measures and new policing efforts, and the formation of the resulting human Resistance movement. The later webisodes focus on humanity's earlier struggle to keep the Cylons from victory in the first Cylon War. The large-scale struggle, similar to that portrayed in the regular series, introduces the Cylon War through the eyes of rookie pilot William "Husker" Adama. These brief stories make key events shown in the regular series more personal to the audience by telling the story through the lives of new characters, including those written just for the first webisodes as well as the little-known (and thus "new") young "Husker" Adama featured in the second group of webisodes.

THE FIRST WEBISODES

Moore and Eick's devotion to their fanbase can be seen by the mere fact that the webisodes exist, as well as their high production values. Never intending them to be released on television, the creators nevertheless chose to spend time and money to film additional scenes for ten brief webisodes (about thirty minutes of total screen time). Moore and Eick filmed the webisodes in the same big-budget, high-quality style as the TV series. Bradley Thompson and David Weddle, who penned several episodes, among them "Act of Contrition," "Downloaded," the two-part "Exodus," and "Maelstrom," wrote the scripts for the online minisodes, which were then guided by "Dirty Hands" director Wayne Rose.

The webisodes were a success with fans: the first received 1,380 "digs," or positive comments, on digg.com, as well as favorable reviews on popular fan forums such as Television Without Pity,

Sci Fi Channel's *Battlestar Galactica* boards, and private blogs. The well-written webisodes fed avid fans' admitted addiction for *Battlestar Galactica* and provided new insights about how Season Two led into Season Three.

Although not every major character from the TV series is included, some notables, such as Tigh, Tyrol, and Cally, appear in the online mini-episodes. The webisodes follow two new characters on Cylon-occupied New Caprica: Duck and Jammer. The two former Viper pilots' daily struggles establish a human tone to the series: Duck's wife rushes to the market to buy rare fresh greens, Jammer is trying to find a wife, Duck is trying to become a father, and both former pilots look for new jobs. The show's dedication to showing humanity's glory and failings by highlighting small, everyday goals is just as strong in the webisodes as in the TV series.

Quite a bit of the early story revolves around the temple and activities within. The temple is nothing more than a tent with a rough altar inside, but it is extremely significant to the human community. Cally and Tyrol dedicate their baby son to the gods. People come to pray, and a priestess tends the temple. Because it is holy ground, the Cylons leave the temple alone until the Resistance movement, a group of humans trying to win their freedom from the Cylons, hides weapons inside. When the Cylons find out and raid the temple, they kill ten humans in the process. One of the dead is Duck's wife, and Cally and baby Nicholas are spared only because she falls to the ground. The temple's destruction recruits more people to the Resistance's cause.

The webisodes also focus on the buildup of both a Cylon police force and the Resistance movement. Duck and Jammer agree that anyone who joins the police is a Cylon collaborator. The Resistance, however, is far from innocent concerning human deaths. Tigh, in particular, hopes that the temple and a resulting massacre will help the Resistance movement grow. Jammer becomes disillusioned with the Resistance movement and, as we learn in a Season Three episode, joins the police force. Duck, at first reluctant to join the movement because of his wife and their hopes of having a child, becomes a spy for the Resistance after his wife is murdered in the temple. The Resistance movement hopes for even more civilian casualties and massacres, specifically to draw more people to its side. They plan attacks and plant weapons caches near vulnerable targets, including the hospital, so that the Cylon raids will get ugly and create outrage within the human community on New Caprica. Escalation is an important part of the online story.

Instead of offering trailers, commercials, and teasers enticing fans to wait until the next season's episodes, the webisodes moved the story forward. Moore and Eick knew what fans wanted, and they delivered.

Although the webisodes aren't vital to viewers' enjoyment of Season Three, they fill in some important gaps and show what is important in the characters' everyday lives. We learn more about the role of religion within the series, through the scenes of a baby's dedication and a wife urging her husband to pray with her at the temple so she'll get pregnant. We learn about the stigmas regarding the proper use of the temple and the "best" way to express religious viewpoints. These small, personal touches are crucial to the plot of each short webisode, but they might slow down the action or seem awkward in full-length TV episodes.

The Second Series

Whereas the first webisodes featured a large cast of characters and multiple storylines, the second series focuses on William "Husker" Adama. The minisodes lack familiar faces from the TV series, mainly because events take place during the first Cylon War, forty years before the TV series begins. Adama's love life is shattered when his lover is almost killed during an attack on a Cylon target. As a result, when Adama receives his combat orders, he ruthlessly hunts down Cylon raiders. After the destruction of a battlestar, Adama pursues the Cylon raiders that destroyed it, following them to a planet. He collides with a raider and plummets toward the surface.

TV episodes often portray Adama as a stern commander haunted by specters of his past; through these webisodes fans meet the specters. Adama is a dynamic young pilot, and many of his early battle experiences help shape his later command decisions.

Although we won't know until Season Four whether this background information is as important to the series as the Resistance movement was to Season Three, we gain insight into one of the most enigmatic characters on *Battlestar Galactica*. After watching these webisodes, we can better understand how Adama was prepared for the next Cylon War, even though most Colonials never thought the Cylons would attack again. We now realize why Adama never wanted to "upgrade" the *Galactica*; his early war experiences helped him think of the Cylons differently than the way most of his compatriots did.

Just like the webisodes between Seasons Two and Three, these minisodes before *Razor* help keep fans interested in the series during a long TV hiatus. In particular, the new webisodes provide more action and an intriguing backstory for one of the series' most important, and interesting, characters.

The TV series tends to focus on the *Galactica*, the president's politics, and the military's difficulties. The first webisodes gave Moore and Eick a much-needed outlet to further illustrate the characters' daily lives, allowing them to get away, even for brief moments, from the military and political plotlines that so often monopolize the *Battlestar Galactica* story. The recent webisodes' emphasis on Adama develops a leading character's backstory in a way not possible during a regular episode; scenes of Adama during battle also feed fans' need for the action sequences more often saved for a bigger screen.

The webisodes reward fans with new information while keeping them hooked on the regular series. Just as *BSG* has been innovative in other aspects of TV programming, Moore and Eick may be starting a new trend for series development online during a TV hiatus. Fan response to these webisodes may help make them standard online fare—at least for series whose creators (and network) want to keep the fan base happy between new TV episodes.

Chapter Thirteen

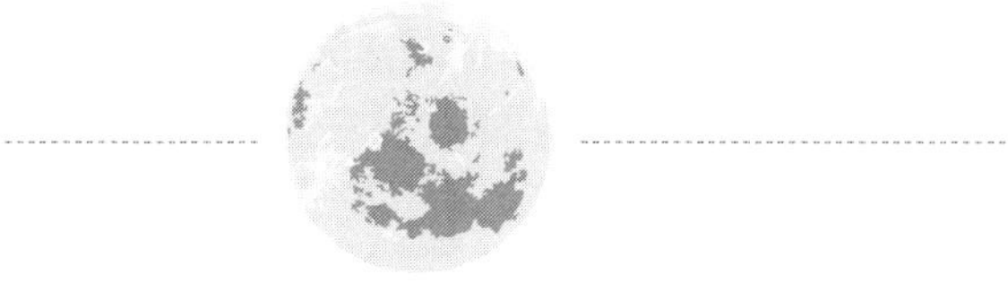

THIS *RAZOR'S* EDGY

Admiral Helena Cain has never been a sympathetic character. Before the November (December in the UK) 2007 debut of the movie *Razor*, she had bullied her way through three regular season episodes ("Pegasus" [2.10]; "Resurrection Ship, Parts 1 and 2" [2.11–2.12]). Lesser series might have used *Razor* to soften the Admiral or make her more sympathetic, but *BSG*'s Ronald D. Moore and David Eick did neither. If anything, one reason *Razor* is so edgy is Cain's unrelenting nature. She seeks and destroys, she takes no emotional or physical prisoners, she does whatever it takes—but she also is more than the sum of all these clichés.

Like the euphemism "a man's man" that could easily be applied to her counterpart, Bill Adama, Helena Cain is as tough as a "man's man," but she's also a "woman's woman"—at least in *BSG* terms, where Cylon lovers often masquerade as human. Cain is as savvy as the other strong female characters on this series, including President Laura Roslin and Kara "Starbuck" Thrace. Like them, she also has a more loving side. Her love interest—surprise—is the Cylon infiltrator Gina Inviere (whose name means, appropriately, "resurrection"), and, like Starbuck, whom Cain briefly mentors in "Resurrection Ship," she often leaves emotional and physical havoc in the wake of her romances.

Love and violence sometimes go hand in hand, or fist to fist, in *BSG* relationships, as Kara and Lee Adama can attest (e.g., their love/hate boxing match in "Unfinished Business," [3.9]), but Cain takes everything to another degree. Taking Gina's breach of her trust as the ultimate betrayal, Cain commands Gina's interrogator to use whatever it takes to break her—"pain, degradation, fear, shame." She sometimes visits Gina's cell to see the results of the interrogator's handiwork, but she never again talks with the "thing" she dared to love. Cain's protégé, Kendra Shaw, gradually turns into a razor—as cold, unfeeling, and deadly as the knife Cain, and later Shaw, carries. She later tells her new commander, Lee Adama, "I am Cain's legacy," and seems intent on being a harshly efficient XO, who Adama, Sr., grudgingly admires as "tougher than Saul Tigh." Cain's legacy, in the lives of her surviving crew and the military logs she and Adama write to document humanity's history, seems to secure her memory as a ruthless tactician who always accomplished her mission.

Razor also goes above and beyond the typical "extended episode" or movie, even if it isn't as pleasant or as accommodating as casual fans might like. The plot makes FTL jumps among Lee Adama's command of *Pegasus*, Helena Cain's rule in the aftermath of the Cylon attacks, and Bill Adama's run-in with Cylons experimenting with early-stage hybrids during the First Cylon War. Instead of just providing a gap-filler (or audience pleaser) until new episodes arrive in April 2008, *Razor* requires audiences to know plenty about the *Battlestar* saga if they are to connect the movie's scenes with previous episodes without any further explanation.

For the initiated, the payoff is worth the whiplash. *Razor* provides new perspectives on characters we know and, mostly, love. As Stephanie (Kendra) Jacobsen told *Sci Fi*, *Razor* is designed to "spin the audience perspective round on these characters that they've known for five years and [will] also be a pivotal point of the series."[108] Michelle (Cain) Forbes approves of

Razor's edginess: "[*Razor*] hits you with these tough moral questions and then doesn't answer them because there *are* no answers."[109] It also hints at Season Four's possible direction and leaves fans wanting more.

Moore and Eick initially released scenes cut from the TV version (but available on a December-released "unrated" DVD) to the Sci Fi Channel to be broadcast during October episodes of *Flash Gordon*. After *Razor* was broadcast, the deleted scenes also became available at SciFi.com. Seeing the deleted scenes in or out of context doesn't dilute *Razor*'s sharpness. It well represents the reimagined *BSG* franchise, but it also plays with audience preconceptions not only about Cain but more "acceptable to like" characters Starbuck, Apollo, and Adama.

FOUR REASONS TO LIKE *RAZOR*

Although the production quality, strong writing, and excellent cast are enough reasons to watch *Razor*, it more importantly indicates that, going into its final season, *BSG*'s still got it. Although the special effects are now expected and viewers may be desensitized to bloodbaths, *Razor* also offers a deeper understanding of why the *Pegasus* story is important to the entire *Battlestar* mythology. Here are four additional reasons to like a movie that violently illustrates how far people will go to "achieve victory" in wartime:

1. STRONG FEMALE CHARACTERS

Continuing the tradition of strong female characters, *Razor* showcases not only Cain but also her protégé, Kendra Shaw. She becomes the pivotal character in the movie; her presence spans Lee Adama's first command on the *Pegasus*, the Cylon invasion, and Admiral Cain's rule. Kendra follows Cain's example and becomes a razor, a finely honed fighting machine capable of anything (but, apparently, humanity). Her final act of disobeying her commanding officer, Lee Adama, and holding Kara Thrace at gunpoint, leads to her redemption; Kendra replaces Kara as the one to destroy the Cylon ship designed to protect an early human-Cylon hybrid. The wounded Kendra admits to this hybrid "god" that she does indeed want to be forgiven for the civilian murders committed in the name of war. As Kara later tells Lee, perhaps Kendra just figured her time had come, or even that she "had it coming" in light of her *Pegasus* past.

Only women are truly razors in this movie. The men who question Cain's authority either die immediately at her hand (she shoots her XO with his own weapon when he refuses to order what he believes is a suicide mission) or placate her to save themselves. Even Lee Adama, whose order to nuke his own team on the Cylon ship is belayed by his father, ultimately backs down from willfully killing his own kind. Razors have no such qualms. Gina loves but betrays Cain, withstanding the resulting torture until she can kill her former lover ("Resurrection Ship, Part 2," [2.12]). Kendra becomes like the Admiral until she can find a way to self-destruct honorably. Kara, who next inherits Cain's trademark knife, occasionally seems capable of becoming a razor, but so far has been "weakened" by her humanity; whether she is next in line to become, as the hybrid prophesizes to Kendra, the "herald of the apocalypse" and "harbinger of death" is the stuff legends in Season Four may be made of.

2. A Combination of Old and New

Razor blends old and new, a fitting way to lead into the fourth, and final, season. As *iF*'s senior editor—and long-time *BSG* viewer—Sean Elliott explained in his review, "One of the parts that made my toes tingle was a shot of the interior of a Cylon viper, with the three Cylons led by a gold leader issuing commands and the pilot responding 'by your command.' It took me back to watching the original series as a kid and made me pretty much yell out loud."[110]

A two-hour movie that can span three time periods, including a remnant from the original series, might not be a good idea to attract new viewers. Long-time fans of the old and reimagined series, however, should find plenty of interest in each time period. *Razor* attempts to bring elements of the old into the new *Battlestar*verse, instead of completely ignoring the 1970s series.

3. The Death of "God"

The hybrid guarded aboard the Cylon ship proclaims he is what his children call "god," although he seems unsure whether he is man or machine. He does seem to know a lot about Kendra and Starbuck, and his prophesy, before Kendra kills him with a nuclear bomb, sets off its own aftershocks. If the Cylons' one god can be so easily destroyed, what does that say about their religion—or religion in general? If the hybrid is yet another Cylon ploy, perhaps set up by one of the Final Five who knew of Adama's early experiences with "hybrid" experiments, are fans being set up to believe a lie instead of a prophesy? After all, Kendra's aborted message to *Pegasus* didn't tell Lee all the hybrid/god said. Whatever the truth behind the hybrid, his scenes alone make *Razor* worth watching.

4. Starbuck

Declaring that "April can't come soon enough," the *Miami Herald*'s TV critic praised not the special effects or wide-ranging story as the rationale for this declaration. Instead, "the best part comes in the last few minutes, and it has nothing to do with gee-whiz special effects. ... It has more to do with Starbuck's fate and a decision that Commander Lee "Apollo" Adama, who has been her lover, has to make."[111] Only Kendra's intervention saves Kara from Lee's order to stay behind and manually detonate a nuclear bomb on the Cylon ship. If the hybrid's prophesy is correct,

Starbuck will lead humanity to its destruction. Perhaps Lee's impulse to see her die in a blaze of glory wasn't horrific; by saving Kara, Kendra may have killed the human race. Safely back on *Pegasus*, Kara sarcastically complains that her CO keeps trying to kill her. "I have a destiny," she smugly tells Lee. "You're stuck with me until the end." Starbuck fans may breathe a sigh of relief at this declaration. Whether she ends the series as humanity's savior or silencer, Starbuck continues to be the key to *BSG*'s future.

* * *

Razor is discussion-making television. Although its violence may be difficult to watch and its rapid-fire shifts in story headache inducing, for long-time *BSG* fans, it hurts so good.

TAKING THE LAST SHOT: THE ENDINGS OF BATTLESTAR EPISODES (THE REIMAGINED SERIES [2003–])

TV shows sometimes develop signature episode endings. Five minutes before the end of each and every *Full House*, the sentimental music rose in preparation for delivery of the sappy moral that took us out of each and every ultra-predictable episode. In the final moments of a *Grey's Anatomy*, week after week after week, Meredith Grey, in far-too-neat, sometimes embarrassingly didactic voice-overs, explains the significance of the drama we have just seen (usually taking special pains to explicate the episode's title themes).

Any regular viewer of *Battlestar Galactica* is likely to have taken notice of the distinctive endings of each of its fifty-plus episodes. In keeping with its overall commitment to quality television—in writing, acting, production design, special effects—the reimagined *BSG* takes great care, week after week, with its final shots. Assiduously avoiding the predictable and prefab finishes of so much film and television, *Battlestar* engages in a fascinating "narrative eschatology"—eschatology being the branch of theology that studies "the end," "final things." The cute, the glib, prepackaged (all loose ends tied up, with a bow on top)—*BSG* will have none of these.

Instead, we exit each individual segment on distinctive images, most often of its characters' great faces filled with agony, perplexity, guilt, yearning, happiness, but also of spacescapes, landscape, and forces at war. Each refuses to tell us what to think about it. Each leaves us with matters to ponder. Each is memorable.

Not surprisingly, "the face of Edward James Olmos" (Adama) about which we have written earlier in this volume, appears in final shots no less than sixteen times, while Starbuck (twelve), Sharon Valerii in her various manifestations (ten), Colonel Tigh (nine), Gaius Baltar and Laura Roslin (both with seven) are also frequently the focus.

As we write, we have, of course, not yet seen the ultimate *Battlestar* ending. When the final episode of the final season of the new *BSG* airs on Sci Fi, a fictional universe will come to an end. We predict, with virtual certainty, that that final final shot will be memorable, as memorable as the series it culminates.

MINISERIES

Part 1—Adama's face as the realization sets in that his son is dead.

Part 2—An aerial shot of the Cylons gathered at Ragnar Station, including Sharon Valerii (who has just insisted "Don't worry. We'll find them").

SEASON ONE

33 (1.1)—Laura Roslin's smiling face after she has added one to the official count of surviving humans (now 47,973) after the birth of a child.

Water (1.2)—A very suspicious-looking Boomer walking down a hallway of the *Galactica*.

Bastille Day (1.3)—Apollo's face after Laura insists she can count on him.

Act of Contrition (1) (1.4)—Starbuck plummeting through the atmosphere of an asteroid behind her Viper and the Cylon Raider with which she crashed.

You Can't Go Home Again (2) (1.5)—Starbuck's troubled face in her hospital bed after a touching visit from Adama.

Litmus (1.6)—Chief Tyrol's face after being snubbed by Boomer.

Six Degrees of Separation (1.7)—A zoom away from the *Galactica* and the Colonial Fleet in deep space.

Flesh and Bone (1.8)—Adama's face as he digests Laura's insistence that there is nothing wrong.

Tigh Me Up, Tigh Me Down (1.9)—Baltar's lab, with hundreds of test tubes spread out on a table, and the doctor at the center.

The Hand of God (1.10)—Baltar on the deck of his lakeside Caprican house as he accepts his role as "the hand of god."

Colonial Day (1.11)—Caprica Sharon's agonized face as Helo flees from her.

Kobol's Last Gleaming, Part 1 (1.12)—Adama's face just after he answers Tigh's query concerning Starbuck's destination with one word: "Home."

Kobol's Last Gleaming, Part 2 (1.13)—Adama, gut shot by Boomer, sprawled on a CIC console, surrounded by his son, Tigh, Dualla.

SEASON TWO

Scattered (2.1)—A Cylon centurion, with a final close-up on its red visor.

Valley of Darkness (2.2)—Tigh's worried face as he keeps a vigil beside the wounded Adama.

Fragged (2.3)—After declaring martial law in a press briefing, Tigh surreptitiously taking a swig from his flask (hidden in his boot).

Resistance (2.4)—In extreme close-up, a drop of blood from the dying Boomer, held by Chief, splattering on the floor.

The Farm (2.5)—Anders, his back to the camera, walking back to the Caprican Resistance headquarters after saying goodbye to Starbuck.

Home, Part 1 (2.6)—Dualla smiling after hearing Adama's declaration that "This ends now."

Home, Part 2 (2.7)—Baltar looking over Six's naked shoulder as she embraces him.

Final Cut (2.8)—D'Anna Biers face as she is revealed to be a Cylon.

Flight of the Phoenix (2.9)—Chief's face as he speaks on a brig phone with Caprica Sharon.

Pegasus (2.10)—The forces of the *Pegasus* and *Galactica* facing off between the two battlestars.

Resurrection Ship, Part 1 (2.11)—Starbuck's astonished face as Adama orders her to "shoot Admiral Cain in the head."

Resurrection Ship, Part 2 (2.12)—Adama's face after he has been promoted to Admiral and kissed Laura Roslin.

Epiphanies (2.13)—A close-up of the nuclear device Baltar gives to Gina.

Black Market (2.14)—A despondent Apollo sitting with his father drinking.

Scar (2.15)—Starbuck standing over Helo, victorious in a playful sparring match.

Sacrifice (2.16)—Sharon, pregnant, as she lies wide awake on her bed.

The Captain's Hand (2.17)—Baltar smiling as Six mock-applauds his announcement that he is now a candidate for President.

Downloaded (2.18)—Maya cradling Hera on a Raptor as it docks on a ship of the Colonial Fleet.

Lay Down Your Burdens, Part 1 (2.19)—Starbuck's forces taking heavy incoming as they attempt to rescue the Caprican Resistance.

Lay Down Your Burdens, Part 2 (2.20)—Starbuck's face as she announces the plan: "Fight 'em until we can't."

SEASON THREE

Occupation/Precipice (3.1–2)—Cally fleeing a Centurion firing squad.

Exodus, Part 1 (3.3)—Adama's face after he has given his Saint Crispin's Day speech.

Exodus, Part 2 (3.4)—A *Galactica* hallway, after Adama exits (post shave).

Collaborators (3.5)—The Chief and Gaeta (whose life has just been spared) eating silently together.

Torn (1) (3.6)—Caprica Sharon's face after discovery of the road to Earth and the realization they are surrounded by Cylon basestars.

A Measure of Salvation (2) (3.7)—Adama looking at Laura after she responds to his "I think we are on the right trail [to Earth]" with "So are the Cylons."

Hero (3.8)—Adama pouring Tigh a drink as they sit down to talk about what happened to Ellen.

Unfinished Business (3.9)—Bloody Apollo and Starbuck embracing in the boxing ring after pummeling each other.

The Passage (3.10)—Starbuck's face, in tears as she looks at Kat's photo on the memory wall (Apollo in the background).

The Eye of Jupiter (1) (3.11)—Laura, Tigh, and Adama looking at each other as the Admiral authorizes the use of nuclear weapons.

Rapture (2) (3.12)—A wide shot of a myriad of rebirthing pods in the resurrection ship.

Taking a Break from All Your Worries (3.13)—Adama standing besides Laura's bed after she insists on giving Baltar his trial.

The Woman King (3.14)—Helo kissing Sharon (who holds their baby).

A Day in the Life (3.15)—Adama's face after he has put his wedding photo away for another year.

Dirty Hands (3.16)—Ensign Seelix smiling broadly as she heads off for flight instruction.

Maelstrom (3.17)—Adama in tears (after destroying his model tall ship), distraught because of the death of Starbuck.

The Son Also Rises (3.18)—Baltar reading a letter in jail from Romo Lampkin.

Crossroads, Part 1 (3.19)—Tigh's face after he announces that "It's [the music] in the frakkin' ship."

Crossroads, Part 2 (3.20)—Earth seen from space after Starbuck tells Apollo she will take them there.

Razor—Lee Adama walks away toward the camera from a conversation with Starbuck in which they discuss the reasons behind Kendra Shaw's death and Kara's announcement that she wants to transfer back to *Galactica*.

APPENDIX A

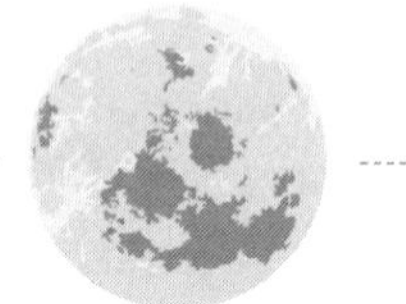

BATTLESTAR GALACTICA EPISODE GUIDE

***Battlestar Galactica*, 1978–1979**				
Episode Number	**Title**	**Airdate**	**Writer(s)**	**Director(s)**
1.1	Saga of a Star World, Part 1 (pilot)	9/17/78	Glen A. Larson	Richard Colla
1.2	Saga of a Star World, Part 2 (pilot)	9/17/78	Larson	Colla
1.3	Saga of a Star World, Part 3 (pilot)	9/17/78	Larson	Colla
1.4	The Lost Planet of the Gods, Part 1	9/24/78	Donald Bellisario	Christian I. Nyby II
1.5	The Lost Planet of the Gods, Part 2	10/1/78	Larson & Bellisario	Nyby
1.6	The Lost Warrior	10/8/78	Herman Groves & Bellisario	Rod Holcomb

Episode Number	Title	Airdate	Writer(s)	Director(s)
1.7	The Long Patrol	10/15/78	Bellisario	Nyby
1.8	The Gun on Ice Planet Zero, Part 1	10/22/78	Bellisario, Leslie Stevens, & Michael Sloan	Alan J. Levi
1.9	The Gun on Ice Planet Zero, Part 2	10/29/78	Bellisario, Stevens, & Sloan	Levi
1.10	The Magnificent Warriors	11/12/78	Larson	Nyby
1.11	The Young Lords	11/19/78	Bellisario, Lupo, & Paul Playdon	Bellisario
1.12	The Living Legend, Part 1	11/26/78	Larson	Vince Edwards
1.13	The Living Legend, Part 2	12/3/78	Larson	Edwards
1.14	Fire in Space	12/17/78	Jim Carlson & Terrence McDonnell	Nyby
1.15	War of the Gods, Part 1	1/14/79	Larson	Daniel Haller
1.16	War of the Gods, Part 2	1/21/79	Larson	Haller
1.17	The Man with Nine Lives	1/28/79	Bellisario	Holcomb
1.18	Murder on the Rising Star	2/18/79	Bellisario, Carlson, & McDonald	Holcomb
1.19	Greetings from Earth, Part 1	2/25/79	Larson	Holcomb

Episode Number	Title	Airdate	Writer(s)	Director(s)
1.20	Greetings from Earth, Part 2	2/25/79	Larson	Holcomb
1.21	Baltar's Escape	3/11/79	Bellisario	Winrich Kolbe
1.22	Experiment in Terra	3/18/79	Larson	Holcomb
1.23	Take the Celestra	4/1/79	Carlson & McDonnell	Haller
1.24	The Hand of God	4/29/79	Bellisario	Bellisario

Galactica 1980,[112] **1980**				
#	**Title**	**Airdate**	**Writer(s)**	**Director(s)**
1.1	*Galactica* Discovers Earth, Part 1	1/27/80	Glen A. Larson	Sidney Hayers
1.2	*Galactica* Discovers Earth, Part 2	2/3/80	Larson	Hayers
1.3	*Galactica* Discovers Earth, Part 3	2/10/80	Larson	Hayers
1.4	The Super Scouts, Part 1	3/16/80	Larson	Vince Edwards
1.5	The Super Scouts, Part 2	3/23/80	Larson	Edwards
1.6	Spaceball	3/30/80	Jeff Freilich, Larson, & Frank Lupo	Barry Crane
1.7	The Night the Cylons Landed, Part 1	4/13/80	Larson	Sigmund Neufeld, Jr.
1.8	The Night the Cylons Landed, Part 2	4/20/80	Larson	Neufeld
1.9	Space Croppers	4/27/80	Robert McCullough	Daniel Haller
1.10	The Return of Starbuck	5/4/80	Larson	Ron Satlof

The Reimagined Series (2003–)				
#	Title	Airdate	Writer	Director
1	Pilot/*Battlestar Galactica* Miniseries—Part 1.0	12/8/2003	Ronald D. Moore & Glen A. Larson	Michael Rymer
1.5	Pilot/*Battlestar Galactica* Miniseries—Part 1.5	12/8/2003	Moore & Larson	Rymer
2	Pilot/*Battlestar Galactica* Miniseries—Part 2.0	12/10/2003	Moore & Larson	Rymer
2.5	Pilot/*Battlestar Galactica* Miniseries—Part 2.5	12/10/2003	Moore & Larson	Rymer
1.1	33	1/14/2005	Moore	Rymer
1.2	Water	1/14/2005	Moore	Marita Grabiak
1.3	Bastille Day	1/21/2005	Toni Graphia	Allan Kroeker
1.4	Act of Contrition (1)	1/28/2005	Bradley Thompson & David Weddle	Rod Hardy
1.5	You Can't Go Home Again (2)	2/4/2005	Carla Robinson & Thompson	Sergio Mimica-Gezzan
1.6	Litmus	2/11/2005	Jeff Vlaming	Rod Hardy
1.7	Six Degrees of Separation	2/18/2005	Michael Angeli	Robert M. Young
1.8	Flesh and Bone	2/25/2005	Graphia	Brad Turner
1.9	Tigh Me Up, Tigh Me Down	3/4/2005	Vlaming	Edward James Olmos
1.10	The Hand of God	3/11/2005	Thompson & Weddle	Jeff Woolnough

#	Title	Airdate	Writer	Director
1.11	Colonial Day	3/18/2005	Robinson	Jonas Pate
1.12	Kobol's Last Gleaming, Part 1	3/25/2005	Moore	Rymer
1.13	Kobol's Last Gleaming, Part 2	4/1/2005	Moore	Rymer
2.1	Scattered	7/15/2005	Thompson & Weddle	Rymer
2.2	Valley of Darkness	7/22/2005	Thompson & Weddle	Rymer
2.3	Fragged	7/29/2005	Nicole Yorkin & Dawn Prestwich	Mimica-Gezzan
2.4	Resistance	8/5/2005	Graphia	Kroeker
2.5	The Farm	8/12/2005	Robinson	Hardy
2.6	Home, Part 1	8/19/2005	David Eick	Mimica-Gezzan
2.7	Home, Part 2	8/26/2005	Moore & Eick	Woolnough
2.8	Final Cut	9/9/2005	Mark Verheiden	Young
2.9	Flight of the Phoenix	9/16/2005	Thompson & Weddle	Michael Nankin
2.10	Pegasus	9/23/2005	Anne Cofell-Saunders	Rymer
2.11	Resurrection Ship, Part 1	1/6/2006	Rymer	Rymer
2.12	Resurrection Ship, Part 2	1/13/2006	Rymer, Moore	Rymer
2.13	Epiphanies	1/20/2006	Joel Anderson Thompson	Hardy
2.14	Black Market	1/27/2006	Verheiden	Rymer & James Head

#	Title	Airdate	Writer	Director
2.15	Scar	2/3/2006	Thompson & Weddle	Nankin
2.16	Sacrifice	2/10/2006	Cofell, Saunders	Reynaldo Villalobos
2.17	The Captain's Hand	2/17/2006	Jeff Vlaming	Mimica-Gezzan
2.18	Downloaded	2/24/2006	Thompson & Weddle	Woolnough
2.19	Lay Down Your Burdens, Part 1	3/3/2006	Moore	Rymer
2.20	Lay Down Your Burdens, Part 2	3/10/2006	Verheiden & Cofell-Saunders	Rymer
	Special. *Battlestar Galactica*: The Resistance (Web series)	9/5/2006	Thompson & Weddle	Wayne Rose
3.1	Occupation	10/6/2006	Moore	Mimica-Gezzan
3.2	Precipice	10/6/2006	Moore	Mimica-Gezzan
3.3	Exodus, Part 1	10/13/2006	Thompson & Weddle	Félix Enríquez Alcalá
3.4	Exodus, Part 2	10/20/2006	Thompson & Weddle	Alcalá
3.5	Collaborators	10/27/2006	Verheiden	Rymer
3.6	Torn (1)	11/3/2006	Cofell-Saunders	Jean de Segonzac
3.7	A Measure of Salvation (2)	11/10/2006	Angeli	Bill Eagles
3.8	Hero	11/17/2006	Eick	Rymer

#	Title	Airdate	Writer	Director
3.9	Unfinished Business	12/1/2006	Michael Taylor	Young
3.10	The Passage	12/8/2006	Jane Espenson	Nankin
3.11	The Eye of Jupiter (1)	12/15/2006	Verheiden	Rymer
3.12	Rapture (2)	1/21/2007	Thompson & Weddle	Rymer
3.13	Taking a Break from All Your Worries	1/28/2007	Taylor	Olmos
3.14	The Woman King	2/11/2007	Angeli	Rymer
3.15	A Day in the Life	2/18/2007	Verheiden	Hardy
3.16	Dirty Hands	2/25/2007	Espenson & Cofell-Saunders	Rose
3.17	Maelstrom	3/4/2007	Thompson & Weddle	Nankin
3.18	The Son Also Rises	3/11/2007	Angeli	Young
3.19	Crossroads, Part 1	3/18/2007	Taylor	Rymer
3.20	Crossroads, Part 2	3/25/2007	Verheiden	Rymer
	Razor	11/24/2007	Moore	Alcalá

Appendix B

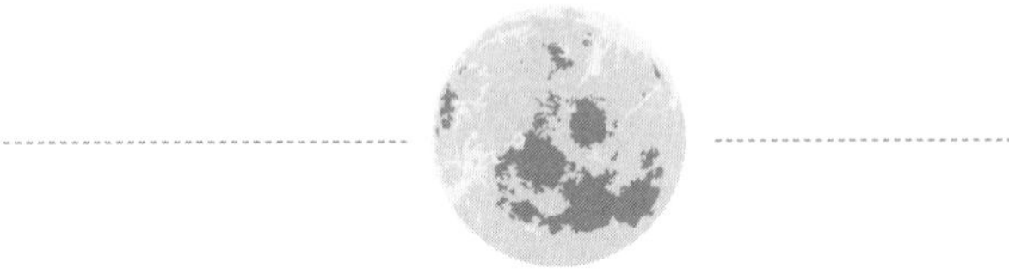

BATTLESTAR GALACTICA: R & D TV LOGOS

—Compiled by Christopher Smiley

Animated logos, ordinarily appearing at the very end of a TV episode and announcing the series' production company, have become yet another way in which small screen creators have established their signature while simultaneously generating buzz about their brand. The "Bad Robot" of J. J. Abrams (*Felicity*, *Alias*, *Lost*), Joss Whedon's "Grr Arg" monster (announcing the work of Mutant Enemy—*Buffy the Vampire Slayer*, *Angel*, *Firefly*) have become minor TV celebrities. But the wonderfully intertextual logos which end *BSG* episodes (see our discussion in "The Swirl") are inarguably the most ingenious we have yet seen. A catalogue of these inspired, gruesome gems can be found below.

"LOGOS"			
Ep. #	**Episode Title**	**Logo Title**	**Description**
1.1	33	*Batter Up!*	David responds to Ron's jabbering by beating him repeatedly with a baseball bat.

Ep. #	Episode Title	Logo Title	Description
1.2	Water	*Mahnkee*	David's idea only manages to inspire Ron to set a gorilla on him.
1.3	Bastille Day	*Hoop*	Ron crushes David into a small ball and shoots him through a basketball hoop.
1.4	Act of Contrition	*Window*	David violently shoves a blabbering Ron through the office window and into a stream of traffic.
1.5	You Can't Go Home Again	*Smack*	David screams like a child when his idea to blow a raspberry lands him a smack in the face from Ron.
1.6	Litmus	*Whistle*	David makes Ron scream for mercy by whistling in a shark to eat him.
1.7	Six Degrees of Separation	*Wand*	Ron opts to pick the bones out of David rather than his idea, using a magic wand to make his skeleton completely disappear and his body slump to the ground like an empty suit.
1.8	Flesh and Bone	*Pop Stars*	Ron's attempt to sing out his idea *American Idol*–style ends abruptly when David rips off a piece of his shirt.
1.9	Tigh Me Up, Tigh Me Down	*Chivalry*	David's killer idea leads Ron to bring in a medieval knight to split his head open with a mace.
1.10	The Hand of God	*Lethal Script*	Again failing to work from the same page, David uses his to slice up Ron's face with a series of vicious paper-cuts.
1.11	Colonial Day	*RPS*	After suggesting a game of "Rock, Paper, Scissors," David learns the hard way that rock really does beat scissors when Ron squashes him with one.

Ep. #	Episode Title	Logo Title	Description
1.12	Kobol's Last Gleaming, Part 1	*Witch*	Ron's shocking idea is nothing compared to the shocking experience David inflicts upon him; turning him into Martha Stewart by shooting lightning from his fingers.
1.13	Kobol's Last Gleaming, Part 2	*Delivery*	As both men seem ready to suggest an idea, a courier enters the scene delivering them each a special package; carnivorous Jack-in-the-Boxes that proceed to eat them.
2.1	Scattered	*Wild West*	When Ron dons a cowboy hat and proclaims he has an idea, David slaps him, knocking his face off and revealing him to be a *Westworld*-style robot.
2.2	Valley of Darkness	*Popular Mechanics*	Ron swoops off in time, but the idea-stricken David is gunned down by a passing Cylon centurion.
2.3	Fragged	*Whistle*	[Repeat of animation from Episode 1.6]
2.4	Resistance	*Pressed for Thought*	When Ron proclaims to have a hot idea, David teaches him the true meaning of "hot" by melting his face with an iron.
2.5	The Farm	*Wand*	[Repeat of animation from Episode 1.7]
2.6	Home, Part 1	*Penmanship*	David has an idea and asks Ron to "jot this down". Ron coolly agrees, picks up a pen, and violently carves "THIS" into David's forehead. David's response: "Jeez."
2.7	Home, Part 2	*Chivalry*	[Repeat of animation from Episode 1.9]

Ep. #	Episode Title	Logo Title	Description
2.8	Final Cut	*Phone Etiquette*	Upset when Ron answers the phone while he is trying to tell him his idea, David grabs the phone, stabs it into Ron's ear, and asks into it, "Can you hear me now?" Ron yelps affirmatively.
2.9	Flight of the Phoenix	*Broken Speech*	When David says he has a jaw-dropping idea, Ron shows him his jaw-dropping left hook, hitting him so hard that his head spins complete revolutions and his jaw literally drops off.
2.10	Pegasus	*Pigskin*	When David hands Ron a football rather than listening to his idea, Ron is sacked so violently by a suddenly appearing football player that he is decapitated. When the head breaks loose, David is forced to call a fumble.
2.11	Resurrection Ship, Part 1	*Bulletin*	Ron interrupts David's idea with a weather alert warning of lightning. Unfortunately for David, he does not get the warning in time and is split in two by a bolt of lightning stemming from the sticker Ron threw onto the board above him.
2.12	Resurrection Ship, Part 2	*Verdict*	When Ron asks for David's verdict on an idea, it turns out to be a damning one. Suddenly dressed as a British judge (complete with wig), David drops an oversized gavel on Ron so hard that it folds him like an accordion.
2.13	Epiphanies	*Pervert*	When David suddenly gooses Ron, Ron makes him pay by severing the offending arm with a sword. David does not seem discouraged.

Ep. #	Episode Title	Logo Title	Description
2.14	Black Market	*That Thing You Do*	In response to Ron's idea of "monsters," David turns into the monster from John Carpenter's *The Thing* (complete with dog) and attacks him.
2.15	Scar	*Holiday*	David suggests a Valentine's episode, but Ron instead shows his proclivity for Halloween by killing David with a Jack-O-Lantern and eating some candy.
2.16	Sacrifice	*Pigskin*	[Repeat of animation from Episode 2.10]
2.17	The Captain's Hand	*Penmanship*	[Repeat of animation from Episode 2.6]
2.18	Downloaded	*Apple*	David interrupts Ron's idea by offering him an apple. As Ron brings it to his lips, David pulls out a bow and reimagines the William Tell legend by shooting an arrow straight through the apple and into Ron's face.
2.19	Lay Down Your Burdens, Part 1	*Scenery*	Ron rewards David's idea of new scenery by snapping his fingers and transporting them both to an arid, rocky landscape. Ron runs off, but David seems to appreciate it until he is violently mauled by a velociraptor.
2.20	Lay Down Your Burdens, Part 2	*Charmed*	Ron's request for a "moment of Zen" to reflect on Season Two is denied when a flute-playing David gets revenge for the velociraptor attack by charming a giant cobra to devour him.
3.1-2	Occupation/ Precipice		After Ron says he feels gloomy, David plays guitar and Ron melts (like the wicked witch of the west in *The Wizard of Oz*).

Ep. #	Episode Title	Logo Title	Description
3.3	Exodus, Part 1		After David announces "This will mark your territory," Ron, now in astronaut gear on the lunar surface, stabs him (thereby claiming the Moon) with an R & D TV flag.
3.4	Exodus, Part 2		When Ron light bulbs "more religion," David morphs into Regan from *The Exorcist* and projectile vomits into his mouth.
3.5	Collaborators		When David light bulbs "more rebels," Ron morphs into Randall Patrick McMurphy from *One Flew Over the Cuckoo's Nest* and starts choking David, who has become Nurse Ratchet.
3.6	Torn (1)		When Ron offers gibberish ("Blah-da-bleh-da-blah"), he is clubbed by a Cyclops.
3.7	A Measure of Salvation (2)	*Scenery*	[Repeat of animation from Episode 2.19]
3.8	Hero		David hands Ron a life preserver against a *Sgt. Pepper's Lonely Hearts Club Band* backdrop featuring characters from *BSG* and from past R & D TV logos.
3.9	Unfinished Business	*Penmanship*	[Repeat of animation from Episodes 2.6 and 2.17]
3.10	The Passage	*Verdict*	[Repeat of animation from Episode 2.12]
3.11	The Eye of Jupiter (1)		TBA
3.12	Rapture (2)	*Whistle*	[Repeat of animation from Episode 1.6]

Ep. #	Episode Title	Logo Title	Description
3.13	Taking a Break from All Your Worries		[Repeat of animation from Episode 3.8]
3.14	The Woman King		[Repeat of animation from Episode 3.1]
3.15	A Day in the Life		[Repeat of animation from Episode 3.3]
3.16	Dirty Hands		TBA
3.17	Maelstrom		As Ron is about to announce a new idea, a muppet-ish "Ronnie Monster" appears, and before he can finish asking "What's a Ronnie Monster?" it begins taking bites out of his head.
3.18	The Son Also Rises		[Repeat of animation from Episode 3.5]
3.19	Crossroads, Part 1		In a slight variation on 3.6, when Ron again blubbers gibberish, David announces "He's doing it again," and a Cyclops clubs Ron.
3.20	Crossroads, Part 2		Ron announces "I kill him" to a light bulbing David, to which he replies "No way!," but then a Ray Harryhausen skeleton (from *The Seven Voyages of Sinbad*) appears and ends a sword fight with David by stabbing him in the gut.
	Razor		Ron squeezes David's "big head," from which bells and whistles pop.

Notes

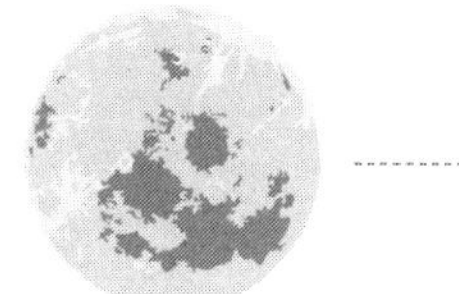

1. That Was Then...

[1] Harwood, Jim. "Laurette Spang." *Us*, October 17, 1978, p. 27.

[2] Harwood, Jim. "Lorne Greene: Reluctant Hero of TV's New 'Star Wars.'" *Us*, October 17, 1978, p. 24.

[3] Rich, Joshua. "'Star' Burst." *Entertainment Weekly*, September 21, 2001. http://www.ew.com/ew/article/0,,254692,00.html.

[4] Stabiner, Karen. "Can 'Battlestar' Ride the Sci-Fi Wave?; Can 'Battlestar' Ride the Wave?" May 13, 1979. *New York Times*. http://www.buck-rogers.com/film_and_series/articles/glen_larson.html. The lawsuit was also mentioned in Harwood, p. 24.

[5] Harwood, p. 24.

[6] Roddenberry's famous line has been repeated in numerous articles in the past forty years, such as "Introduction to *Star Trek*" at StarTrek.com, http://www.startrek.com/startrek/view/features/intro/.

[7] As with most sci-fi series, most critical recognition comes through technical awards, and the new *Battlestar Galactica*, like its predecessor, has received many awards, among them Saturn and Peabody awards as well as numerous Emmy nominations, but neither series, to date, has won in more mainstream categories, such as best actor/actress or series, at the Emmys. The new

series' actors, however, have done much better at the ALMA Awards, where Edward James Olmos won as best actor in 2007, and the Saturn Awards, where Katee Sackhoff and James Callis both won in 2006, and the series was named Best Syndicated/Cable Television series in 2006 and 2007.

8 "Awards for *Battlestar Galactica* (1978)." IMDB.com. http://www.imdb.com/title/tt0076984/awards.

9 Vulkon fan convention, Orlando, FL. November 2000.

10 Singh, Arune. "*Battlestar Galactica* #0 Debuts in *TV Guide*." CBR News, The Comic Wire, May 15, 2006. http://www.comicbookresources.com/news/newsitem.cgi?id=7331

11 Dynamite Entertainment. http://www.dynamiteentertainment.com/htmlfiles/titles.html

12 Jankiewicz, Pat. "Apollo's View." *Starlog*, February 2005, p. 80.

13 Hatch's website, http://www.richardhatch.com/battlestar_galactica/bsgtsc.html, provides photos from the film and further description of it.

14 "Battlestar Wars." *Cinescape*, July/August 1999, p. 10.

15 *Veronica Mars* even used the term. Young, Susan. "Stellar Show Warps into Pop Culture." *Oakland Tribune*, October 5, 2006. Reprinted at http://findarticles.com/p/articles/ mi_qn4176/is_20061005/ai_n16776048.

16 Composer Williams received Academy Awards and Grammy Awards for the soundtrack, which also went platinum, an achievement recognizing the music's critical and popular acclaim.

17 Fansite *Battlestar Wikipedia* notes that Larson is credited on screen and in print (for *BSG* books) under the pseudonym Christopher Eric James (http://en.battlestarwiki.org/wiki/Glen_A._Larson).

18 An occasionally irreverent explanation of Larson's credits on the new series can be found at Gary Westphal's Bio-Encyclopedia of Science Fiction Film, "Larson, Glen A.,"

http://www.sfsite.com/gary/lars01.htm.

19 Bassom, David. "Wolf in the Fold." *Dreamwatch*, March 2005, 58.

20 Jonja.net. "A Candid Interview with Dirk Benedict." April 26, 2006. http://jonja.net/forums/viewtopic.php?t=1228.

21 Benedict, Dirk. "Lost in Castration." Feb. 7, 2006. http://www.dirkbenedictcentral.com/home/articles-readarticle.php?nid=5. Benedict, now a book author as well as actor, posted a well-written opinion about the new series and the nature of the TV business. The quoted section doesn't do justice to the entire essay; Starbuck and/or *Battlestar Galactica* fans should read it, whether they agree or not with Benedict's opinion, simply because it clarifies the argument against the new Starbuck, as espoused by many fans as well as the actor who originally played the character.

22 Jankiewicz, Pat. "Space Nightengale." *Starlog*, 2001, posted at http://www.laurettespang.com/home/opinion-archive.php (Laurette Spang's official website).

23 Nuytens, Gilles. Interview with Katee Sackhoff. The SciFi World. Posted February 25, 2007, at http://www.thescifiworld.net/interviews/katee_sackhoff_01.htm.

24 Kraus, Bruce. "Cylon." *Encyclopedia Galactica: From the Fleet Library Aboard the Battlestar Galactica*. New York: Windmill Books and E. P. Dutton, 1979.

25 Kraus, Bruce. "Lucifer." *Encyclopedia Galactica: From the Fleet Library Aboard the Battlestar Galactica*. New York: Windmill Books and E. P. Dutton, 1979.

26 "Galactites Arise!" *Space Wars*, September 1979, pp. 19–20.

27 Lorenzen, Michael, "*Battlestar Galactica* and Mormonism," http://www.michaellorenzen.com/galactica.html; this essay is insightful not only because of Lorenzen's analysis but his many references to previous publications, mostly in print and not online, that also explain similar connections. Lorenzen's bibliography lists the most important references,

including Ford, James E. "Battlestar Galactica and Mormon Theology." *Journal of Popular Culture* 17 (1983):83–87.

28 Martin, Walter R. *The Kingdom of the Cults*. Minneapolis: Bethany Fellowship, 1965, p. 178, cited in Lorenzen, Michael, "*Battlestar Galactica* and Mormonism," http://www.michaellorenzen.com/galactica.html.

29 Kraus, Bruce. "Ibley." *Encyclopedia Galactica: From the Fleet Library Aboard the Battlestar Galactica*. New York: Windmill Books and E. P. Dutton, 1979.

30 Vulkon. Columbus, OH. July 15, 2007.

31 O'Brien, Steve. "Battlestar Britannia." *SFX*, Christmas special 2004, p. 58.

32 Huddleston, Kathie. "Behind Every Good Woman ..." *SciFi*, October 2007, p. 17.

33 DiLullo, Tara. "A Season of Hope." *SciFi*, October 2006, p. 42.

34 O'Brien, Steve, and Dearsley, Jayne. "Cylon Running." *SFX*, December 2004, p. 74.

35 Bassom, David. "Battle Cry!" *Dreamwatch*, January 2004, p. 59.

36 O'Brien and Dearsley, "Cylon Running."

37 DiLullo, "A Season of Hope."

38 Young, "Stellar Show Warps into Pop Culture."

39 "Retuning Shows. *Battlestar Galactica.*" *SciFi*, October 2007, p. 40.

40 Huddleston, "Behind Every Good Woman ...," p. 17.

3. Piloting a Series

41 Interestingly enough, during *Battlestar Galactica*'s last first-run season in the U.S. (2007–2008, with *Razor* in November and the fourth season in January), U.S. television again embraced escapist programming, much of it fantasy based, in much the same way as television did in the late 1970s. A respite from "heavy" fare and "relevant" series of the late 1960s and early 1970s gave way to fluff and humor for a few years, a move recurring in 2007. In its fourth season, *Battlestar Galactica* is much darker than most new series, a

notable exception being Eick's reimagined *Bionic Woman.*

[42] "Galactites Arise!" *Space Wars*, September 1979, p. 21.

[43] Moore later disparagingly commented that his pilot episode didn't need the unnecessary distraction of visiting the "casino planet." Indeed, many scenes seemed more *Star Wars* bar homage than critical plot development. Ryan, Maureen. "An Interview with Ronald D. Moore." January 19, 2005. The Watcher, *Chicago Tribune.* http://featuresblogs.chicagotribune.com/entertainment_tv/battlestar_galactica/index.html.

[44] Larson, Glen A., and Thurston, Robert. *Battlestar Galactica.* New York: Berkeley, 1978, p. 21.

[45] Phillips, Mark. "The New Apollo." *Starlog*, February 2005, p. 76.

[46] Kraus, Bruce. "Baltar" entry. *Encyclopedia Galactica: From the Fleet Library Aboard the Battlestar Galactica.* New York: Windmill Books and E. P. Dutton, 1979.

[47] Bloch-Hansen, Peter. "John Colicos—The Quintessential Klingon." *Starlog*, #138, January 1989. Republished on John Larocque's *Battlestar Galactica* site, http://members.tripod.com/john_larocque/tns/colicos.html.

[48] Bloch-Hansen, "John Colicos—The Quintessential Klingon."

[49] Bloch-Hansen, "John Colicos—The Quintessential Klingon."

[50] Bassom, David. "Confessions of a Dangerous Mind." *Dreamwatch*, February 2005, p. 31.

[51] Bassom, "Confessions of a Dangerous Mind."

[52] Eramo, Steven. "Secrets and Lies." *Starburst*, November 2005, p. 23.

[53] Eramo, "Secrets and Lies."

[54] Eramo, "Secrets and Lies."

4. From the Buffyverse to the *Battlestar*

[55] For a more in-depth defense of Jane Espenson as an auteur, please take a look at my chapter, "Understanding the Espensode," in *At Sixes and Sevens:* Buffy the Vampire Slayer

in the UPN Years

[56] Espenson has a history with Moore. According to his podcast, he heard her first pitch and bought her first script in his days on *Star Trek: The Next Generation* (Larocque).

[57] DiLullo, "A Season of Hope."

[58] Jozic.

[59] "02 May 2006."

[60] "09 March 2006."

[61] "23 February 2006."

[62] "03 October 2006."

[63] For a fine examination of Espenson's investigation of such issues of identity, please take a look at "'Wait Till You Have an Evil Twin': Jane Espenson's Contributions to *Buffy the Vampire Slayer*" by my former student, Laura Kessenich, in *Watcher, Junior.* at http://www.watcherjunior.tv/03/kessenich.php.

Jump: Michael Rymer: More Than a Go-To Guy

[64] *Haunted* went on to become a TV series but was cancelled after airing six episodes (excluding the pilot). The remaining six episodes were never aired. The lead actor was none other than a pre-*Lost* Matthew Fox.

[65] Nuytens.

[66] p. 169.

[67] Bordwell and Thompson 483.

[68] This device was later used by Joss Whedon in the opening sequence of the movie *Serenity* (2005) to introduce characters already established in the ill-fated series *Firefly*. The "oner" (as it's known in the world of TV) is a favored device of Whedon's.

[69] It should be noted that Rymer is credited—"Teleplay by"—for "Resurrection Ship, Part 1" (2.11).

5. R & D: Ronald D. Moore and David Eick as Collaborators

70 Gruber, Howard. "Which Way Is Up? A Developmental Question." In *Adult Cognitive Development*. Ed. R. A. Mines and K. S. Kitchener. New York: Praeger, 119.

71 Rogers, Adam."Captain's Log: Want to Understand *Battlestar Galactica?* Eavesdrop on Its Writers" in *Slate*, November 29, 2006 http://www.slate.com/id/2154625.

Jump: Under the DRADIS

72 The following essays and reviews on/about *Battlestar Galactica* are referred to in this chapter:

Ackerman, Spencer. "*Battlestar*: Iraqtica" *Slate* October 13, 2006. http://www.slate.com/id/2151425/.

Havrilesky, Heather. "Darkness Becomes Them." Salon, October 6, 2006. http://www.salon.com/ent/tv/ review/ 2006/10/06/ battlestar/.

___. "I Like to Watch." *Salon*, March 26, 2007. http://www.salon.com/ent/tv/iltw/2007/03/26/finales/.

McFarland, Marjorie. "On TV: Far from Earth, *Battlestar Galactica* Continues to Strike Close to Home." *Seattle Post-Intelligencer*, October 6, 2006. http://seattlepi. nwsource.com/tv/287715_tv06.html.

Miller, Laura. "The Man Behind *Battlestar Galactica*." *Salon*, March 24, 2007. http://www.salon.com/ent/feature/ 2007/03/24/battlestar/.

___."Space Balls." *Salon*, November 10, 2006. http://dir.salon.com/story/ent/feature/2005/07/09/ battlestar_galactica/index.html.

___."Where No TV Show Has Gone Before." *Salon*, July 7, 2005. <http://www.salon.com/ent/feature/2005/07/09/ battlestar_galactica/html>.

Patterson, Troy. "Apocalypse Noir: The Gloomy Charm of *Battlestar Galactica*." *Slate*, October 13, 2006 http://www.slate.com/id/2151426/.

Tucker, Ken. "Battlestar Galactica." Entertainment Weekly, September 6, 2006, TV Review. http://www.ew.com/ew/article/review/tv/0,6115,1540545_3_0_,00.html.

Weiss, Joanna. "Moral dilemmas pulled into *Battlestar* Galaxy." *Boston Globe*, October 5, 2006 http://www.boston.com/ae/tv/articles/2006/10/05/moral_dilemmas_pulled_into_battlestar_galaxy/.

73 In awarding *Battlestar* the Buffy, Lauerman directly addresses the neglect:

But others of you—and we're addressing you, Emmy voters, directly here—ignore us like the petulant little pills you are. Having never watched a single episode of *Battlestar*, you picture bad fight scenes on cheap green screens with fake laser beams. You think *Battlestar* is some anti-Republican thing, and you think awards shouldn't reward politics (silly, silly you). Sure, that guy who pads around the office in fuzzy clogs loves the show—and he's a geek. Plus, you saw Allison Janney at the mall once, and she seemed really nice, so you've decided to vote for *The West Wing* over and over and over again, until they pry the remote from your dead, cold hand.

74 It must be noted that Moore insists on the "Occupation/Precipice" podcast that Iraq was only one of many historical referents for the Cylon rule over New Caprica. Israel's occupation of Palestine, England's rule over its colonies, even an unspecified Roman example were all discussed in the writers room.

75 As Eick would further explain: "That's the phrase that we use to apply to all the violence taking place in this part of the world that we're so neck deep in. …" The situation, however, Eick adds, calls to mind the conundrum that "One person's

freedom fighter is another person's terrorist. It all depends on what your frame of reference is, and on what side of the ledger you're on."

Jump: In the Name of God(s)

76 *Blue Fire* 38-39.

77 "Psychology: Monotheistic or Polytheistic" 127-28.

78 "Psychology: Monotheistic or Polytheistic," 113.

79 "Psychology: Monotheistic or Polytheistic," 124.

80 Moore 37-38.

81 We are indebted here to the discussion of "Cylon Religion" in the *Battlestar* Wiki: http://en.battlestarwiki.org/wiki/Cylon_Religion#_note-0.

82 "Psychology: Monotheistic or Polytheistic," 136.

Jump: The Face of Edward James Olmos

83 Havrilesky, "I Like to Watch," January 8, 2006.

84 Bassom, 126.

Jump: Red Spines and Hot Sex

85 Although Six is, by any measure, one of *BSG*'s most interesting creations, not all critics find her relationship with Baltar worthy of continued attention: "His endless seduction by Number Six (Tricia Helfer) seems to be drawing to a close as well—a relief, after more than a season of the same breathy, imagined encounters with the Amazonian blonde that have been the only repetitive, predictable element in the series" (Havrilesky).

86 Clute, John and Nicholls, Peter, eds. *The Encyclopedia of Science Fiction.* New York: St. Martin's Griffin, 1995.

8. Women on Top

87 Cooke, Sam, Alpert, Herb, and Adler, Lou. "Wonderful World." Keen Records, 1957.

88 Phillips, Mark. "A President among the Stars." *Starlog*, April 2005, p. 27.

89 Sassone, Bob. "*24* Has a New President, and It's a Woman." July 21, 2007. http://www.tvsquad.com/ 2007/07/21/24-has-a-new-president-and-its-a-woman/.

90 Ausiello, Michael. "Exclusive: *24* to Elect Female Prez?" Ausiello Report, *TV Guide* Editors' Blogs, June 21, 2007. http://community.tvguide.com/blog-entry/TVGuide-Editors-Blog/Ausiello-Report/Exclusive-24-Elect/800017368.

91 "The Women of Battlestar." Q&A. Sci Fi Wire. Exclusive. July 2007. http:/video.scifi.com/player/?id=150561.

92 Bassom, David. "Six Degrees of Separation." *Dreamwatch*, February 2005, p. 31.

93 "The Women of *Battlestar*."

94 Bassom, "Wolf in the Fold," p. 57.

95 "Change Is Good. Now They're Babes!" *Battlestar Galactica* Season 1 DVD, Disc 5.

96 "The Women of *Battlestar*."

JUMP: THE SWIRL

97 See "Is There an (Ancestor) Text on This Island?" in *Lost's Buried Treasures.*

9. BLOOD WILL TELL

98 Sega's videogame, entitled *Blood Will Tell*, requires players to fight demonic beings to regain a samurai's missing (human) body parts and learn why he was turned into a weapon.

99 Dana Stabenow's mystery novel, published in 1997; Carlton Smith's 2003 true crime novel about "marriage, murder, and fatal family secrets"; a 2007 *Star Trek* novel about Klingons, written by Scott Tipton and David Messina; and Gary Cartwright's 1979 story of the real-life murder trials of T. Cullen Davis all prominently feature *Blood Will Tell*

as the leading words in their titles. The many literary genres represented by these titles indicate the public's continuing familiarity with this concept of the importance of bloodlines.

100 Although several sources spell the name *Zak*, Glen Larson's original character's name is spelled Zac, which is used throughout this chapter.

101 During Season Two, when Hera's lack of blood type is determined, no one has any idea that Chief Tyrol will be revealed as a Cylon by the end of Season Three. His son renders Hera "unique" only in the sense that she's the first female human-Cylon known to both the Cylons and humanity.

11. "KOBOL'S LAST GLEAMING"

102 All Moore quotations are from his podcasts to the episodes.

12. CYLON-VÉRITÉ

103 To be assigned "final cut" means to have the ultimate say in post production with decisions made during the editing process.

104 Riefenstahl (1902–2003) was, of course, the German filmmaker who propagandized on *Der Führer's* behalf in *Triumph des Willens* (*Triumph of the Will*, 1934) and *Olympia* (1938).

105 On the podcast, Moore reveals that to "discover things I didn't know" about the *Galactica* crew had been part of his charge to Verheiden.

106 Here's how Ephraim Katz defines the term in *The Film Encyclopedia*: "Cinema *verité* (literally cinema truth). A style of film-making the practitioners of which attempt to capture truth on film by observing, recording, and presenting reality without exercising directorial control or otherwise utilizing conventional film techniques to affect the veracity of a situation."

107 It is worth noting that Biers is bored by the quotidian reality of *Galactica's* life. When Dualla points out the functioning of "an oxygen recirc unit," she facetiously tells her camera man to "Get a close-up of that." When Dualla shows her "vegetable stores and canned goods," she responds that she "didn't come all this way to interview the soup of the day."

13. This *Razor's* Edgy

108 Huddleston, Kathie. "Razor Sharp." *Sci Fi*, December 2007, p. 60.

109 Logan, Michael. "Razor's Edge." *TV Guide*, November 26, 2007, p. 52.

110 Elliott, Sean. "Review: Battlestar Galactica Special Movie *Razor*." *iF*, November 23, 2007. http://www.ifmagazine.com/review.asp?article=2172

111 Darling, Cary. "TV Review: *Battlestar Galactica: Razor* Will Please Fans." *The Miami Herald*, Nov. 21, 2007, http://www.miamiherald.com/776/story/316165.html

Appendix A: Episode Guide

112 The series later changed its title to *Battlestar Galactica.* Although the switch made the new series seem like a continuation of the old, the 1978–79 original and 1980 spin-off really were conceived as two separate TV series.

Bibliography

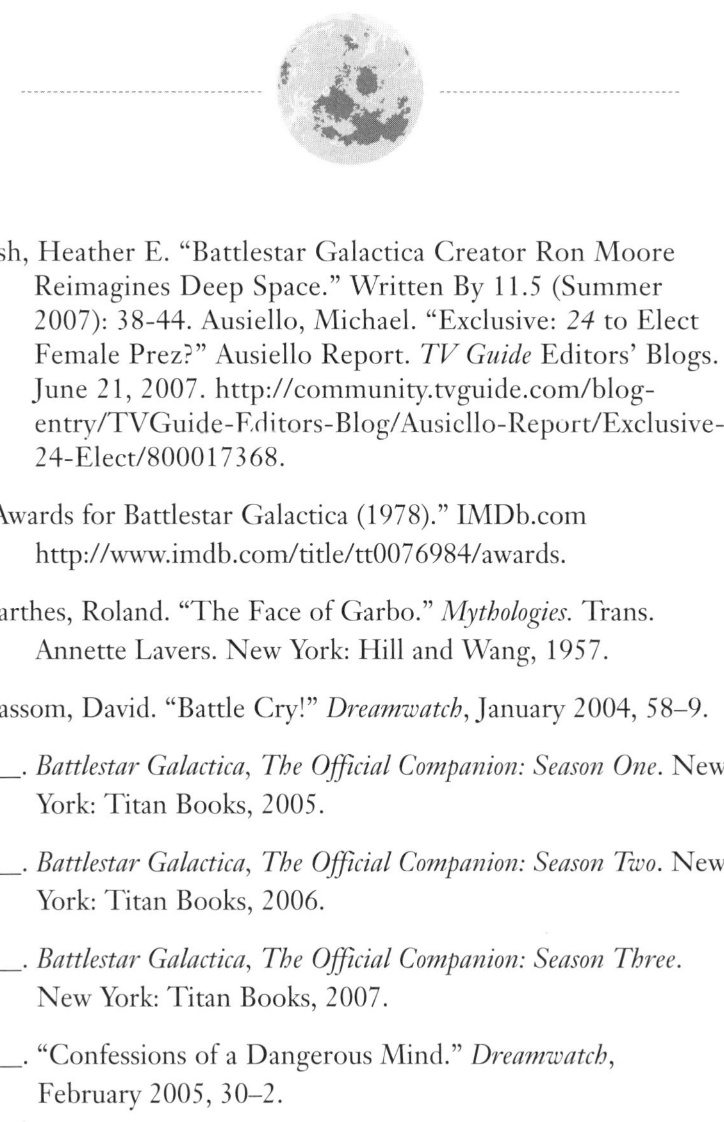

Ash, Heather E. "Battlestar Galactica Creator Ron Moore Reimagines Deep Space." Written By 11.5 (Summer 2007): 38-44. Ausiello, Michael. "Exclusive: *24* to Elect Female Prez?" Ausiello Report. *TV Guide* Editors' Blogs. June 21, 2007. http://community.tvguide.com/blog-entry/TVGuide-Editors-Blog/Ausiello-Report/Exclusive-24-Elect/800017368.

"Awards for Battlestar Galactica (1978)." IMDb.com http://www.imdb.com/title/tt0076984/awards.

Barthes, Roland. "The Face of Garbo." *Mythologies.* Trans. Annette Lavers. New York: Hill and Wang, 1957.

Bassom, David. "Battle Cry!" *Dreamwatch*, January 2004, 58–9.

___. *Battlestar Galactica, The Official Companion: Season One*. New York: Titan Books, 2005.

___. *Battlestar Galactica, The Official Companion: Season Two*. New York: Titan Books, 2006.

___. *Battlestar Galactica, The Official Companion: Season Three.* New York: Titan Books, 2007.

___. "Confessions of a Dangerous Mind." *Dreamwatch*, February 2005, 30–2.

___. "Six Degrees of Separation." *Dreamwatch*, February 2005, 32–3.

___. "Wolf in the Fold." *Dreamwatch*, March 2005, 58.

"Battlestar Wars." *Cinescape*, July/August 1999, 10.

Benedict, Dirk. "Starbuck: Lost in Castration." Feb. 7, 2006. http://www.dirkbenedictcentral.com/home/articles-readarticle.php?nid=5.

Bloch-Hansen, Peter. "John Colicos—The Quintessential Klingon." *Starlog*, #138, January 1989. Reprinted online at http://members.tripod.com/john_larocque/ tns/colicos.html.

"Change Is Good. Now They're Babes!" *Battlestar Galactica* Season 1 DVD, Disc 5.

Cooke, Sam, Alpert, Herb, & Adler, Lou. "Wonderful World." Keen Records, 1957.

DiLullo, Tara. "A Season of Hope." *SciFi*, October 2006, 38–42.

Dynamite Entertainment. http://www.dynamiteentertainment.com/ html-files/titles.html.

Eramo, Steven. "Secrets and Lies." *Starburst*, November 2005, 23–5.

"Galactites Arise!" *Space Wars*, September 1979, 16–22.

Harwood, Jim. "Laurette Spang." *Us*, October 17, 1978, 27.

___. "Lorne Greene: Reluctant Hero of TV's New *Star Wars*." *Us*, October 17, 1978, 24.

Hatch, Richard. Interview July 8, 2007. SciFi World. http://www.thescifiworld.net/interviews/richard_hatch_01.htm.

Hillman, James. *A Blue Fire: Selected Writings by James Hillman.* Ed. Thomas Moore. New York: HarperCollins, 1989.

___. "Psychology: Montheistic or Polytheistic?" *The New Polytheism: Rebirth of the Gods and Goddesses.* Ed. David

Miller. Dallas: Spring, 1981.

Huddleston, Kathie. "Behind Every Good Woman ..." *SciFi*, October 2007, 17.

Jankiewicz, Pat. "Apollo's View." *Starlog*, February 2005, 80.

___. "Space Nightengale." *Starlog*, 2001. Reprinted at http://www.laurettespang.com/home/opinion-archive.php.

Jonja.net. "A Candid Interview with Dirk Benedict." April 26, 2006. http://jonja.net/forums/viewtopic.php?t=1228.

Kraus, Bruce. *Encyclopedia Galactica: From the Fleet Library Aboard the Battlestar Galactica*. New York: Windmill Books and E. P. Dutton, 1979.

Larson, Glen A., and Thurston, Robert. *Battlestar Galactica*. New York: Berkley, 1978.

Moore, Thomas. "Introduction." *A Blue Fire: Selected Writings by James Hillman*. Ed. Thomas Moore. New York: HarperCollins, 1989.

O'Brien, Steve. "Battlestar Britannia." *SFX*, Christmas special 2004, 56–9.

O'Brien, Steve, and Dearsley, Jayne. "Cylon Running." *SFX*, December 2004, 74.

Phillips, Mark. "Battle Ready." *Starlog*, January 2005, 82–5.

___. "The New Apollo." *Starlog*, February 2005, 75–9.

___. "A President among the Stars." *Starlog*, April 2005, 26–9.

"Retuning Shows. *Battlestar Galactica*." *SciFi*, October 2007, 40.

Ryan, Maureen. "An Interview with Ronald D. Moore." January 19, 2005, The Watcher, *Chicago Tribune*. http://featuresblogs.chicagotribune.com/entertainment_tv/battlestar_galactica/index.html.

Sassone, Bob. "*24* Has a New President, and It's a Woman." TVSquad. July 21, 2007. http://www.tvsquad.com/2007/07/21/24-has-a-new-president-and-its-a-woman/.

Singh, Arune. "*Battlestar Galactica* #0 Debuts in *TV Guide*." CBR News, The Comic Wire, May 15, 2006. http://www.comicbookresources.com/news/newsitem.cgi?id=7331.

Spragg, Paul. "Cylon Running." *TV Zone*, #184, 2004, pp. 28–32.

Vulkon fan convention, Columbus, OH. July 2007.

Vulkon fan convention, Orlando, FL. November 2000.

"The Women of Battlestar." Q&A. Sci Fi Wire. Exclusive. July 2007. http:/video.scifi.com/player/?id=150561.

Young, Susan. *Oakland Tribune*, Oct. 5, 2006. "Stellar Show Warps into Pop Culture." http://findarticles.com/p/articles/mi_qn4176/is_20061005/ai_n16776048.

INDEX

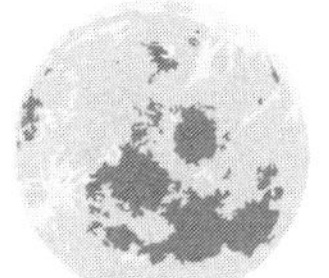

In this index, (O) refers to the original series, and (R) refers to the reimagined series

D

E

U

V

W

Y

Z